Race

Language, Power and Social Process 7

Editors

Monica Heller
Richard J. Watts

Mouton de Gruyter
Berlin · New York

Race and the Rise of Standard American

by
Thomas Paul Bonfiglio

Mouton de Gruyter
Berlin · New York 2002

Mouton de Gruyter (formerly Mouton, The Hague)
is a Division of Walter de Gruyter GmbH & Co. KG, Berlin.

♾ Printed on acid-free paper which falls within the guidelines
of the ANSI to ensure permanence and durability.

Die Deutsche Bibliothek — Cataloging-in-Publication Data

Bonfiglio, Thomas Paul:
Race and the rise of standard American / by Thomas Paul Bonfiglio.
– Berlin ; New York : Mouton de Gruyter, 2002
(Language, power and social process ; 7)
ISBN 3-11-017190-2
ISBN 3-11-017189-9

Cover design: Christopher Schneider.
Printed in Germany.

For Gina

Acknowledgements

The realization of this project was facilitated by a sabbatical leave from the University of Richmond, generous grant support from the Faculty Research Committee, and the unwavering interlibrary loan services of the Boatwright Library in obtaining the most obscure of materials. For their interest, continual encouragement, and valuable comments, I am indebted to my colleagues at the university, especially those in the Department of Modern Languages and Literatures. I am also grateful to Richard Watts, Monica Heller, and Lesley Milroy for their indispensable help with the manuscript. Further thanks go to Oliver Pollak for supplying valuable documents from Harvard University and to The Museum of Fine Arts, Houston, The Amon Carter Museum, The Enoch Pratt Free Library, The National Cowboy and Western Heritage Museum, The Frederic Remington Art Museum, The Buffalo Bill Historical Center, The New York Public Library, and The Brandywine River Museum for reprints and reproduction permission.

Contents

Contents

Introduction

In the first half of the twentieth century, Americans began to view the accent of the midwest and west as a "general American accent" that represented a standard for pronunciation. In the second half of the twentieth century, American linguists began to reject the rubrics of *midwestern* and *general American* and to problematize the status of a standard American speech in itself. This had little or no effect upon the popular consciousness; folkish notions of a standard American and (mid)western accent continued throughout the century and were extended to include network broadcast speech, as well. Indeed, Americans came to recognize the pronunciation of network announcers as a (mid)western norm. The general features of this accent are readily identifiable; the phoneme /r/ is pronounced both before and after vowels, there is no intrusive /r/, as in "I 'sawr' her standing there," diphthongs like /ay/ and /aw/ are not monophthongized, and the phoneme /æ/ is used in words like rather, bath, and calf. Americans came to recognize obvious deviations from these sounds as nonstandard and regional, such as the dropping of /r/ after vowels in New York and Boston, the Bostonian pronunciation of "rather" so that it rhymes with "father," and the southern pronunciation of "right" as /ra:t/.

The question as to why and how this (mid)western accent rose to be perceived as the standard has neither been satisfactorily answered nor engaged in a systematic way. The discourses of popular social science and popular opinion have been content with tangential and impressionistic explanations for the evolution of standard American pronunciation. The discipline of sociolinguistics has not fared much better in this regard. It has either avoided the issue, offered its own insufficient explanations, or made some late inroads, most notably in the research done in the recently emerged field of perceptual dialectology (folk linguistics).

Explanations for the etiology of standard American pronunciation have been riddled with misprisions from the onset. Some of the major ones are:

–American English pronounced the /r/ after vowels in order to differentiate from British speech, not from other forms of American speech.
–Because America is a democracy, the speech of the average person was taken as a standard. Two-thirds of the country pronounced the /r/ after vowels in the 1920's; the standard was simply the pronunciation of the majority.
–The standard that arose was simply the pattern of speech that was most pleasing to the greatest spectrum of radio listeners.
–The early radio announcers were from the midwest. This caused the mid-western pronunciation to become imitated and standardized.
–American English has no real standard pronunciation. There are many speech areas and differing pronunciations within any given speech area.
–There is no such thing as "general American" or even "mid-western" pronunciation.

This study progressively engages and deconstructs these myths in the process of developing its thesis.

My curiosity on this subject was stimulated by the observation that the process of standardization in the United States occurred in a fashion quite dissimilar from standardization in other countries, especially as regards phenomena of economic, social, and cultural power. Economic power is an important determinant of the status of a kind of speech and generally marks the difference between a language and a dialect. There are some jokes in linguistics that demonstrate this; one is that a dialect becomes a language when the dialect speakers get rich; another is that a language is a dialect with an army. In general, the standard language of a nation will derive from the speech area that is also the center of economic and cultural power in that nation. Examples of this are the British "received pronunciation," which derives from upper-class London speech; similarly, Parisian is the hegemonic standard for French, and the standard for German is generally associated with the northern industrial centers. It is highly uncommon that standard pronunciation should be taken from rural or agrarian areas. It would be strange to imagine British emulating the speech of Yorkshire or German emulating the Alpine dialects. Yet, this is basically what happened in the standardization of American English. The pronunciation of the economic and cultural centers of power was not taken as a model. Instead, the pronunciation of a largely rural area, the midwest and west, was preferred.

New York was clearly the American center of economic power at the turn of the twentieth century. It had a metropolitan population of nearly four million, at a time when there were only two other American cities with populations over a million, and was the cultural center of the country as well. Along with Boston, it centralized the power of the northeast, which was clearly the most influential part of the country at that time. The combined population of New York and the New England states comprised one-sixth of the national population in 1900 and had comprised one-fourth of the national population in 1850. The most distinctive phonetic feature of this area was the marked dropping of postvocalic /r/. Why then did this feature not develop into the national standard? Some massive cultural counterforce must have been at work here that was strong enough to override the power of the patrician pronunciations of New York and New England, which remained the determinants of American stage pronunciation in the first half of the twentieth century. This stage pronunciation generally replaces postvocalic /r/ with a schwa. The diction of Katharine Hepburn is a prime example of this type of speech, and one would have well expected it to rise to the status of a national standard, especially in view of the cultural power of such figures as Hepburn and of the New York milieu with which they are associated. Even though this was also the pronunciation for radio plays, it eventually yielded to the (mid)western pronunciation for radio broadcast speech.

The period of standardization of American pronunciation coincided with the growth of radio, and these developments also occurred during and in the aftermath of the passing of 12 million immigrants through Ellis Island, New York (1892–1924). Most of this immigration was from southern and eastern Europe. In 1907, 75% of immigration was from those regions. By 1910, 75% of the population of New York and Boston was comprised of immigrants or the children of immigrants, and 25% of the population of New York consisted in Russians and Italians. 1907 was also the year that the American congress started looking into the restriction of immigration. This culminated in the Immigration Quota Acts of 1921 and 1924, which reduced the average southern and eastern European immigration from an average of 783,000 per year to a maximum of 155,000 in 1921 and 25,000 in 1924 (Chermayeff 1991: 70, 17). The cultural and economic national capitals of New York and Boston came to be seen as sources of contamination of the "purity" of America. This was especially true of New York, which saw the immigration of 2.3 million eastern European Jews, and which became the focus of extreme antisemitism. This aversion to the large cities may be compared to similar phenomena in the prefascist movements in Germany at the turn of the century that idealized the rural German as an unspoiled, uncitified, and unsemiticized noble man of the soil. For similar reasons, Americans began to emulate the (mid)-westerner; he was the Nordic man, be he of native Anglo-Saxon or immigrant northern European "blood."

Major shifts in the cultural values of a nation will be reflected in the language of that nation. This brings me to my thesis: the adoption of western speech patterns as the preferred norm was influenced by the xenophobic and antisemitic movements of the early twentieth century. Thus Americans gravitated toward the pronunciation associated with a "purer" region of the country, and they did so in a largely non-conscious manner. Consequently, this study gradually moves toward the reintroduction of the regional terms *western* and *midwestern,* which linguistics discarded after 1945 as overgeneralizations. This study shows that the ideological construction of the categories *western* and *midwestern* was a prime agent in the process of the standardization of American pronunciation.

Thus this study coordinates a dialogue between the waxing xenophobia of the early twentieth century and the discussion of American pronunciation, linking the two via the common discourses of empowerment, disempowerment, and the articulation of identity. The dynamics of pronunciation that I am trying to illuminate by using models of ethnocentrism are largely unconscious. While the antisemitic and racial statements themselves were clearly conscious, if not shameless, the evolution of pronunciation itself was not one that was consciously mapped out, nor was it the product of a conscious, unified decision. It is analogous to the phenomenon of the post-war "white flight" to the suburbs, which was a process of gradual and incremental gravitation, the ethnocentrism of which can generally be read only on the level of submerged or coded discourse.

While this study is clearly indebted to the work done by William Labov on the changes in the speech patterns of New York City, it reviews that work, however, within an alternative methodology. Labov's findings, produced by an inquiry that is categorically linguistic in nature, are rearticulated here in a broader sociohistorical and sociocultural context, which enables this study to arrive at different causal explanations than those offered by Labov. While Labov speculated that the shift in the pronunciation of postvocalic /r/ could be coordinated with the role of the United States in World War II, this study demonstrates that the determining factors for the change were already operative well before the decade of the forties and corresponded to radically different social phenomena.

It is not the purpose of this inquiry to offer a detailed description of the phonetics of American English. Indeed, such an endeavor would be an impediment to the objective at hand. I am concerned instead with the larger cultural causes for the popular perception and valorization of regional accents and with describing the cultural milieu that gave rise to positive and negative value judgments. For this study will seek to demonstrate that it was the prejudices of nonlinguists that created the idea of standard American pronunciation. In his work on perceptual dialectology, Preston (1999) has pointed out that it is imperative to study "the triggering mechanisms of language regard among the folk and through such study the potential influence of such regard on the more general process of variation and change" (xxxviii). In his studies of the perceptions of standard United States English, he emphasizes that "research puts the weight of describing SUSE precisely where it belongs–in the mind, out of the mouths, and from the word processors of nonlinguists" (29). And this evidence can answer the questions as to how and why American English pronunciation standardized as "network standard" or, informally, "midwestern" in the twentieth century.

It should be emphasized, however, that the phenomenon of a standard language cannot be reduced to pronunciation alone, which is but a subset thereof; nor can it be claimed that postvocalic /r/ constitutes a whole variety in itself. This study views pronunciation, especially that of postvocalic /r/, rather as a reduction, as a symptomatic and metonymic indication of a preferential shift in prestige discourse, and not as constituting prestige discourse in itself.

In order to illuminate the cultural milieu that generated the popular perception and evaluation of regional accents, this study focuses on the linguistic, racial, and ethnic ideologies of influential figures in the United States, among them statesmen, writers, philologists, speech trainers, and historians. It also investigates the perception and reception of the accents of major American actors, announcers, and political figures. The ideologies and receptions of such influential figures are not only symptoms, but also determiners of the national consciousness of pronunciation as it relates to race, class, and power. With that in mind, the study discusses the findings of linguistic experiments on attitudes toward various American accents, for explicating the influence of the kinds of American figures mentioned above can help reveal the larger socio-cultural background that determined the results of those experiments and place the data in a larger interpretive context.

Consequently, the investigation will concern itself with phonemes that have high cultural visibility and that can be focused upon as diagnostic markers of the migration and legitimation of accent. The most central and pivotal of these phonemes is the characteristic American /r/; it was a principal marker of the difference between British and American, as well as between inland and coastal American speech. This phoneme became a major point of contention in pronunciation debates, invested with the ideologies of the first half of the twentieth century, and supercharged with linguistic capital and cultural significance.

The standard American postvocalic /r/ is referred to in this study variously as continuant, constricted, alveolar, retained, and rhotic. (The category of retroflex is reserved for the /r/ of the inland, i.e. non-coastal south, which includes the southern mountain, south midland, and Texas areas.) All of these designations refer to the same phoneme; it is the unmistakable sound of /r/ heard in the diction of standard network broadcasters from Lowell Thomas to Walter Cronkite and Dan Rather. It is peculiar to the United States and Canada. It is contrasted with the coastal postvocalic /r/, which is referred to here as dropped and non-rhotic. Among the other strong phonemes discussed are the more constricted retroflex /r/ of the inland south, the phoneme /oy/ if the New York and Tidewater areas, the back vowel /ɑ/ of the northeastern coast, found in the Boston pronunciation of *dance* as /dɑnts/, and the inland standard low front vowel /æ/. This last vowel is also a very strong marker of the characteristic American pronunciation.

It will be emphasized throughout this study that the phonemes in question have no essential value in themselves. The history of post-Saussurean linguistics has firmly held that there is no natural or ontological connection between a sign and its referent. This means that signs in themselves do not possess any particular intrinsic value or meaning; their value is gotten by virtue of their relationship to other signs. Thus value is culturally constructed by an associative network of signs. Sounds will gain value in the same fashion. A certain sound becomes associated with a certain positive or negative sign or image. Then, the relationship becomes reciprocal, not unlike a conditioned response, with the sign evoking the sound image and the sound image evoking the sign. Finally, the relationship becomes iconic, and the sound image is held to convey the value in itself. Network standard speech, which arose by the power of its association with midwestern and western speech, came to evoke positive personality images, i.e. to "sound better." Thus the characteristic phonemes of that speech came to indicate these positive personality values. To say that these phonemes in themselves already had *a priori* the requisite positive connotations would be untenable and would contravene the progress of linguistics in the twentieth century.

Chapter one of this study develops a social theoretical construct for analyzing the legitimation of accent, reviews the recent literature on language standardization, and develops a working concept of standard American English, especially in the context of power, race, and class. It also accounts for the differing regional pronunciations of postvocalic /r/ and the origins of those differences. Chapter two focuses on the relationship between pronunciation and ideology in the eighteenth, nineteenth, and early twentieth centuries and demonstrates that the prescriptive discussion of proper American pronunciation does not exist in a vacuum, but is instead buttressed and rationalized by ideological interests of morality, class, race, and ethnicity. It also shows how fundamental ideologies of race and immigration were instrumental in determining the modes of the broadcast voice. In order to illustrate the socio-cultural context that generated prescriptions on pronunciation, the methodology of chapter two departs from the realm of the purely linguistic. These excursions, however, are always intended to be viewed for their sociolinguistic implications, for the purpose of this study is to demonstrate that there is, in the United States, a long historical tradition of confounding the linguistic and the extra-linguistic and of configuring pronunciation within a matrix of race and class. Chapter three examines the relationship between immigration to the eastern seaboard and migration to the western regions and correlates this relationship with a phonemic shift away from New England and New York toward western and midwestern prestige patterns. It also shows how this shift precipitated a reversal in the speech patterns of New York City itself.

The (mid)western accent was constructed and desired by forces external to the area itself that projected a preferred ethnicity upon that region and defined it within a power dynamic of difference, i.e. it was precisely *not* the speech of the ethnically contaminated areas of the northeast metropolis and the south. Prior to a discussion of the social, cultural, and historical contexts of the discourses of race, ethnicity, and standardization in the United States as they existed in the popular sphere, it is necessary to develop an operative model of pronunciation as a strategic social phenomenon that is determined by factors of economy, prestige, status, and power.

Chapter 1
The legitimation of accent

1. Power, pronunciation, and the symbolic

It was Karl Marx who first formulated the relationship between structures of economic power and structures of thought. Marx argued that ideas do not have an independent existence, but are instead generated and maintained by the material, economic, and commercial conditions that humans live and experience. In *The German Ideology,* he held that human history began at that point when humans started to produce their own means of material existence; this is the point at which humans left the animal state, and the ideas that they created have always been subsequent to and fashioned by material necessity.

For Marx, all modes of thought are the direct result of observable material behavior, and the language of politics, law, morality, religion, metaphysics, etc.–indeed all human representations–have their origin in the material and economic interests of their producers. In any given epoch, there will be certain ideas that take precedence and dominate over others; these will be the ideas of the dominant class. Thus the class that is in possession of material power will also be in possession of intellectual power, and the ideas manufactured by the dominant class will act to preserve and protect the power of that class. Both the problem and the beauty of this system lie in the fact that those ideas will appear as abstract, independent, and universal, i.e. they will lose their visible connection to their generating economic base, appear to have their own existence, and also appear to be generally valid for the good of the whole population. A given structure of material power will thus generate cultural symbols that support that system and the class that benefits from the extant structure. Marx referred to these ideas as sublimates from a material substrate, thus employing a chemical metaphor to explain a social process. For instance, just as alcohol bears no ostensible connection to the grain base that produced it, so do cultural symbols lack a visible connection to the dynamics of power and class interest that created them. Just as the chemist can trace the process of sublimation from grain spirit back to grain, so can the social historian trace the process of sublimation from the spiritual/intellectual back to the material.

An example of such a creation of cultural symbols from an economic and political substratum can be taken from the dominant political situation in the United States, which have long celebrated the advantages of individualism and weak, decentralized government. From a Marxist perspective, one could argue that the interests of an affluent American entrepreneurial class are well served by an ideology of economic liberalism and laissez-faire politics, which ideology then must of necessity desire a form of government that is non-interventionist and non-regulatory, and that levies minimal taxes. Such an ideology will then view a large governmental system as ominous, sinister, invasive, etc., and it will also view the free exercise of individual power as moral, proper, and curative. This particular kind of political economy will then generate cultural symbols and artifacts that reflect and support its ideology. A primary example would be the classic American narrative of the self-made man who triumphs in the face of overwhelming opposition. This nuclear tale then becomes retold in numerous permutations, one of which is the American film *Star Wars,* the fable of the rustic Luke Skywalker and rugged individual Han Solo who destroy the massive evil empire. Such tales are basically retellings of the American war of independence, in which a tiny colony of individuals triumphed over a taxing empire.

Such cultural manifestations will, however, as Marx said, have no ostensible connection to the political and economic substratum that generated them and will instead appear in abstract form as the independent and innocuous ideas of, for instance, a writer, screenwriter, or director. In addition, they will appear in generalized form, i.e. they will be taken for granted as ideas that serve the general good, and that are thus resistant to criticism. Thus the heroic resolution of *Star Wars* will appear as politically and socially moral.

This supplies a model for viewing cultural artifacts as commodities generated by and dependent upon economic and class interests. Among such signs of cultural capital, language is certainly to be found, especially in its ideological, discriminatory, and divisive manifestations. Like all ideologies, the linguistic ideology will also appear to be abstract and general, and will not readily reveal an ostensible connection to its generating infrastructure. Certain locutions will appear to be "proper," "good," pleasant," "elevated," "strong," etc., and others will appear to be lacking in or opposed to those qualities. In addition, the absence or presence of these qualities will be expressed and evaluated on an ethical watershed; i.e., a transparent morality will be assigned to the presence of these qualities and their associated speech patterns. Techniques of linguistic archeology will be necessary in order to expose the infrastructural ideological mechanisms that generate these values and assign them to certain speech patterns. While Marx himself never discussed the symbolic function of language in this regard, some social historians who were influenced by him have investigated language from this perspective and formulated theories of speech patterns as certain kinds of commodities, ones that have the value of symbolic capital.

In *Language and Symbolic Power* (1991), The French social theorist Pierre Bourdieu has formulated a complex theory of language as symbolic capital that, while clearly influenced by Marxist concepts, also supersedes the strict economic determinism characteristic of much of Marxist theory. For Bourdieu, there are many forms of capital and many kinds of markets, only one of which is the economic. He prefers to see phenomena of economic symbolic capital, cultural capital, linguistic capital, etc., as each having a certain autonomy, although they are interrelated, and he resists the strict Marxist view that sees all forms of capital as permutations of the economic. In addition, he also departs from the Marxist notion of class, saying that it is too abstract, general, and monolithic in nature, and substitutes instead the more specific notion of group; i.e. there are divisions and competitions among numerous groups, even though the groups may be of the same social class. This has clear value for studies of differences in sociolect.

It is Bourdieu's concept of linguistic capital that is of primary importance for the purposes of this study. Linguistic capital is the capacity to tailor specific locutions to the demands of specific markets. Just as there is an uneven distribution of capital in the Marxist model, so is there an uneven distribution of linguistic capital in Bourdieu's model. Certain individuals have more linguistic power at their disposal than others and can use their fluency to a social advantage. In the act of exercising this social advantage, which is itself the instantiation of status, an element of power is ineluctable and increases as a function of the discrepancy in status between and among speakers. Bourdieu holds that "the relations of communication *par excellence*–linguistic exchanges–are also relations of symbolic power in which the power relations between speakers or their respective groups are actualized" (Bourdieu 1991: 37). He describes the mechanisms of power at work in the standardization of French, in which the dialect of Paris was adopted as the official language and implemented in schools, so that it effectively suppressed regional dialects. There was, clearly, an implicit intimidation, coercion, and violence present in the domination of Parisian speech patterns over regional *patois*. He also holds, however, that official adaptation is not the sole condition of power and domination; these may also exist in social settings that juxtapose a standard and a nonstandard speaker and a given standard and nonstandard pronunciation. Such a situation could occur, for instance, between a French speaker using the received uvular /r/ and one using the *patois* alveolar /r/. Depending on the relationship between the two speakers, this may involve a certain inevitable intimidation, "a symbolic violence which is not aware of what it is (to the extent that it implies no *act of intimidation*)" (51). This violence "can only be exerted on a person predisposed (in his habitus) to feel it, whereas others will ignore it" (51). This would posit a person aware of the implications of status and power within the symbolic exchange: "The cause of the timidity lies in the relation between the situation or the intimidating person ... and the person intimidated" (51). It is important to emphasize that the violence involved in such symbolic exchanges at the level of pronunciation will be ostensibly innocuous:

The factors which are most influential in the formation of the habitus are transmitted without passing through language and consciousness, but through suggestions inscribed in the most apparently insignificant aspects of the things, situations, and practices of everyday life. Thus the modalities of practices, the ways of looking, sitting, standing, keeping silent, or even of speaking ("reproachful looks" or "tones," "disapproving glances" and so on) are full of injunctions that are powerful and hard to resist precisely because they are silent and insidious, insistent and insinuating. (51)

Here, Bourdieu has astutely isolated the dynamics that determine standardization in an unregulated environment. In a situation in which there is no official prescribed language, no language that would have a kind of legal status, one of publicly accessible laws, there still remains a powerful class-conscious notion of acceptability and unacceptability, of locutionary standardness and nonstandardness. It is this notion that indicates societal group membership, and it should be emphasized that the rules that determine membership in the most influential social and cultural groups are never explicit, never spelled out, but instead always intuited by those included and, often, by those excluded, as well. Their formal decipherment is the task of the social scientist. Bourdieu indicates that this type of communication proceeds as a "secret code" (51) implicitly understood by its interlocutors. Thus the most powerful factor is the most subtle one; it is the strength of the silent implications in a social situation.

Bourdieu discusses a situation of social coercion that has a direct application for this study: "The recognition extorted by this invisible, silent violence is expressed in explicit statements, such as those which enable Labov to establish that one finds the same *evaluation* of the phoneme 'r' among speakers who come from different classes and who therefore differ in their actual *production* of 'r'" (52). Bourdieu is referring to Labov's 1966 study of the social evaluation of rhotic and non-rhotic /r/ in New York City speech, a study that is discussed at length below. The body of this study will demonstrate that the mechanisms of implicit coercion that Bourdieu discusses are those that, in their class-conscious and race-conscious forms, determined the standardization of American pronunciation in the twentieth century. In this process, the postvocalic /r/ was a pivotal phoneme, hypersaturated with the social dynamics and significance that Bourdieu illuminates.

There are certain lacunae, however, in the writings of both Bourdieu and Marx. While Marx's system facilitates the discussion of cultural symbols as products of the dynamics of class and power and also offers a basis for the inclusion of the mechanisms of race and ethnicity, Marx himself did not fully develop these connections. Similarly, Bourdieu makes little mention of the role of race and ethnicity in the formation of social divisions; this is certainly missing when he discusses the divisions that are also inscribed by linguistic demarcations. It is important to emphasize that, when a certain locution becomes stigmatized and avoided by a given group, it is because of the associations and connotations of that locution. When one asks the question as to what is really being avoided in the stigmatizing of a given speech form, the answer often points to the associations of that locution with a specific ethnic or racial group. It is important to construct a model that includes race, ethnicity, class, and power within the discourse of standardization.

It was Friedrich Nietzsche who first formulated the relationship among morality, race, and class as a function of a differential of power. In *On the Genealogy of Morals,* he works within the basic dyad of good and evil and seeks to show how these categories are based on class and race. For Nietzsche, morality originated when the upper classes held their comportment to be "proper" in an act of differentiation from the lower classes. Their behavior then became the locus of good, and that which was simply other became the locus of evil. In speaking of the upper classes, Nietzsche refers to them by using the adjective *vornehm,* which contains the meanings of elegant, proper, noble, and elevated. His choice of term indicates that the modes of behavior of those in power came to signify that power itself. Those modes of action then became codified in a basic act of segregation from the plebeian class that was seen as "low" and undesirable. Thus Nietzsche holds early on that the designations of good and evil have no ontological referential value, and that their value emerges from their moment of difference from the other. Nietzsche also argues that the segregation and subjugation of the other exists not only in the interests of the maintenance of power and property, but also in an act of racial prejudice. Using the Indian caste system as a model and observing the general European prejudicial valorization of lighter complexion over darker, he argues that the Indo-European migrations and conquests instituted a system of racial stratification that maintained well into his time, and that added the aspect of race into the matrix of class and power. Thus that which signifies good, high, noble, mannerly, etc. not only also signifies power and wealth, but, as well, the "proper" race and ethnicity, visible in the notion of "good breeding." This sets up a possible chain of substitutions among the signs of value, power, class, and race, which means that an element of a set or subset of signifiers from one phenomenon can substitute for an element of a set or subset of signifiers from another phenomenon.

Nietzsche displays a kind of linguistic idealism, in that he sees the seigneurial privilege (das Herrenrecht) of bestowing names as an indication of the very nature of language as an articulation of the power of the ruling classes. He makes use of etymologies–some fanciful, but nonetheless illustrative of his points–to underpin his arguments and argues that the connection between the German *schlicht* (simple, common) and *schlecht* (bad) is a linguistic attestation of the connection between class difference and morality. He argues that the perception of someone as being a "simple" or "common" person is the product of the interested and skewed gaze of the viewer, who, for Nietzsche would be a spokesperson for the class in power. This apprehension makes the object of its perception also the object of its prejudices. A similar argument could be made for the English term "mean;" that which is average becomes that which is base. Thus those terms designating the class of commoners then generate metaphorical extensions that contain meanings of evilness. Conversely, those terms designating the class of nobles generate metaphors of goodness.

This discussion of Marx, Nietzsche, and Bourdieu provides a model for situating speech within a signifying matrix of race, class, and morality. Qualitative, evaluative, and prescriptive assessments of pronunciation reveal themselves as ideological judgments that supersede the realm of language in itself. They contain a symbolic hierarchy of empowered and disempowered cultural artifacts and

reflect a competition for desired commodities, as well as a devaluation of undesirable ones. The class of signs that comprise cultivated
or "proper" elocution, as well as any of the characteristic phonemes
of that type of elocution that is held to be proper and elevated, are
pronouncements of linguistic capital and contain resonances of other
elements of the signifying system of race, class, and morality.

2. Standard ideology

In the work *Eloquence and Power*, John E. Joseph opens with the
following words:

> Within a group of communities that define themselves as a unitary region,
> it is impossible for all these communities to be precisely equal in political
> power ... Only one community will be recognized as the region's capital,
> leading to a further centralization of political and cultural institutions. Even
> in the most egalitarian-spirited of regions, then, one community will
> emerge as first among equals ... sheer pragmatics make it likely that the
> dialect of this dominant community will be used in any function which
> concerns the region as a whole. (Joseph 1987: 1–2)

Joseph uses "the rhetorical term synecdoche" (2) for the process that
bestows the name of the dominant dialect upon the region as a
whole. Synecdoche normally designates the relationship between the
part and the whole, in which the part serves to represent the totality.
The use of the term in current rhetoric largely derives from the studies of Kenneth Burke (1969), and, subsequently, Harold Bloom
(1979). Its use, however, is generally limited in scope, concerns a
nearly ideal system of paradigmatic vertical substitutions, and does
not include signifiers that are laterally and tangentially associated
with the signifier in question. It is useful to augment synecdoche
with the trope of metonymy, also a productive critical tool, that goes
beyond the vertical substitution of part for whole and thus can access the associative network of signs that are related to the phenomenon under investigation in a syntagmatic manner as displacements, substitutions, partial correspondences, inductive leaps, etc. In
this study of American English, it shall be demonstrated how the
process of metonymy or displacement generated the folk designa-

tions "western" and "midwest(ern)" to indicate the American standard, both in terms of pronunciation as well as identity.

Joseph also states that the linguistic standard must be "associated with prestigious cultural realms" (6). Here, the dynamics are largely metonymic, as the perception of prestige arises largely by association: "Prestige is transferred to attributes of the prestigious persons other than those on which their prestige is founded, and these prestigious-by-transfer attributes include things which others in the community may more easily imitate and acquire, if they so choose. Language is one of these" (31). Thus a particular dialect or pronunciation has no ontological status per se; its status is acquired by its association with prestigious images and figures. The language of the dominant class will acquire prestige by its association with the power of that class. With few exceptions, the standard language will arise from the metropolitan center of economic power. The linguistic hegemony of London, for England, and Paris, for France, serve as two premier examples of this rule. Joseph discusses two exceptions:

> The standard is usually associated with upper-class speech, but in Iceland the prestigious dialects upon which the standard is based were originally those of lower-class rural speakers, thought to be closer to the "pure" Icelandic of an earlier era than was the Danish-influenced upper-class speech of the time at which the standard was formed. Similarly in Senegal rural Wolof is valorized over urban Wolof because the latter is felt to be tinged with "the harmful influences of the city and above all of contact with French." (1987: 58) (see also Aléong 1983: 270–271; Haugen 1968: 278)

Joseph adds that "one thing is constant: it is the people with power and prestige who determine the prestigious dialect. The Icelandic case is unusual only in that prestige was at a given moment defined by Romantic notions of racial purity rather than by the usual class-capital hierarchies of post-Renaissance Western culture. In social and geographical terms, prestige usually means upper-class and urban" (59). It can be shown that, alongside the unusual example of tiny Iceland, one can place the unusual example of the massive United States, for a similar romantic ideology of racial and rural purity motivated the migration of prestigious American English in a westward direction away from the eastern urban metropolises. Although Joseph and others are suspensefully close to unlocking the key to the rise of standard American English, they stop on the precipice of doing so.

The pronunciation that eventually emerges as the standard–de facto and otherwise–will then determine the kind of speech that is used on radio and television, and a "standard accent" will thus establish itself in the media. This is the most powerful instantiation of the accent perceived to be standard. When it attains systemic media presence, it then becomes an organism that operates reflexively, in and of itself, as the vocal embodiment of the values of the dominant class, and it will suppress speech patterns that signify an opposition to those values. Joseph also discusses the American network standard: "In the twentieth century, the literary norm has given up a fair amount of ground to what in America is commonly called 'network standard,' the usage of national radio and subsequently television broadcasters, and especially newscasters. These media have the advantage over literature of covering the phonological spectrum fully" (119). No attempt, however, is made at a larger correlation.

Joseph hardly countenances the popular myth that broadcasters coincidentally determined the nature of standard American pronunciation by virtue of the fact that they just happened to be from the midwest. His work does not offer, however, a dynamic connection among network speech, geographic region, and cultural power, even though his discourse actually juxtaposes these three elements: "The fact is that newscasters do not determine rules and norms; the rules and norms determine the newscasters. Individuals are chosen for the position largely on the basis of their linguistic traits–including voice quality–and how great a cross-section of the audience these traits are likely to appeal to. No one could rise to the position of Cronkite or Rather if his or her usage deviated more than mildly from the general aristocratic-Midwest norm" (119). Here, he generates the golden phrase "aristocratic-Midwest norm," but he leaves it uninvestigated. How is it that a rural area came to be "aristocratic" and to determine the standard network speech? He invokes the image of Walter Cronkite, generally known by the apocryphal attribute "the most trusted man in America." How is it that Cronkite's phonemes were invested with the attributes of trustworthiness? It is the task of this study to answer that question. The causal sequences of this process are, however, clear: the phonemes of the area called "the west" or "the midwest" acquired prestige status and determined who was chosen as a broadcaster and how *he*–for it was, in this case, a male voice that was preferred–was (trained) to speak.

The process of standardization is also linked to the interests of language purism, which is, in turn, related to larger social and psychological issues of cultural purism. In *Linguistic Purism,* George Thomas observes:

> Not only do periods of strong national sentiment tend to co-occur with purism, but where associated with xenophobia they almost invariably share the same targets. While there are such languages as English and Polish, where national fervor and pronounced xenophobia did not on the whole lead to a puristic movement, it is hard to think of an instance of purism which is not motivated by some form of cultural or political nationalism. (G. Thomas 1991: 43)

In the United States, however, the period of greatest xenophobia in the twentieth century, namely the decades of the twenties and thirties, was coeval with a rising interest in linguistic purity and in protecting the language from foreign influence (see also Shapiro 1989; Bakhtin 1981). That this did not take place "on the whole," as Thomas says, is a factor that would support exception of the English and Polish languages. The process did, nonetheless, take place unofficially, and also on the state and local governmental levels, and it did express itself as a movement away from urban eastern speech, which became associated with the undermining of national identity. Indeed, Thomas sees the fundamental importance of the matrix of national identity and national language: "Since the native language, as component of this national culture, serves as a card of national identity, it must be carefully differentiated from any other. In the process a national language, with which its speakers can identify, is created" (43). Thomas holds that "this differentiation can be achieved through purism. In other words, purism can be motivated by a search for, or the need to preserve, national identity" (43–44).

In *Eloquence and Power,* Joseph's prefatory words observe that "in modern linguistics, the phenomenon of language standardization has not been a central interest" (Joseph 1987: vii). He notes that "linguistic scholars have often been content with *ad hoc* and incomplete definitions of 'standard language' ... said to be merely a dialect or variety on a par with other varieties" (vii). What motivates linguists to orient themselves in this way is the massive distinction between prescriptive and descriptive linguistics, the former being largely the domain of popular journalists and the latter of scholarly linguists. Since standardization smacks of prescription, linguists have tended to let its study lie fallow. The British work on standardization, however, tends to have a political orientation. Since the institutionalizing of a standard works to undervalue and suppress other varieties of pronunciation, many British scholars have sought to deconstruct its power and status in a gesture of democratic support of heteroglossia. In the United States, this tension tends to express itself almost exclusively in the debates on the instruction of Ebonics and bilingual education (see Taylor 1989). These debates are discussed in the afterword below.

Thus qualitative assessments of proper speech have tended to be underrepresented in linguistic investigation when, in fact, they should be studied as correlates of sociolinguistic phenomena. For example, Pyles writes:

> In February, 1947, the United Press reported that the Linguaphone Institute of America, "authority on American speech," has awarded the palm for "the most perfect speech," which I assume would be the "purest," to Dallas, Texas, with New York ranking only thirtieth. Cities other than Dallas which won the Institute's accolade were Los Angeles, Chicago, and Mason City, Iowa ... what does it all mean? I haven't the faintest idea. (Pyles 1952: 284)

Pyles's prescriptive and glib agnosticism is indicative of a generation of scholars who sought to dismantle the idea of a single standard American language or a single correct pronunciation. This generation demonstrated that variation persists even down to the level of idiolect, but it did not seek to deconstruct the ideology that erected, maintained, and still maintains the notion of a standard speech, thus obfuscating the analysis of the process of standardization and the submerged fascination with images of power within that standardization.

In his "Studies of American pronunciation since 1945," Pederson lists four major "characteristics marking a degree of maturity that was the exception, rather than the rule, in earlier works" on American pronunciation before the end of World War II. Included among these is the "rejection of the 'general American' descriptor" (Pederson 1977: 288). Pederson quotes Pyles's "good advice that 'the old assumption of a homogeneous 'General American' pronunciation, spoken everywhere save the South and eastern New England, must be once and for all discarded'" (Pyles 1952: 289). Post-war linguistics discarded this umbrella term, as its research had discovered a plethora of variations within this supposed category. A similar reconfiguration took place in the categories of midwest and west, as those areas, under further scholarly scrutiny, displayed variations that rendered these geographical designations of little concrete utility. While scholarship dismissed these categories outright, as they were not the product of rigorous study, scholarship failed to account for the construction of these geographical generalizations in the first place; i.e., it did not ask why the terms "general American," "west," and "midwest" were–and still are in non-scholarly circles–preferred categories. Are we to simply assume that these generalizations were the accidental products of a dearth of scholarly scrutiny? This seems unlikely. While scholarship has done well to dismantle these terms, it has not attempted to deconstruct them: in other words, it has not attempted to study their ideological origins. The lack of investigation of the ideological utility of these terms is similar to the lack of investigation of the ideological origins and utility of the notion of standard American pronunciation. Post-war linguistics has, and justifiably so, shunned the specter of prescriptivism; in doing so, it has become so thoroughly descriptive and particular in its methodology that it occasionally fails to account for the origins of the categories that it has determined to be illusory. This has persisted in spite of the fact that the research in the field of perceptual dialectology has shown not only the persistence of these and other folkish categories in the popular consciousness, but also the importance of these categories as determiners of conceptions of language, accent, and even language change. This is, in part, due to the fact that perceptual dialectology was a very long time in the making and did not really emerge until the nineties, when scholarship started to reveal a mounting interest in the study of standardization, both in the United Kingdom and the United States, and to reexamine the continued presence of prescriptivism, especially as it relates to phenomena of social power.

In *The Role of Prescriptivism in American Linguistics, 1820–1970*, Glendon F. Drake investigates the persistence of prescriptivism:

> The 20th-century in linguistics is the move away from traditional 18th-century notions and 19th-century historical emphasis into the scientific and relativistic structural linguistics, and finally, at the present time, into transformational theory. Each of these two modern developments, structuralism and transformational theory, although contrasting fundamentally in method, eschews prescriptivism. Yet, the evidence suggests that the prescriptive notion remains dominant in the consciousness of the large majority of intelligent and educated people to this day. (Drake 1977: 31–32)

Drake also points out that prescriptivism persists in the popular consciousness despite "the powerful contrary and corrosive force of relativism and the scientific ethic of the 20th-century" (32).

More recent scholarship, however, has shed new light on the complex of standardization, descriptivism, and prescriptivism. In the recent article, "The Consequences of Standardization in Descriptive Linguistics," James Milroy points out that the success of the standard or canonical forms of languages such as Latin, Greek, Sanskrit, English, Spanish, French, and others "has arisen, not from the superiority of their grammatical and phonological structures over those of other less successful languages or from the great poetry that has been composed in them–but from the success of their speakers in conquering and subduing speakers of other languages throughout much of known history" (J. Milroy 1999: 16). In the examples supplied by Milroy, an actual physical conquest by the speakers of the languages was, indeed, the cause of the success of those languages. Clearly, when a given language or dialect suppresses or marginalizes another language or dialect, military force is not an indispensable component of that process. An element of power, however, and, consequently, status certainly is. There is nothing in the particular language in itself that determines its worth: it is the connection of the language in question to the phenomena of power that determines the value of that language and that contributes to the standardization process. The language *in* and *of* power then becomes an ideal: "Standard languages are high-level idealizations, in which uniformity or invariance is valued above all things. One consequence of this is that no one actually speaks a standard language. People speak vernaculars which in some cases may approximate quite closely to the idealized standard; in other cases, the vernacular may be quite distant" (27).

Here, Milroy aptly captures the complexities surrounding the phenomenon of standardization. It is basically a paradoxical situation, in which speakers presume the existence of a standard that, in reality, does not exist. It can perhaps be clarified by characterizing it as asymptotic in nature. In mathematics, an asymptote characterizes the relationship between a straight and a curved line, in which the straight line continually approaches but never meets the curved one. The incommensurability present in the notion of a tangent at infinity does not preclude its use as a viable mathematical function. It may be helpful to view the phenomenon of standardization in the same way: the unattainability of the standard should not proscribe its viability as a linguistic concept.

There remains, however, a larger question: what does one do with and within the space of incommensurability? The language purists attempt to close it with rigid definitions of proper language that deny the problem of incommensurability *a priori*. From their perspective, linguistic discrepancies and aberrations are the result of faulty education and/or logic and are fully amenable to amelioration. For the social theorists or relativists, on the other hand, the space of incommensurability should be magnified so as to draw attention to the fact that all language forms are dialect variations of equal value. There is, however, another option for dealing with the problem of incommensurability.

The most common criticism of the concept of standardization is that it is exclusionary and elitist in nature, and that it is simply a linguistic medium of class consciousness that serves to demarcate and maintain class boundaries. In order to mark and preserve its identity, status, and power, a group will arbitrarily select and canonize certain linguistic features as standard or prestigious. These linguistic elements—be they grammatical, lexical, or phonetic—then become codes, a form of secret exclusionary language, which is not very secret and cannot remain so for very long. The result is that prestige forms must therefore be transitory and must pass from fashion, so that they may be replaced by the most current indication of separate status. This means that the standardization process has no fixed center and that, as an elusive phenomenon, it must remain dynamic. This precludes any fixed description of the standard language *a priori* and may well help account, at least in part, for the eluctability of the notion of standardization in the first place. It may also help account for the stable structure but fluid content of prescriptivist recommendations.

Milroy makes another observation that is quite valuable for the present study. Noting that scholarship lacks a nuanced understanding of the relationship between prestige and standardization, he says, "The idea of prestige is still used rather routinely, and there are many instances in the literature where it is assumed that a scale of prestige parallel to a scale of social status is the same thing as a scale from non-standard to standard" (37). He says, basically, that the group with the highest social prestige is not necessarily the group with the highest linguistic prestige: "Salient forms that are generally viewed as standard, or mainstream, are not necessarily those of the highest social class" (39). These observations are especially applicable to the process of standardization in the United States, where the accent of an area that was not associated with a high level of prestige rose to be perceived as the norm. This is the inland northern area, and its perceived association with the west and midwest introduce elements into the standardization process that are not usually associated with phenomena of social prestige: rustication, purity, openness, simplicity, honesty, etc.

These issues may be further illuminated by a comparison of the emergence of standard American English pronunciation with the emergence of standard British English pronunciation in view of the dynamics of class origin, official imposition (in the case of England), and unregulated development (in the case of America). In *Authority in Language,* Milroy and Milroy observe that "although the Received Pronunciation of Standard English has been heard constantly on the radio and then television for over 60 years, only 3 to 4% of the population of Britain actually speak RP ... the promotion of standardization through official and centralized channels is less widely effective than is generally believed" (Milroy and Milroy 1985: 29) (see also Trudgill and Hannah 1982). The authors are referring to the well-known existence of RP, or the received pronunciation of Great Britain, which was, as they say, promulgated through official and centralized channels and became the standard pronunciation of the national broadcast media. Even though it did not represent the mode of speech of the majority of the population, it nevertheless assumed a normative position. It arose from the upper-class speech of the national, political, and economic capital of London and was originally a vehicle of exclusionary class identity:

> English RP was maintained between the late nineteenth century until well after the Second World War as an élite and exclusive accent partly through ties formed by members of the élite group at school, university, clubs, in the army and so on ... this common language was maintained because of the common interests of these groups. (Milroy and Milroy 1985: 58)

Thus RP arose as an in-group class marker, the usage of which signified class membership *a priori* as an instantiation of status. It was not intended as a vehicle of democratic leveling, but, on the contrary, as a marker of class boundaries, a linguistic code that communicated the fact of group membership. In the second half of the twentieth century, RP became "the official language, used by government; it is codified in dictionaries and grammar-books; it is appealed to as the norm in the educational system. These facts give it a *legitimacy* that other varieties do not usually have and make it *potentially* accessible to all citizens" (58). Thus RP arose as an exclusionary class-code and then was institutionalized via government channels as the acceptable national norm. While it still carries with it the ring of aristocratic status, it is nonetheless, in theory and principle, adoptable by all. If a speaker from a disenfranchised class, however, had used it before it became nationally visible, this usage would have been seen as perhaps transgressive, egregious, suspect, and subject to interpretation. Since the emergence of RP as a kind of standard and its mediation via radio and television, its usage by non-elite strata has become much less transgressive.

The norms of acceptable American English in the twentieth century emerged from different social and political structures. As the peculiar American system of political economy guarantees the long-term existence of a less involved government, phenomena such as official national standards of speech or even national educational policies are excluded from discourse *a priori* as contraventions of democracy. The government is not supposed to prescribe speech standards or represent or advocate any particular form of linguistic behavior at all. It is generally held, in America, that such advocacy would only enforce a class system, strengthen the advantages of one class, and increase the disadvantages of others. The non-involvement of government in issues of class and the reluctance of government to champion the interests of one race, class, or gender over another does not mean, however, that the interests of a certain race, class, or gender do not, in effect, dominate and possess greater status than the interests of the other(s). This can be applied, as well, to linguistic behavior.

Here, a comparison with studies on race and ethnicity could help illuminate this murky area between science and ideology. Decades ago, anthropology jettisoned the concept of race as a useful category of human taxonomy and has substituted other classificatory terms, such as family. Race is the product of a perception of differences in skin color. The anthropologist Mark Cohen observes that skin color is based on no more than four to ten pairs of genes out of the 50,000 to 100,000 pairs of genes needed to produce a human being:

> "Races" as imagined by the public do not actually exist. Any definition of "race" that we attempt produces more exceptions than sound classifications. No matter what system we use, most people don't fit ... studies of the human family tree based on detailed genetic analysis suggest that traits such as skin color are not even good indicators of who is related to whom, because the traits occur independently in several branches of the human family. (Cohen 1998: B4)

Should one thus conclude that there is no such thing as racism because there is no such thing as race? Had one done so, there would never have been an American civil rights movement. Clearly, it is imperative to study how race operates as an ideology and not a biological given. Similarly, it is imperative to study how the terms *standard, midwestern,* and *general American* function as linguistic ideologies, even if their empirical status is problematic, for it is through their existence as ideologies that they have had a determining influence on linguistic behavior.

The nonexistence of official national speech and pronunciation standards does not mean that there is no social hierarchy of speech in the United States, nor does it mean that no one pronunciation has greater social and economic status than another. We all judge others by their discourse, especially by their modes of pronunciation, and most educated middle-class speakers of American English are aware of the relationship among pronunciation, status, and power– especially pertaining to employment interviews–, and these same educated middle-class speakers have come to share a comparatively common pronunciation.

It is productive to observe, however, that the common pronunciation of American English arose in a manner structurally similar to the rise of British RP before it became a kind of national standard. RP was communicated and shared among members who also shared the same interests of class, race, and gender, and it spread in an imitative, deregulated, and largely undeliberate fashion as a marker of social position. This process also describes the rise and systematization of (network) standard American within a deregulated political economy. It is shared and imitated by those who have similar class interests.

There is, however, one important distinction to be made between the rise of British RP and the rise of (network) standard American: the former was a marker of social station, while the latter is a marker of both social mobility (i.e. upward mobility) and social station. In other words, the use of standard American can signify both station within the upper middle class and the process of accession to that class. For these reasons, one will generally find it supraregionally within the suburban upper middle class and especially among college students at prestigious institutions. This will generally occur regardless of the regional origin of the students. At representative high-status colleges and universities, which invariably draw their pools of students on a national and intentionally non-local basis, one tends to find *a priori* a general accession to network pronunciation, in spite of the fact that the students may arrive from Dallas, New York, New Orleans, or Charleston.

One of the most astute observations on standardization has been made by Susan Ramsaran in her recent article "RP: fact *and* fiction:"

> Whatever the reasons, educated speakers of English do not speak with the broadest (or purest) forms of their local accents and the modifications are generally towards RP. So it can be argued that RP displays itself as a kind of standard, not necessarily deliberately imposed or consciously adopted, not a norm from which other accents deviate, nor a target toward which foreign learners need necessarily aim, but a standard in the sense that it is regionally neutral and does undoubtedly influence the modified accents of many British regions. (Ramsaran 1990: 182–183)

The decisive factor that determined the status of RP-like accents was, paradoxically, that it ceased to be identified solely with one class. Ramsaran notes that

> by the end of the last century, this accent was characteristic of the speech of members of the upper class throughout England, perhaps throughout Britain. It is no longer possible to talk in such clear-cut terms of social classes; nor is there any longer so straightforward a correlation between social background and profession or type of education in present-day society. (178)

Thus it became acceptable for other social classes to use RP-like accents, thus generating a kind of norm that exists in Britain until this day.

In the recent "Standard English: what it isn't," Peter Trudgill discusses these discrepancies. Under the subheading "Standard English is not an accent," he holds that "Standard English has nothing to do with pronunciation" (Trudgill 1999: 118), but then he says, "From a British perspective, we have to acknowledge that there is in Britain a high status and widely described accent known as Received Pronunciation (RP)" (118). While this may seem paradoxical, he goes on to say, "It is true that in most cases Standard English speakers do not have 'broad' local accents, i.e. accents with large numbers of regional features which are phonologically and phonetically very different from RP, but it is clear that in principle we can say that, while RP is, in a sense, standardized, it is a standardized accent of English and not Standard English itself" (118). From these observations, one might be led to conclude that speakers whose accents are perceived as standard tend to exhibit speech patterns that allude to RP, without actually fully conveying the speech patterns of RP *per se.*

In *'Talking Proper:' The Rise of Accent as Social Symbol,* Lynda Mugglestone makes use of Ramsaran's arguments and notes that "notions of 'standard' and 'non-standard,' 'good' and 'bad' still continue to be fostered in the face of linguistic reality and linguistic change" (Mugglestone 1997: 330). She also offers the clever observation that "ideologies of a standard remain ... in good health. The process of standardization, on the other hand, can and will only reach completion in a dead language" (330). This is not only due to the fluid nature of living languages, but also to the dynamics of class interaction discussed above. There was even great variability and indeterminacy in the construction of RP itself. Mugglestone describes how [ɑː] as in *bath* and *path* began as a cockney variant that was initially condemned by purists and rejected by the upper class. Instead, [æ], a phoneme that became more characteristic of American speech, was preferred. Subsequently, [ɑː] became the RP standard (90–98). The same is true of the loss of [r], which was initially deemed a Cockneyism. The term "Cockney rhymes" was applied to such pairs as *Italy* and *bitterly, morn* and *dawn, fought* and *sort.* Keats used such rhymes and was initially criticized for doing so, especially by Gerard Manley Hopkins (100–101) and Alfred Tennyson (102). Some of Keats's rhymes, such as *farce* and *grass* contravened both the recommendations against the backed /a/ and dropped /r/. She holds that dropped /r/ started appearing in the mid-eighteenth century and became imitated by RP speakers in the nineteenth century.

Mugglestone notes that, in Britain, radio broadcasts were seen as an ameliorative medium for objectionable pronunciations. She quotes J. C. W. Reith in his *Broadcast over Britain*: "One hears the most appalling travesties of vowel pronunciation. This is a matter of which broadcasting may be of immense assistance" (Reith 1924: 161). And there were, indeed, some curious customs employed to insure proper verbal behavior. For instance, she reports that radio announcers were instructed to wear dinner jackets for their evening broadcasts (Mugglestone 1997: 324).

Mugglestone also offers a viable account of the interplay of class and status in this context. Noting that "it was, however, 'class' and not ethnicity which commonly came to operate as the basis of these divisions" (70), she observes that "class, as both historians and sociologists have stressed, is formally an economic determinant alone ... Disraeli's 'two nations ... who are formed by a different breeding, are fed by a different food, are ordered by different manners' can all be seen to encode the economic realities of social difference in nineteenth century society" (75). After defining class in economic terms, she then introduces the qualification that wealth alone, especially acquired wealth, does not insure upper-class membership (76). Thus the economic, while initially the origin of class distinctions, is not always the sole determiner thereof, but may function, instead, as a valuable symptom or attribute of class difference; i.e. money itself was not sufficient; indicators of status were introduced as complementary criteria. She holds that one of these indicators consisted in the difference of accent, which became an important marker used to instantiate and reinforce class membership in light of the insufficiency of the economic in that regard. She says of Disraeli's statement: "People are regularly aligned into social groupings on grounds such as these, irrespective of their pecuniary level" (77) and concludes that "the relevant terms are, in effect, those of 'status', not of 'class'" (78).

Mugglestone's taxonomy of accent, class, and status is helpful in situating pronunciation as a powerful marker of social group membership and non-membership. It is interesting, however, to note that, even here, concepts of class cannot be divorced from those of race and ethnicity. Language itself will not free one from those traces. In reviewing the passage from Disraeli, one sees that the first two examples in the citation have bodily and racial correlates. It is "breeding" that can characterize the "breed." Only the third example, that of manners, is exclusively one of status, but, on the other hand, judgments of manners, especially in their negative manifestations, are often confounded with notions of ethnicity.

Mugglestone's perspectives are well supported in the work done by John Honey, a scholar of and major apologist for RP. In *Does Accent Matter?*, Honey offers the following description of the social function of RP from 1870 onward:

> It was the public school system in this new sense which made possible the extension of RP throughout the top layers of British society, and indeed to many people below the top. There is little evidence that, in boys' public schools at least, it was systematically taught. New boys with local accents were simply shamed out of them by the pressure of the school's "public opinion." (Honey 1989: 27)

The fact that it was not systematically taught, but instead simply assumed to exist, emphasizes its role as a divisive sign of status. Indeed, Honey shares Mugglestone's characterization of the function of status:

> The most easily manageable, if superficial, index of public school status was accent. By the end of the nineteenth century a non-standard accent in a young Englishman signaled non-attendance at a public school, whereas if he spoke RP he was either a genuine member of the new cast of public school men or he had gone to some trouble to adjust his accent elsewhere, thus advertising the fact that he identified with that caste and its values. (28)

RP eventually ascended to the level of official sponsorship: "The central government's Education Department prescribed in 1898 the correct method of teaching vowel sounds, and teacher-training colleges offered instruction in elocution" (29). Honey relates some anecdotes that underscore the value of RP as a proper indicator of status and class membership. For instance, an RP accent was a major criterion for assuming the rank of an officer in Word War I. The progress of the war, however, necessitated the promotion of officers from lower ranks and, consequently accents of lower prestige. At a public school in 1919 (Lancing), Evelyn Waugh actually organized a demonstration in protest against the accent of such an officer who was inspecting the cadets (Honey 1989: 30–31). Also, the actor Dirk

Bogarde claims that he was promoted to officer in World War II solely based upon his RP accent (31). The promulgation of RP through official channels affected radio speech from the very beginning. Honey notes that, in the twenties, the BBC carefully chose announcers with RP accents, and in 1926, the BBC Advisory Committee on Spoken English was established to insure proper pronunciation (31). These measures, however, started changing in the sixties, and the BBC relaxed some of its policies (32).

While Honey's scholarship on received pronunciation is quite reliable, it reveals, however, some peculiar ideological underpinnings. He does not stop at the level of descriptive and evaluative inquiry, but reveals himself to be a prejudiced supporter of standardized RP. He discusses "vernacular Black English in the USA" and says, "the adoption of such speech forms often goes hand in hand with hostility to education, with blatant forms of sexism, and with forms of discrimination against those fellow black pupils who co-operate with the schools and resist pressures to steal, smoke, take drugs, and indulge in other forms of criminality" (160–161). Thus the lack of a standard language leads to drug consumption, while the presence thereof, at least its regular instruction, is supposed to ameliorate social ills. In this discussion, he foregrounds the presence of a black Pentecostalist pastor in England whose use of RP serves as an ameliorative example, presumably religious as well as social, for young West Indians (161). Also, in the recent *Language is Power*, he offers a singular and very curious account of the rhetorical success of Martin Luther King and says that the "historic speech 'I have a Dream' achieved its impact because it was in standard English" (Honey 1997: 41). What one sees in Honey's discourse is the persistence of ideology in the advocating of standardization, not in the description of its processes. Indeed, it seems that, in the conversations on standardization, description tends to turn to ideology at the point of prescription and advocacy.

In "Standard English and language ideology in Britain and the United States," Lesley Milroy offers the very useful observation that the concept of a standard language is best viewed in a negative sense:

People find it easier to specify what is *not* standard than what is; in a sense, the standard of popular perception is what is left behind when all the non-standard varieties spoken by disparaged persons such as Valley Girls, Hill-billies, Southerners, New Yorkers, African Americans, Asians, Mexican Americans, Cubans and Puerto Ricans are set aside. In Britain, where consciousness of the special status of RP as a class accent is acute, spoken standard English might similarly be described as what is left after we remove from the linguistic bran-tub Estuary English, Brummie, Cockney, Geordie, Scouse, various quaint rural dialects, London Jamaican, transatlantic slang and perhaps, even conservative RP as spoken by older members of the upper classes. What remains is sometimes described as English spoken with "no accent." (L. Milroy 1999: 174)

Thus the absence of perceptible dialect variations is seen as the presence of the standard language. But this presence is also seen as a kind of neutrality, not only one of accent, but also one of character, because it is perceived as the absence of objectionable traits. This means that change and variation will then be equated with adverse characteristics: "Yet, the standard ideology holds that far from being a morally neutral fact of social life, language change equates with language decay, and variation with 'bad' or 'inadequate' language. Metonymic shift (or perhaps guilt by association) provides the logical slippage for such negative judgments to be expressed in terms of undesirable moral, intellectual or social attributes of groups of speakers" (175). The phrase "metonymic shift" is very valuable here, as it indicates that the listener will tend to move associatively between accent and character, and that the accents in question will then become coded for objectionable or unobjectionable attributes that correlate with "substandard" or "standard" accents respectively. The result of this is that the championing of a single standard will be informed by a surreptitious ideology whose aims, at bottom, are exclusionary and protective:

Thus, when we hear proclamations by Republican senators in the USA along what lines that it is common sense that English should be the only language used in the official documents of the US federal government, or by Cabinet ministers of the last British Tory government that standards of English will improve since common sense is back in fashion, we can be sure that they are being driven by an unacknowledged ideology. (176)

The ideological foundations of the "English only" movements in the United States are not readily visible in their recent manifestations, as Milroy implies, but this was not the case in their initial historical forms, in which the expression of the real operative agenda was not as subject to mechanisms of repression and displacement as it is today.

It has been said many times in numerous social analyses of the United States and Great Britain, that the social divisions in those countries tend to be demarcated along lines of race and class respectively. These operative divisions have held in sociolinguistic analyses as well. While these broad distinctions do, indeed, have their usefulness, they are by no means mutually exclusive. Class-conscious and race-conscious evaluations and descriptions of American pronunciation have both alternated and coexisted throughout the history of the United States and the American colonies. Milroy's contrastive analysis of the dynamics of the standardization process in the United States and Great Britain is very useful for this inquiry, especially as concerns the classic distinction between race and class. She observes that

> in both countries, the upper layers are formed by relatively standardized speakers, with respective layers below of rejected and disparaged social groups ... In Britain, speakers of stigmatized urban dialects constitute the lowest layer of all, while in the United States that position is occupied by AAVE speakers, and perhaps also some Spanish speakers. It is these differences ... particularly at the top and the bottom, which give rise to the stereotypical perception that America is classless and Britain free of racial animus. (183)

This is an interesting observation on the role of stereotyping. The image of standard American is clearly associated with white speech and not black vernacular. Furthermore, it is not readily seen as "high class." It is merely seen as neutral and as not being, in the main, the property of marginalized ethnic groups. This then leads to the perception that the process in question is, in the United States, race-related. This observation could be complemented to include a similar process of stereotyping vis-à-vis Britain. RP is represented in British popular culture as a characteristic of members of the upper class. This association then leads the observer to conclude that dialect differences are class-based. There is, however, a certain interplay of race and class issues in both countries, as is evident in the following comment by Milroy: "Certainly there does not exist in America a focused and identifiable class accent corresponding to Received Pronunciation in Britain, although some might argue that network American and the famous Brahmin accent of Boston are candidate varieties" (202). Clearly, there *is,* however submerged, a dynamic of class distinction involved in the phenomenon of network standard. The older "Boston Brahmin" accent, however, has sustained a degradation of status and is no longer a marker of elevated or cultivated speech. On the contrary, the loss of /r/ in coastal Massachusetts is more a marker of lower middle or working class status. Milroy adds that "we need to acknowledge that the focus on race and ethnicity in the United States is mediated by class" (176). Beginning with chapter 2.3. below, "Class and race in the nineteenth century," it will become clear in this study that, while race and ethnicity have been dominant factors in the ideology of standard American, their relationship to class concerns has also been symbiotic; they have both mediated and augmented each other.

Milroy is among the first to see the consciousness of race and ethnicity as an agent in the determination of the American standardization process. In discussing the ideology of standardization, she moves comparatively between the situations in the United States and Great Britain and observes that, in the United States,

in the early twentieth century we find both a parallel and a contrast to the British situation. The parallel lies in the widespread but intemperately expressed fear of engulfment. However, the groups which are seen to threaten the social fabric are not an urban proletariat speaking varieties of English rooted in historically established dialects, but immigrants who are speakers of languages other than English. (192)

She offers an explanation of the origin of this dynamic: "The bitter divisions created by slavery and the Civil War shaped a language ideology focused on racial discrimination rather than on the class warfare which erupted particularly fiercely in Britain in the early years of the twentieth century" (204). While this is true to a certain extent, it will be demonstrated in chapter two of this study that there are major race-based notions of language even during the antebellum period. In the main, however, race-consciousness, in its most widespread and damaging forms, appeared in the postbellum period. This was aided by the massive immigration to the eastern seaboard, as Milroy also observes: "heavy immigration to northern cities between 1880 and 1920 gave rise to conflicts for dominance between immigrant groups and older elites. Labor conflicts and America's emergence as a capitalist economy par excellence with the associated money-making ethos had the effect of crowding out democratic ideals of equal rights in both north and south" (197). Thus it was the legacies of the American Civil War and of massive immigration that determined the folkish, i.e. non-scholarly linguistic geography of North America:

> It seems reasonable to suggest that the beliefs reported to Preston derive from the major historical divisions ... notably the Civil War conflict between (what is perceived to be) an urban, progressive north and a rural, conservative slave-owning south. The status of New York City as the first destination of the poorest immigrants may well be the source of its negative image. (203)

She is here referring to the work on perceptual dialectology done by Dennis Preston, which is discussed at length in section 1.4. below, "Heartland rules." She is correct in noting that the speech areas that are the most marginalized in the United States are those of the rural south and of New York, as has been demonstrated in surveys from those done by Wilke and Snyder in the forties to those done by Preston in the nineties. The following tenet is, however, a bit problematic: "In America the urban dialects of industrial cities generally do not seem to be as stigmatized as the speech of the South, which is associated not only with an historic and divisive conflict but with rural poverty ... British attitudes to urban industrial accents are particularly negative and are rooted in class consciousness" (203). The problem is that there are few speech patterns in the United States that can be identified as "urban industrial." Moreover, the American accent that is perceived to be the norm, as demonstrated by Preston and others, is that of the inland northern area, which comprises the historically great industrial centers along the Great Lakes. Indeed, one may risk the utterance that the only American accent readily associated with an urban area is that of New York City, with Boston being perhaps a second possibility. In addition, the "speech of the south" is not monolithic. There are two general speech areas, the southern coast and the inland south, which includes Appalachia, the south midland, and Texas; it is the accent of the coastal area that is now waning (see the afterword below).

In the twenties and thirties in the United States, national identity and ethnic purity were prime concerns; this is attested by the hysterical reactions to the massive immigration and the presence of immigrants in those decades. During this period, radio was acting to make Americans more aware of regional pronunciations and to standardize pronunciation as well. Thus a relationship begins to congeal here: nationalism, linguistic, cultural, and ethnic purism, radio, prescriptivism, and the standardization of pronunciation are all elements balanced in a large equation–an equation that revolves around the presence of the immigrant.

This period saw a waxing national consciousness of race and contamination as well as racial and rural purity. Since the dominant national consciousness has been determined by the northern states–at least since the end of the American Civil War–, there was only one way for that consciousness to proceed. It had to move in a westward direction, and it had to acquire the signs of that western movement. A signification system arose that opposed western migration to eastern immigration.

The rise of radio as a popular medium in the thirties saw an unprecedented rise in the number of articles on pronunciation in such journals as *The English Journal* and *School Review,* where there had been but a scant few in the twenties. The ideology of proper pronunciation congealed in the thirties and created and utilized three categories as strategic devices: 1) New England and New York, 2) southern, and 3) western, midwestern and general American. An article in *The English Journal* in 1933 entitled "Speech at the National Broadcasting Company" offers a telling and oversimplified summary of the "typical dialects of Yankee, Western, Southern, and foreign" (Sutton 1933: 457). The operative ideologies of the period constructed the substitution of *western* for *American* and bequeathed prestige status to the speech patterns of the west, especially the continuant /r/. These phonemes were thus invested with linguistic and cultural capital, emerged as accents of transparent power, and became signs of "proper" American ethnicity, class, and morality. It is necessary, however, to demonstrate the sources and chronologies of the different geographical pronunciations of /r/ before proceeding with further studies of the roles of race, religion, and ideology in the valorizing process.

3. The story of r

Noah Webster (1758–1843) was the most influential and prominent American philologist of his era and author of *An American Dictionary of the English Language* (1828), editions of which have been continually published ever since. He is not only a premier source of descriptive information on the English language in the United States in the late eighteenth and early nineteenth centuries, but also a mirror of the linguistic ideologies of that era, which are discussed in more detail in chapter two below. In *Dissertations on the English Language*, Webster says of the pronunciation of /r/:

> Some of the southern people, particularly in Virginia, almost omit the sound of *r* as in *ware, there*. In the best English pronunciation, the sound of *r* is much softer than in some of the neighboring languages, particularly the Irish and Spanish; and probably much softer than in the ancient Greek. But there seems to be no good reason for omitting the sound altogether; nor can the omission be defended on the ground, either of good practice or of rules. It seems to be a habit contracted by carelessness. (Webster 1789: 110)

Later, in *The American Spelling Book*, Webster says, "R has one sound only, as in barrel" (Webster 1831: 10). Webster's word choice here is quite judicious, as it isolates the sound between two vowels. In such an intervocalic position, it would be most likely to have rhotic value in all American speech areas. His differentiations from Irish, Spanish, and Greek would indicate that the sound as he hears it would be neither flapped nor trilled, but simply constricted. His characterization of the dropping of /r/ before consonants as the result of carelessness is among the first of such formal explanations. This incidental remark was destined to become an increasingly more frequent perception of the source and significance of dropped /r/ in the history of American pronunciation. It was the attribution of a sign of lassitude to dropped /r/ that was to contribute to its demise as an American prestige marker.

Webster's recommendations on the pronunciation of /r/, however, are not of great descriptive dependability, as has been noted by George P. Krapp in *The English Language in America:*

> /r/ was not heard finally and before consonants in the New England speech of Webster's day as universally as Webster's remarks in general would indicate. With the grammarian's reverence for the letter, Webster would certainly prescribe a /r/ wherever the spelling gave him the slightest warrant for hearing one. (Krapp 1925: 219)

Webster's observations on /r/, along with Krapp's observations on Webster, reflect the difficulties involved in trying to ascertain the phonetic value of a transcribed sound. We have the same orthographic symbol today but only an acoustic vestige of the earlier value of that symbol. This makes the historical reconstruction of an earlier kind of pronunciation a highly problematic endeavor, for speech, as in the case of any other natural occurrence, is highly sensitive to environmental changes. The presence of alien pronunciation within a given speech area can precipitate changes that are very difficult to determine and that make the process of linguistic reconstruction of an earlier accent very problematic. An example can be found in Robert Howren's "The Speech of Ocracoke, North Carolina." This is the first linguistic study of the speech of Ocracoke Island, which lies off the coast of North Carolina, south of Cape Hatteras. Isolated for centuries from the mainland, this island was, and still is, to some extent, believed to have preserved the speech patterns of the original Elizabethan settlers of the area. Howren's study shows, however, that the islanders themselves had started noticing changes in the local dialect already in 1910; this was due to the daily arrival of mail boats that had begun in 1900 (Howren 1962). More recent studies (Wolfram and Schilling-Estes 1997) have shown the diverse geographic origins of the island's initial population and thus finally laid to rest the myth of Elizabethan English on Ocracoke Island.

In spite of these uncertainties, one can make probable arguments for the earlier value and evolution of the phoneme /r/. Krapp provides an abundance of data to show the widespread occurrence of dropped /r/ in coastal New England. He lists some early rhymes in New England speech, such as learn:man, first:dust, nurse:us, and morning:dawning (Krapp 1925: 220) and also observes that "Webster, who never lost an opportunity to reprehend any trait of speech that had a British flavor, says nothing about the omission of /r/ as being characteristically British" (227). Krapp also observes that the loss of postvocalic /r/ is noted in British as well as American English at the same time, namely at the end of the eighteenth century, and characterizes this notation as "a coincidence in the critical record of historical development" (227). Krapp rightfully holds that the loss of postvocalic /r/ is a common derivation of southern British English, which can be attested: "The naive spellings, however, of early town records indicate a loss of *r* which must have been much more general than the mere numbers of spelling with *r* omitted might lead one to suppose" (228). Thus he finds seventeenth and early eighteenth century town records with the following misspellings: *fouth* for *fourth; clack* for *clerk, woned* for *warned, Bud* for *Bird, Passen* for *Parson, lebity* for *liberty,* etc. Interestingly, he also finds *Bostorn* for *Boston, Linkhorn* for *Lincoln* (which appears in the discussion of genealogy of Abraham Lincoln's family) *charmber* for *chamber, northen* for *nothing, methord* for *method,* etc. (228–229).

The orthographic omission of the postvocalic /r/ clearly indicates that it was dropped, and its insertion where it does not belong only serves to reinforce that indication. On the insertion of the non-etymological letter, Krapp concludes that the "*r* was silent and merely intended as a mechanical clue to the pronunciation of the vowel" (229). Thus postvocalic /r/ was not perceived as a separate phoneme in this speech area, and its presence after a vowel seems to have been perceived as an indication of the length of that vowel. Thus the pronunciations of *pot* and *part* in this speech area would be phonetically transcribed as /pat/ and /pa:t/; the letter *r* served only as a marker of vowel length. Krapp concludes that such a use of the letter *r* non-etymologically was "a custom which could have arisen only after *r* had established itself as a silent letter" (230). Also, in his *The Pronunciation of Standard English in America,* he says that "it is true that /r/ is regularly omitted by some speakers, especially in the East and South in America, when it is final or stands before another consonant, the difference between *taw* and *tore, pot* and *part,* so far as there is one with such speakers, being altogether a difference of vowel quality or length" (Krapp 1919: 22).

In the same work, he provides an early definition of the concept of standard American English and says that "standard may best be defined negatively, as the speech which is least likely to attract attention to itself as being peculiar to any class or locality" (ix). Subsequently, this definition came to be partly true. Standard was formed negatively in a gesture of avoidance of "peculiar" areas. It also embodied a phonetic non-offensiveness, but only by virtue of the fact that the sounds of some speech areas were prejudicially assigned offensive values. It was not, however, perceptually unlocatable in region or class; on the contrary, it was associated with and achieved its status via the valorizing of the midwestern and western regions.

Krapp provides what seems to be the most compelling answer to "the difficult question why *r*'s are pronounced in the Western or General type of pronunciation and not in the Eastern and Southern in America" (Krapp 1925: 230). The loss of postvocalic /r/ in the latter two areas is an aspect of "the cultivated speech of both regions inherited from the same type of speech as that which has produced London and southern British speech" (230–231). It is interesting to note that he characterizes the dropping of /r/ in those regions as still cultivated in 1925, a time period on the threshold of the standardizing influence of radio. Although postvocalic /r/ is not pronounced in seaboard speech, Krapp notes that "between the Connecticut and the Hudson a speech exists which is noticeably different from that of Eastern Massachusetts and the seaboard generally, and in this speech the pronunciation of *r* final and before consonants is a common feature" (231). Krapp does not observe that Noah Webster was native to this region, hailing from Hartford, and would have been motivated to prescribe the speech of that area. This may be the chief reason why Webster sees a fully sounded /r/ and a full correspondence between the orthography and pronunciation of the letter. This area provided the bulwark of immigration to the western states and brought with it the continuant /r/. In addition, the population of the western states included a lot of Irish, Scotch, and Northern English settlers, all of whom had fully active /r/ in all points of articulation.

Until the early modern period, the English language had both prevocalic and postvocalic continuant /r/. It was either constricted, trilled, or an alveolar flap that had the quality of a current British stage pronunciation of /r/ in *very*. In the article "Early Loss of /r/ Before Dentals," Archibald A. Hill finds that the loss of postvocalic /r/ before dental consonants had become systemic in some English dialects about 1300. He also notes some episodic or perhaps even anomalous instances from the eleventh century. During the early modern period, English began to drop the postvocalic /r/ in a very uneven fashion. Some speech areas retained the consonant, and others dropped it. During the nineteenth century, the dropping became systemic in England. The consonant was retained, however, in the outlying areas, e.g. Scotland and Ireland (A. Hill 1940).

English North America was colonized by speakers from different speech areas of England and the United Kingdom. Some of them had postvocalic /r/, and some did not. Thus there are some American speech areas where postvocalic /r/ is pronounced and some where it is not. It is generally dropped along the eastern seaboard from Maine through Georgia, excepting parts of the mid-Atlantic area. Some scholars hold that the non-rhotic /r/ arrived on the eastern seaboard along with the colonists to that area. Others argue that the colonists arrived with the consonant intact, and that the dropping was a nineteenth century import, a product of trade between the eastern seaboard and England. This study is skeptical of the latter explanation and demonstrates that there were periods of simultaneous colonization from British speech areas with and without postvocalic /r/.

Similarly, Hans Kurath, in "The Origin of the Dialectical Differences in Spoken American English" observes that "the dialectical differences in the pronunciation of educated Americans from various sections of the country have their origin largely in the British regional differences in the pronunciation of Standard English" (Kurath 1971a: 20). Kurath holds that the eastern seaboard was populated by settlers from southern England who had no postvocalic /r/. In the early eighteenth century, settlers from Scotland and Ireland populated western New England. After the French evacuation of North America in 1763, which was a result of their defeat in the French and Indian War, this population poured into Upstate New York and the Western Reserve of Ohio. The opening of the Erie Canal in 1825, also known as the New York State Barge Canal, facilitated the massive migration to the Great Lakes states and the upper midwest (see below). Thus the high phonetic affinity among the speech patterns found, for example, in Rochester, Cleveland, Chicago, and Madison, most notable in the raising of /æ/ to /i/ with an offglide, so that *bad* and *mad* come to sound rather like combinations of *be* and *add* and *me* and *add* respectively. It is also most notable in the nasalized /ã/ phoneme, as in /gãd/ and /hãt/ for *god* and *hot*. Later, Irish immigrants came to Eastern New England, beginning about 1849, and formed the bases for further western migrations. Thus the northern states supplied the bulk of the immigration to the west, and, for this reason, the pronunciation in the western states has remained largely that of western New England.

Also in the early eighteenth century, settlers from Scotland and Ireland populated the Piedmont of Virginia and the Carolinas and the Great Valley. These Scotch and Irish settlers and later immigrants had an alveolar /r/ in all points of articulation. This population migrated to the southwest, Kentucky, Tennessee, the southern halves of Ohio, Indiana, Illinois, and Missouri and established southern mountain or Appalachian speech in those areas. The retroflex /r/ became distinctive in those areas and resembles the current retroflex /r/ found in Irish English speech. It was also very audible in the diction of Lyndon Johnson. This particular articulation of /r/ is a salient and systemic feature of American country and western music and acts as a marker that differentiates that music from the closely related rock and roll. A good example can be found in the music of Garth Brooks, which is instrumentally almost indistinguishable from rock and roll, and which marks its difference in an almost exclusively phonetic manner. Here, the retroflex /r/ is a major indication of difference. A similar sound is also found in English Canadian speech and derives from the Scotch and Irish settlers of Upper Canada.

The mid-Atlantic states were also settled by speakers who pronounced postvocalic /r/. Among them were Scotch and Irish settlers, and there were numerous Germans, whose /r/ in the eighteenth century was most certainly pronounced with the tip of the tongue and either trilled or flapped. The widespread articulation of postvocalic /r/ surely aided in its adoption as the standard for radio pronunciation, but geographic distribution alone cannot account for the suppression of the speech patterns of the culturally and economically dominant metropolises of Boston and New York.

Charles Hall Grandgent, the Harvard professor of Romance languages and noted Dante scholar, published, in 1920, a thorough investigation of the American /r/. The publication was called "The dog's letter," and refers to a discussion in Shakespeare's *Romeo and Juliet* between the nurse and Romeo (Grandgent 1920). The nurse tells Romeo that Juliet has been making sentimental speculations about the initial letters in the names Romeo and rosemary and says:

Nurse.   Doth not
          rosemary and Romeo begin both with a letter?
Romeo.   Ay Nurse, what of that? Both with an R.
Nurse.   Ah, mocker, that's the dog's name. R is for
          the–No, I know it begins with some other letter–
          and she hath the prettiest sententious of it, of you
          and rosemary, that it would do you good to hear it.
                                        (Act II, Scene 3)

Many scholars, including Grandgent, have interpreted this as an indication that /r/ was then pronounced as a strong consonant and probably trilled apically, i.e. with the tip of the tongue.

Grandgent was a New Englander by birth and identified himself with the culture and letters of that region quite strongly. In this essay, he attempts to account for the weakening of the /r/ from a strong trill to a schwa: "to account for the passage from tongue-tip to uvula it has been suggested that in chilly climates the growth of polished society and the development of indoor conversation may naturally have led to the adoption of less strenuous habits of speech"

(Grandgent 1920: 38). Thus the transformation of /r/ into a semi-vowel and ultimately to a vowel is linked with a certain weakening process, a loss of vigor and vitality, although Grandgent represents it here in a highly hierarchic context as the speech of polite society. Thus the weakening of the sound is not connected to a loss of social, economic, and political power, but is, instead, a sign of that power.

Grandgent is not alone in his interpretation of the history of /r/. In *Language. Its Nature, Development and Origin,* Otto Jespersen says, "There is one change characteristic of many languages in which it seems as if women have played an important part even if they are not solely responsible for it: I refer to the weakening of the old fully trilled tongue-point *r"* (Jespersen 1923: 244). Jespersen sees this weakening as "a consequence of social life: the old loud trilled point sound is natural and justified when life is chiefly carried on out-of-doors, but indoor life prefers, on the whole, less noisy speech habits." The weakened /r/ is a result of "domestic life" and is seen "chiefly in the great cities and among the educated classes, while the rustic population in many countries keeps up the old sound with much greater conservatism" (244). He is referring here to the pronunciation of /r/ in Scotland, Ireland, and parts of North America. While Jespersen's observations on the regional distribution of /r/ are largely correct, his interpretation is nonetheless amusing. In order to agree with him, one would have to conclude that the Scots spend most of their time yelling outdoors, while Londoners occupy themselves with indoor whispers. The real reason for the persistence of the trilled and alveolar /r/ in non-metropolitan areas is due to the conservative nature of rural and colonial speech in general, as opposed to the progressive and innovative nature of urban speech.

Jespersen's curious explanation is, however, of twofold interest. First, this weakening process carries with it a submerged fascination with the sign of the rustic; second, it ascribes the sign of cultural degeneration in part to the presence of the feminine. Jespersen's discussion of the weakening of /r/ takes place in a contorted chapter entitled "The Woman," in which he observes that the stratification of classical Indic into the vulgar Prakrit, spoken by women and the lower castes, and the elevated Sanskrit, spoken by the priestly caste, is related to the fact that "Prakrit is a younger and worn-out form of

Sanskrit" (242). The equation of the weakening of /r/ and cultural feminization and degeneration is, although quite specious, nonetheless one of the main thematic motifs in the rise of network standard and the discussion of standard American pronunciation in the broadcast media, as will be shown in chapter two.

Grandgent's discourse on the loss of /r/ appears to be less ideological than Jespersen's. He observes that "normally, in our southern states, in New England, and in most of Old England, at the present time, *r* is sounded consonant-fashion only before a vowel and then only as a feeble murmur. We say fah, paht, but rat, try, very ... peppa becomes, in proper company, pepper and salt ... fatha's home, but mother isn't" (Grandgent 1920: 41). Here, Grandgent is recommending linking /r/ as an indication of proper, cultivated speech. He also observes that, in his time, the United States had no general standard, and, if there was to be one, it would be shared with Great Britain: "As far as we have any common standard, it is that of the high-comedy stage, which is based on the usage of Southern England" (48). It is important to note here, however, that Grandgent is not stating that the New England-New York speech area should imitate southern England; he is merely stating that, if there is any standard, it would be a shared one.

Of interest is Grandgent's assessment of the nature and status of the extra-coastal rhotic /r/:

> In a great part of the Unites States–a region, let us say, north of the Ohio and stretching from the Hudson to the Rockies–the retracting tendency is exaggerated and the tip of the tongue is curled up toward the middle of the root of the mouth, leaving a curiously shaped passage, which, though very wide, strikingly modifies the acoustic effect of the outgoing breath. A similar pronunciation may be heard in Kent. This strange sound, which seems to afford its utterers an inexplicable satisfaction, does not convey in the least the impression of an *r* to anyone accustomed to either variety of the trill; it suggests merely an obstructed formation of the preceding vowel. The Middle Western *par, court,* for example, impress the unpracticed ear rather as *pa, coat* spoken with one's mouth full. (36–37)

Here, Grandgent seeks to disqualify the western variant from the status of an /r/ per se and to classify it instead as a transformation of the preceding vowel. This is an interesting reaction, because it is precisely the New England postvocalic /r/ that is a modification of the preceding vowel, and a slight one at that, as it serves largely as a length marker. Also, the initial trilled /r/ would not have been used in the New England coastal speech of Grandgent's era either. One wonders indeed what the referent here really is. Even though he admits that this phoneme exists in the largest geographical area of the United States, Grandgent represents it as exotic, aberrant, and as an unpolished breach of elocutionary etiquette. On the other hand, he does admit that the weakening of the /r/ parallels a certain loss of vitality: "sturdiest of the consonants, it has partaken of the softening effects of civilization ... it has weakened and declined" (56). He sees the trilled /r/ as a primary phoneme that persisted "from prehistoric days to the eighteenth century" and was probably used by "Hercules, who strangled snakes in his cradle" (37). Even he must also admit that the /r/ of the midwest and west is connected to a retention of cultural vitality:

> America has, in the main, followed about the same paths as the parent lands; but our enterprising Middle West, unwilling to abandon the *r* tradition, has developed and cherished an *r*-substitute, homely, to be sure, but vigorous and aggressive. What has the future in store? Will decay pursue its course; or will a reaction set in, restoring to the English-speaking world a real *r* of some kind, or a tolerable substitute? (56)

Grandgent's voice is very significant, as he is speaking on the cusp of a major phonetic revolution in the United States. In 1920, radio had not yet begun its programmed broadcasting. Thus knowledge of pronunciation remained largely local, and impressions of the speech of other regions was not gained directly but spread largely by word of mouth. Grandgent can speak ingenuously at this point and assume that the dropped postvocalic /r/ is dominant in his time, as is indicated by his description "in the main," which could either refer to the majority of the population or to the superior status of that sound. Interestingly, in assuming an authoritative voice that describes history and lineage, he tends to disown the continuant /r/ as an adoption, a neologic and transitory surrogate that may serve to bridge the lacuna between the loss of the vital /r/ and its future reinstatement. Grandgent's words are indeed prophetic, as the /r/ of the west and midwest was to rise to become the (network) standard; the discourse of its ascent represented it in similar terms as a reinvigorating and revitalizing force that contravened the decaying force of the east. It is most interesting that Grandgent, in his elaborate descriptions of both non-rhotic and rhotic /r/, should elevate the former over the latter, while simultaneously representing it as decadent and unvital.

In 1926, the noted linguist John S. Kenyon published "Some notes on American r." His operative geographical categories for the variations on /r/ are simply "eastern" and "western" (Kenyon 1926: 329). He observes that "in South England, eastern New England, New York City, and the South, [r] is sounded in cultivated speech only before a vowel ... a great many Westerners suppose vaguely that the Bostonian drops all his *r's*" (Kenyon 1926: 333). It is interesting that Kenyon here does not note exceptions to the dropping of postvocalic /r/ in New York City and New England, where it is a marker of cultivated speech. This indicates that, in 1926, New Yorkers had not yet begun to problematize the pronunciation of /r/ as a marker of prestige. This is one very important aspect of Kenyon's observations: they would prove to be one of the last attestations of the unproblematized pervasiveness of dropped postvocalic /r/ in New York and New England.

Kenyon asks, "Why do Westerners pronounce all their *r's*?" and rightfully agrees with Krapp that "thousands of people from New England and the Southeast migrated across the Appalachians in the forty years preceding 1830, and formed the backbone of the present Western population. They brought their *r's* with them and bequeathed them to their descendants" (338).

Kenyon fields some of the other hypotheses about the presence of rhotic /r/ quite well, especially the question, "Was the use of /r/ only before a vowel once universal in America, and has the influence of the spelling-book, and the school-teacher been sufficient to restore the /r/ before consonants, except in New England and the South?" (338), to which he astutely replies that, if the /r/ had been "restored by educational influences, there would be sure to exist many little speech islands where they had not penetrated. But none such exist in the *r*-regions" (338). His theory about the forces that maintained the dropped /r/ on the eastern seaboard are, however, not as fortunate.

He holds that "at the close of the eighteenth century the commercial and social relations between the East coast and England were far closer than with the new West. The ocean was a highway, while the mountains and the miles of wilderness to the west were a barrier" (338). Kenyon is not alone in this proposition, as has been noted earlier. The problem is that the isogloss between retention and dropping of /r/, i.e. the linguistic border that separated the region that dropped the /r/ and the region that retained it, was not in the "new West;" it was only a few hundred miles inland from the east coast. Rhotic /r/ existed all over Upstate New York in the nineteenth century. To posit that there was more social and commercial intercourse at that time between New York and London than between Upstate and Downstate New York not only defies logic, but data as well. An important historical role of international significance was played by a long and narrow ditch: The Erie Barge Canal, which connected Buffalo on Lake Erie with Albany on the Hudson in 1825. Before the canal was built, goods from the west had to be shipped either overland or by boat up the St. Lawrence River, south of Labrador, around the Gaspé Peninsula, and then down along the east coast. The canal opened a waterway from the Great Lakes to New York City, and the resultant commerce contributed greatly to that city's rise to world prominence.

The importance of the Erie Barge Canal is well documented in Ronald E. Shaw's *Erie Water West: A History of the Erie Canal 1792–1854*. Its significance and promise were clearly indicated in the celebrations of the opening of the thoroughfare from Buffalo on Lake Erie to New York City on Wednesday, October 26, 1825. The *Seneca Chief* entered the canal at Buffalo carrying a retinue of New York State officials and two kegs of "the pure waters of Lake Erie" (Shaw 1966: 184). The embarkation was heralded by the "Grand Salute," which consisted in the firing of a thirty-two-pound cannon that triggered a volley of guns all along the perimeter of the waterway from Buffalo to New York City (184–5). The ship was followed by the *Noah's Ark,* which carried a collection of birds, fish, insects, two young bears, and two Seneca Indian boys (185). It arrived at New York Harbor at 7:00 a.m., Friday, November 4, welcomed by more than eighty ships (188). A keg of the Lake Erie water was carefully poured into the Atlantic Ocean, and a vial of the precious fluid was set aside for the Marquis de Lafayette by Governor Dewitt Clinton, the chief patron of the canal, after whom it was nicknamed "Clinton's Ditch." In addition to the waters of Lake Erie, vials of water from fifteen major world rivers, including the Rhine, the Ganges, and the Nile, were poured into the harbor (189). These were oddly ominous gestures that seem to portend the future of New York City as the premier metropolis of the United States as well as an international crossroads, a destination of a plethora of immigrants, and a locus of diversity.

The effect upon immigration to New York was staggering: in 1825, there were only 9,000 immigrants to the city, as the canal was open for only the last two months of that year. In 1830, the number rose to 30,000; in 1840, to nearly 63,000, in 1848, to nearly 192,000, and in 1852, to nearly 300,000. Altogether, 1.5 million people relocated to New York between 1820 and 1850, many of whom traveled by inland waterway (274). Even though one-third of these migrated beyond New York, they effected an augmentation in population that catapulted the city, already before the American Civil War, to the status of the largest metropolis in the western hemisphere. This migration also had major commercial correlates: in 1826, fourteen thousand bushels of wheat were shipped from the Lake Erie basin to New York City. That number increased to eight million bushels in 1840.

The voices of the era were clearly aware of the causes of the boom in New York population and commerce. In 1832, Samuel B. Ruggles commented, "The flourishing growth of this city must be attributed almost entirely to the Erie Canal" (283). An editorial from the *Albany Argus,* August 12, 1845 offers an appropriate summation:

> To what may this change be attributed? Is it not clearly to the influence of the western trade, which seems to be a mine of wealth and power and population beyond human calculation ... the settlement of Western New-York and Ohio forced the construction of the Erie Canal, which literally united the waters of the western seas with the Atlantic ocean. For only twenty years, the wealth of the teeming West has poured on down that avenue, and already it has placed New-York on an eminence as the Com-

mercial Emporium of America ... so long as New-York remains at the head
of the western trade ... it must irresistibly advance in wealth, influence and
population, until she will be known not only as the great city of America,
but as the *great city of the world.* (Shaw 1966: 283–284)

The population of New York rose from 125,000 in 1825 to 815,000
in 1847, an increase of six hundred percent (Voorsanger and Howat
2000: 4). Clearly, New York must have been exposed, in the nineteenth century, to a massive amount of influence from the western
regions, an influence that must have dwarfed anything resulting
from maritime commerce between New York and London. The
presence of the Erie Canal in the making of New York City is reflected in the recent publication *Art and the Empire City: New York,
1825–1861* (Voorsanger and Howat 2000), which was accompanied
by an exhibition of the same name at the Metropolitan Museum of
Art, held from September 19, 2000 to January 7, 2001. The title itself indicates the historical relationship: it is both the city as an empire in itself, as well as the city as the center of the American empire. The date 1861 indicates that a national unity, centered in New
York, was interrupted by the Civil War. The date 1825 indicates the
Erie Canal as the empire builder: the work opens with the following
words: "On October 26, 1825, the canal boat *Seneca Chief* left Buffalo ..." (3).

Between 1790 and 1820, New York and Brooklyn had added less
than 100,000 people to their stable population. Between 1820 and
1860, the first decades of Erie Canal commerce, they added close to
one million (Jackson 1985: 27). In the decades immediately following the opening of the canal, the New York area grew two to three
times as rapidly as Boston and Philadelphia (Jackson 1985: 316).
Clearly, New York would have been sufficiently exposed to the
postvocalic /r/, which apparently left no measurable impression
upon New York speech. Thus one must conclude that the dropped /r/
of New York City was not the result of British influence in the nineteenth century, but instead the result of the resistance of indigenous
pronunciation to external influences.

The most recent account of the rise of dropped postvocalic /r/ is
found in the very erudite study *Nineteenth-Century English* by Richard W. Bailey, who notes that this phenomenon

affected the prestige variety of southern England, but did not markedly influence English in Scotland or Ireland. Except for a few East Coast cities,
it did not reshape the language in North America either, though the other
varieties of world English share the preference of London. (Bailey 1996:
98–99)

Bailey describes this difference in national and regional terms and
thus prepares for the introduction of nationalistic issues into the bifurcation. He sees the consonant as initially trilled, as it still is in
Scotland. In England, the trill remained prevocalically but weakened
postvocalically and eventually turned into a schwa. This resulted in
a semantic separation; out of one word there arose two, one retain-
ing the /r/, and one dropping it, e.g.: burst, bust; curse, cuss; girl,
gal; horse, hoss (Bailey 1996: 99). The words cuss, gal, and hoss
still persist in less formal discourse. The dropping of /r/ was centralized in London, subsequently became systemic in England, for the
most part, and finally rose to become the preferred national received
pronunciation. In the nineteenth century, however, there was
considerable extra-metropolitan resistance to the more recent
fashion in London.

The anonymous but very influential author of *The Vulgarities of
Speech Corrected; with Elegant Expressions for Provincial and
Vulgar English, Scots, and Irish; for Those Who are Unacquainted
with Grammar* did not endorse this trend:

> [I]t may be remarked in this case that the natives of London leave out the
> "r" altogether in many words where it ought to be sounded, though but
> slightly. We thus hear them say *pul* for "pearl"; *wuld* for "world"; *ghell* or
> *gull* for "girl"; *mal* for "marl"; *cawnt* [sic] for "cant"; and *cawd* for "card."
> (256)

The Birmingham schoolmaster Thomas Wright Hill viewed the loss
of /r/ as a greater transgression:

> Indeed, the *r* of our language, when correctly formed, is among the most
> pleasant of articulate sounds, and ought more carefully to be preserved for
> posterity than can be hoped, if the provincialists of the Metropolis and their
> tasteless imitators be to be tolerated in such rhymes as *fawn* and *morn,
> straw* and *for, grass* and *farce,* &c., &c., to the end of the reader's pa-
> tience. (T. Hill 1860: 22)

Bailey observes that "resistance to the spreading London fashion was, however, not long sustained by Britain" (Bailey 1996: 102). This was, of course, due to the hegemonic power of the capital city. Bailey then returns to the initial observation with which he began the discussion of /r/, namely, that the loss of /r/ did not reshape the speech of North America. He asks, "Why did some regions of the English-speaking community *not* participate?" and speculates that

> the retention of old-fashioned *r*-ful speech in the western reaches of Eng-
> lish along the Atlantic basin arose from a cause identical to that operating
> in Britain. Irish, Scots, and inhabitants of England from the midlands
> northward all resisted the "tasteless" innovation of London and the exam-
> ple of epigones of London in such cities as Belfast, Liverpool, Boston,
> New York, and Charleston. (106)

Bailey holds that the retention of /r/ must have arisen and spread in chauvinistic contradistinction to the metropolitan pronunciation. He has here a potential perspective for observing the true motivator of this change in the United States, but does not have the necessary paradigm for doing so. His own paradigm is London-centered and sees the difference in the pronunciations, for instance, of New York City and Rochester, Boston and Pittsfield, and Charleston and Greenville as colonial reenactments of the British battle of /r/ waged between London and the rest of England "from the midlands north-ward." Here, Bailey's paradigm is stretched well beyond its limits and cannot cover the immense geographical area that he attempts to analyze. Clearly, London, Boston, New York, and Charleston have distinct pronunciations, even in the specific case of dropped postvo-calic /r/, the preceding vowels of which differ quite perceptibly in length, nasality, and point of articulation. Moreover, the notion that the genteel speech of Charleston could be mimetically related to the speech of New York and London would surely be received in Charleston proper as a most curious idea.

The issue of geographical distance also problematizes Bailey's explanation for the retention of /r/ in parts of England and the United Kingdom. While there are clearly nationalistic factors at work in the maintenance of distinct speech in Scotland and Ireland, and while the trilled Scotch and retroflex Irish /r/ are each inextrica-

bly bound to national self-image and identity, it is difficult to argue
that the preservation of these sounds was solely motivated by an act
of resistance to the perceived tastelessness of London. Communications in the nineteenth century could not have easily allowed a
wave-like spread of the London innovation to such peripheral areas.
Geographical distance probably played a role as well. It is also difficult to argue for a consciousness of ethnicity as a determining factor,
as the postvocalic /r/ was retained in southwestern England as well,
i.e. in Cornwall, Devon, Somerset, and Dorset, where there could
not have been a consciousness of ethnic difference vis-à-vis London.
The situation in the United States in the twentieth century was, however, quite different. The perception of ethnic difference became
most marked during the period of massive immigration to the northeastern metropolises, which came to be seen as racially different
from the rest of the country. This caused a bifurcation in national
consciousness that became marked by differences in speech. Moreover, twentieth-century communications would have facilitated the
perception of these significant differences in ethnicity and pronunciation in the United States.

It is interesting to note that, while Joseph and Bailey come close
to seeing the real motivating factors in the evolution of standard
American pronunciation, neither one discusses the necessary mode
of application to the situation of American English. Joseph knows
that the cases of Icelandic and Senegalese Wolof, in which rural
speech was taken as the standard, were produced by a consciousness
of ethnicity and purism that viewed the urban center as a source of
foreign pollution of the native language. Yet, Joseph does not make
the analogic transfer to the case of American English. Bailey offers
an oppositional model of the provincial versus the metropolitan,
both in the United States and the United Kingdom, but he ascribes
the difference to one of fashion and taste and leaves the function of
ethnicity out of the American theater altogether. It seems that Lesley
Milroy (1999) and Rosina Lippi-Green (1997) are the only scholars
who, albeit in very general terms, see the determining function of
race and ethnicity for the American standardization process.

As already stated, both the description and prescription of the
pronunciation of /r/ remained largely local and tended to generalize

based upon the regional custom until the advent of regular radio broadcasts. Non-rhotic /r/ is observed and recommended on the east coast, while rhotic /r/ is preferred in the central states. There are, of course, exceptions to this general pattern, the earliest being the prescriptions of Noah Webster. There is also William Russell's *Lessons in Enunciation, Comprising a Statement of Common Errors in Articulation, and the Rules for Correct Usage in Pronouncing; with a Course of Elementary Exercises in these Branches of Elocution,* published in Boston in 1830. Oddly, Russell argues against dropping the postvocalic /r/, but offers no justification for this exclusion. This is an opinion quite uncharacteristic of the Boston elocutionists of the time.

On the whole, however, local usage tends to be seen as normative. Lewis Sherman's *A Handbook of Pronunciation,* published in Milwaukee in 1885, views continuant /r/ as more customary and dropped /r/ as somewhat exceptional. He notes that "some polite people in some parts of New England suppress the sound of *r*, pronouncing farther as though it were written fahthah" (14). Eugene H. Babbitt's *The English Pronunciation of the Lower Classes in New York and Vicinity,* which Babbitt published in 1896 while teaching at Columbia, notes the currency of non-rhotic /r/ in the speech of New York City: "In general, *r* after vowels is completely silent" (6). Robert Paltry Utter, an English professor at Amherst College, published *Every-Day Pronunciation* in 1918. He seems here to be advocating pronunciation largely based on his local custom. Of postvocalic /r/, he says, "It is practically silent in England and in our Atlantic States. In other parts of the country, it is a subject of controversy, but most careful speakers make it more or less obscure." (19).

Richard Soule and William Wheeler, in *Manual of Pronunciation and Spelling*, writing from the east coast in 1874, prefer "the sound of *r* in *nor, short* (called *untrilled r* or *smooth r*), this sound, which occurs only after a vowel in the same syllable, is much softer than that of initial *r*" (28). The Chicago elocutionist Arthur E. Phillips, in *Natural Drills in Expression,* writing in 1920, says that /r/ in rear, roar, row, oar, and urn are "sometimes incorrectly sounded like a in farther and like aw in awl" (99). Also, he recommends, "Utter in pairs decisively, the mind intent upon the distinction: car, caw; mar, maw; farther, father; leer, Leah; carve, calve; bore, boa" (99). In 1912, Irvah L. Winter, of Harvard University, says, in *Public Speaking, Principles and Practice*, "Among localisms the letter 'r' causes frequent comment. In singing and dramatic speaking, this letter is best formed at the tip of the tongue, In common speech it may be made by only a very slight movement at the back of the tongue" (18–19).

In 1926, Samuel Arthur King published *Graduated Exercises in Articulation* in Philadelphia. In the preface, he complains of slovenly articulation in America and quotes Henry James, for whom such pronunciation was also bothersome. He says that we have allowed our speech "to pick up a living, in fine, by the wayside and the ditch" (vii). He recommends that people should be just as careful with their speech as they are with their dress, and engages in several sartorial metaphors: He advocates "graceful, clear-cut articulation" and says that "it is just as essential to please the ear as the eye" (viii). Interestingly, he eschews both the dropped /r/ and the overarticulated /r/:

> Many tendencies point to the gradual elimination of the soft R in speech. In Southern English it is now omitted entirely ... A barbarous exaggeration in the form of a harsh grating sound resembling a "morose grinding of the back teeth," sometimes made by speakers in certain sections that shall be nameless, cannot be indorsed on the grounds of expedience nor of beauty. This unmusical sound, probably a softening of the Northumbrian "burr" or rough Scotch R, may be characterized as an importation that has not been sufficiently examined at the custom-house; the sooner turned out, the better for the euphony of the language. Another curious aberration from correct standards, owing to the lack of attention to the subject of articulation, is the prevalence of *y* sound for the soft R; e.g., the eayly boyd catches the wuym. (14–15)

The "soft R" is most likely meant to indicate the /r/ heard in the inland northern region, as the southern retroflex /r/ and the dropped /r/ of the coastal areas would have been unacceptable to him. He does not want to hear it, however, in its overarticulated form; it thus becomes "a barbarous exaggeration" that betrays the lack of sophistication and restraint of the speakers, who do not even merit naming here. They are mentionable only in an allusive form. By remaining thus unidentified, they are denied any status at all and are fully marginalized in their "morose grinding of the back teeth," which is also a quote from Henry James (see section 2.4. below). His transcriptions of "boyd" and the like sounds indicate New York City speech. It is interesting to see here the allusion to immigration and also the suggestion, perhaps a bit, but not entirely ironic, that pronunciation could be ameliorated by some sort of border vigilance. The speaker and the pronunciation are both objectified as "importations" that exist as if they were items in a custom house. In King's view, such aberrant pronunciations should not even be allowed in the country.

Improving Your Speech. A Pupil's Practice Book in Speech Training was published in New York in 1934 by Letitia Raubincheck, who was Director of Speech Improvement for New York City Public Schools, and is an interesting late example of a careful attempt to standardize New York City speech, i.e. to create a standard based upon the cultivated speech of New York. This is interesting not only for its recommendations, but also for its omissions. There is no mention at all made of the low vowel [a]. For Raubincheck, the New York and coastal New England [ɑ] is "the lowest back vowel," of which she says, "This is the sound your doctor asks you to make when he wants to look down your throat" (112). She advocates non-rhotic postvocalic /r/ in all environments and makes no mention of intrusive /r/, as in "sawr" [sɔːɹ] for "saw." She actually uses the legendary string "park your car," with elision of the final /r/, as a pronunciation exercise (112). She also recommends [ɒ] in "hot coffee," and "soft spot" (110). She advocates the phoneme [ɜ], with no r-coloring at all, for "first worm" and "worse and worse" (98). She endorses backing the vowel in "ask, dance, laugh" ([ɐ]), so as to differentiate it from [æ] in "bat, had, lamb" (94). She also tends to ameliorate some idiosyncratic regional pronunciations by referring them to their cultivated variants, among them the infamous example of "third" pronounced as if it were "toyd." She claims that [ɜ] is mispronounced "among careless speakers in New York City" (132) as [ʌɪ] in third, thirst, thirty, and that "oil" is mispronounced as [ɜːl], so that it would rhyme with "girl" (134).

Most of these early descriptions of regional differences tend to acknowledge and respect local custom. In 1928, William P. Sanford, of the University of Illinois, and Willard H. Yeager, of George Washington University, published *Principles of Effective Speaking,* in which they seem to diplomatically balance the pronunciations of their respective regions: "Whether one conforms to the usage of New England or of the Middle West in the sounding of *a* and *r* is relatively less important than correctness in the pronunciation of words for which the accepted standard is the same everywhere" (265). Arthur G. Kennedy, in *Current English,* published in 1935, says that "consonantal *r* is a distinguishing feature of Western American pronunciation, whereas in England, as also in New England and the American South, the *r* is vocalized" (157). Thorleif Larsen, in *Pronunciation. A Practical Guide to American Standards* (1931), isolates coastal speech patterns: "In English Received Pronunciation and in New England and Southern American speech the letter *r* is usually mute unless it is followed by a vowel sound in the same or in the following word" (3); he then advocates these over inland ones: "Many would say that English Received Pronunciation, with which New England speech may be loosely grouped, is the more beautiful. It may at least be said that this speech form has certain advantages over General American" (14). Barret H. Clark's *Speak the Speech. Reflections on Good English and the Reformers,* published in Seattle in 1930, displays ambiguous reactions to the contemporary standardization movements. He expresses his bewilderment at the supra-regional standard English of the stage, especially the "World English" movement. He argues against a standard but then curiously claims that an educated coastal New England speech, which he does not describe (12–13), might be a candidate for the standard, while also supporting the "Mid-Western R" (30). William N. Brigance and Ray K. Immel, in *Speechmaking. Principles and Practice* (1938), offer a descriptive approach to dropped or undropped /r/ and say that both are acceptable (135).

Even in the late thirties, the idea of a standard American English had not yet been located in a specific region, and a sort of linguistic relativism in the field of pronunciation prevailed. Alfred H. Holt, in *You Don't Say! A Guide to Pronunciation,* published in New York in 1937, makes no specific recommendations for the pronunciation of /r/ and says, "The East and the South have long objected to the harsh *r* of the West and Middle West. Both sides are compromising" (xiv). This would indicate that the coastal and western regions were equipotent in the status of their respective pronunciations of postvocalic /r/ and stood in a kind of stalemate. But the social, political, and economic power of the coastal regions, however, did not alone suffice to combat the mounting prejudices against them. While not recommending one or the other pronunciation, Holt does say that if one drops the /r/ in *word*, "it slips easily into 'woid.' This is the *origin* of the famous 'toity-toid street' dialect of New York. A curious development of recent years in New York has been to give words like *oil* and *joint* the 'er' stolen from *bird* and *hurt*. When adjourn and adjoin become practically indistinguishable, or go so far as to change places, teachers in the affected areas must go into decisive action" (xiv). While at first seeming to be dispassionate and relativistic, he seems finally to be judgmental against the speech of New York. Holt does rightly observe, however, where the real transformational power of the era lay: "We must recognize that radio and travel are fast making the American people talk alike" (ix).

In 1944, the New York State Department of Education formed a committee to decide on standards of pronunciation to be taught in the public schools (C. K. Thomas 1945). The committee was comprised of over a dozen national language experts, who decided that the pupils should all become acquainted with the three types of American pronunciation: "Eastern, Southern, and General American."

Wilke and Snyder, who investigated perceptions of American regional pronunciations in 1942, also published *Effective Pronunciation: A Phonetic Analysis of American Speech* in 1940. Extrapolating from work done in the late thirties, they predicted that "General American" would win out over "Eastern" and "Southern" by virtue of population numbers alone (60). This seems, however, to be based upon Kenyon's overestimation of the number of speakers of "general American."

Thus the pronunciation of postvocalic /r/ before the advent of radio was largely local and seems not to have been subject to cross-regional imitation to any significant degree. Generally, the differences in the pronunciations of /r/ have their sources in original regional differences in Great Britain itself. In reality, standard British English does not have a parental, but instead a sibling relationship to American English. The international migration of English, especially before the nineteenth century, consisted largely in decentered and disorganized voyages of diaspora, each with its own speech characteristics, which left a network of mutually intelligible heteroglossia. The migration of the American continuant postvocalic /r/ from the western states eastward, its supplanting of the dropped postvocalic /r/ of the east coast, and its rise to standardization began in the twenties and was precipitated by the axis of radio, anti-immigration, and westward nostalgia.

This chapter has attempted to account for the etiology and distribution of rhotic and non-rhotic /r/ in the United States. The remainder of this study is more interpretive and largely concerned with the ideological values of the phoneme in question. The mapping and distribution of rhotic and non-rhotic /r/ can be seen as a litmus test that indicates the social complexion of a given speaker as well as a given speech area. It is a phonetic commodity whose level of usage gauges the level of empowerment or disempowerment of the discourse at hand. As a thematic thread, it unifies the subsequent chapters, which illustrate the ideological values involved in the distribution of /r/ and in its respective prescriptive receptions. In chapter two below, section three describes the relationship of the phoneme to issues of morality and class in the nineteenth and early twentieth centuries. Section four studies the discourse of morality, class, and race in the specific pronunciation prescriptions of Henry James as reflective of some ideologies of the late nineteenth and early twentieth centuries. Section five concentrates on the value of /r/ as a marker of race and gender in the early twentieth century and includes a discussion of its association with the speech of black Americans. (Issues of the black American non-rhotic /r/ and its relationship to the speech of whites are also discussed in the afterword.) Section six discusses the impact of H. L. Mencken's misprisions of the standardization of postvocalic /r/ and his Anglophobic ideology. Section seven shows the persistence of race and gender consciousness in the adaptation of rhotic /r/ for broadcast speech. In chapter three, section two shows the value of rhotic /r/ for the ideologies of the American west, and section three investigates the dropped /r/ of New York City and its subjection to ethnically based prejudices.

4. Heartland rules

The debate on standard American English forms a central point in the research on the speech of the region believed to be the locus of the common standard, and even the proper geographic designation of this area is problematic: midwest, upper midwest, north central, Great Lakes, and inland northern are but some of the terms used. Recent scholarship tends toward usage of the term inland northern, which was acronymed SWINE by Raven McDavid for Standard White Inland Northern English, a characterization that may reflect that scholar's reactions to his difficulties as a southern speaker residing in Ann Arbor, Michigan and Ithaca, New York. The inland northern region extends from Lake Champlain westward to Minnesota and includes most of Upstate New York, Ohio's Western Reserve, and all the major industrial cities along the southern shores of the Great Lakes: Syracuse, Rochester, Buffalo, Erie, Cleveland, Toledo, Detroit, Chicago, Milwaukee, and Minneapolis.

A recent major work on the subject is the anthology by Timothy C. Frazer, *"Heartland" English: Variation and Transition in the American Midwest.* In his introduction, "Problems in Midwest English: introduction and overview," Frazer begins with the following observation: "If the term *General American* is heard less these days, the related belief that the Midwestern United States speaks with a single voice–a single, uniform 'Midwestern' form of English– remains current. Linguists, unfortunately, often seem no better informed than the general public" (Frazer 1993: 1). Frazer makes this observation in reference to the work of Fromkin and Rodman (1983) and Trudgill and Hannah (1982). The latter speak of midwest English in their book *International English,* but, according to Frazer, "the dialect they represent as Midwestern is really Inland Northern, a dialect with a very restricted geography in the Midwest, where it predominates only in Michigan, Wisconsin, and Minnesota, in northern Illinois, Indiana, Ohio, and Iowa, and in enclaves elsewhere" (2).

Frazer's observations are a very good indication of the nature of the misperception of "midwestern" American English. There is a metonymic process at work here that allows a subset of a region to substitute or stand for the region as a whole. While this occurs even in some linguistic studies, it is most characteristic of the misperceptions within the popular sphere. Frazer observes that "anecdotal evidence locates 'Standard English' in an imagined homogeneous Midwest as well" (2). The appropriate phrase "imagined homogeneous Midwest" rings true not only in the linguistic, but also in the ethnic sense as well. The area was perceived as a vast reserve of northern European consanguinuity. It is perhaps this notion of proper ethnicity (itself an imagined construct) that underlies Frazer's characterization of the perception of the speech of this area in the popular consciousness as "something safely sanitized, a measure against which everything else is deviant" (3).

In the first study in Frazer's anthology, "Two heartland perceptions of language variety," Dennis R. Preston, the pioneer of perceptual dialectology, identifies the essential dynamic that determines Standard United States English (SUSE):

> Research puts the weight of describing SUSE precisely where it belongs–in the minds, out of the mouths, and from the word processors of nonlinguists. Of course, linguists (presumably sociolinguists, dialectologists, and ethnographers) will need to do the collection and interpretation, but there should be no confusing of their own feelings with their reports on and interpretations of the opinions of the respondents who count. (Preston 1993: 29)

This is precisely the point: it is the popular construction of linguistic identity that determines the standard. The problem is that detailed linguistic analysis of the actuality of pronunciation almost always shows that the idea of homogeneous speech is erroneous. The illusion of homogeneity is largely a function of a secondary revision that glosses over differences and constructs a linear metanarrative, an overgeneralization that suppresses difference and unites the percepts in a structure of wish-fulfillment; i.e. there is something in the popular consciousness that desires to see a unity of geography, ethnicity, and language.

It is, however, the persistence of the linguist's analysis–the same analysis that Preston qualifies–that hinders the understanding of the construction of the necessary myth. This is evident in the following passages from Preston:

> Regionalisms which are glaringly nonstandard ... continue to remind linguists and nonlinguists alike that the promised leveling of variation which was to have resulted from universal opportunities in education and from the mass-media influence of film, television, and radio did not occur. (23)

> The single standard which the mass media were to evince turned out to be another fiction. Movies, radio, and television exposed an even greater diversity of regional types and allowed further solidifying of stereotypes and caricatures. The supposed single standard of newscasters is bogus, as three major networks in the United States demonstrate. The anchorman for CBS is Dan Rather (South Midland); for NBC, Tom Brokaw (North Midland); and for ABC, Peter Jennings (Canadian). (24)

It would be helpful to rethink these statements from the perspective of the linguistically naïve viewer/listener. Rather, Brokaw, and Jennings all approximate a type of speech that is perceived by the vast majority of television viewers as pleasant, inoffensive, proper, i.e. standard. While it is certainly true that they have vestigial vowel pronunciations that betray their respective regional origins, these regionalisms are largely suppressed and not at all obvious to the average viewer. This is especially clear in Jennings's efforts to downplay the Canadian centralizing of the /aw/ diphthong, such as, for example, in the characteristically Canadian pronunciation of *about* and *house*. None of the television networks has a major anchorperson whose speech is glaringly regional. No anchorperson sounds like Jimmy Cagney, Lyndon Johnson, John F. Kennedy, or the Second City Television's parody of Canadian "Great White North" speech. Regionalisms are suppressed, and when they are suppressed, it is always in one direction: in favor of a pronunciation that approximates the mythic white speech of the linguistic area misnamed and misperceived as the "midwest."

Consonant with his view of widespread difference, Preston holds:

A commonplace in United States linguistics is that every region supports
its own standard variety; that is, no one region is the locus (or source) of
the standard. Historically, that is a fair assessment; no center of culture,
economy, and government such as Paris or London ever dominated. (24)

This is problematic, as the New York-Boston region, which shared
similar speech characteristics, did indeed dominate, especially in
terms of economy and culture; other forces, however, prevented that
area from attaining any form of linguistic domination.

In the body of his study, Preston surveyed the residents of two
regions of the United States about their conceptions of "correct" and
"pleasant" English. The two regions were southern Indiana and
southeastern Michigan. The regions were well chosen, as they
would, in the popular consciousness, both be miscategorized as
"midwest." Southeastern Michigan was settled by migrants from
Upstate New York and northern Ohio, who would have preserved
the original speech characteristics of western New England. Respondents from this area saw themselves as speaking correctly (32).
Southern Indiana, however, was populated by migration from Kentucky northward and preserved the southern mountain speech characteristics of the south midland region. Respondents from this area
were less confident of the status of their own speech and displayed
what Labov called *linguistic insecurity* (Labov 1966). The respondents from both regions associated the speech of the south and of
New York City with incorrect English, and both regions also placed
New York City at the lower end of the pleasantness scale (35).

Both the respondents from Michigan and the respondents from
Indiana made a broad distinction between northern and southern
speech and generally placed the correct speech in the northern states
and the incorrect speech in the southern states. While both groups of
respondents rated midwest (inland northern) speech very highly,
they also tended to rate western speech very highly as well. In Preston's factor analysis of correctness and pleasantness ratings, the
speech of the western states was seen as having a high degree of uniformity. The lines of demarcation tended to proceed from Wisconsin
and Illinois westward, cutting around the borders of Missouri, Okla-

homa, and New Mexico, and thus excluding the south in toto. Most interestingly, both groups located highly correct speech in Washington State. Indiana residents perceived it as the most correct type of speech, while Michigan respondents rated their own speech most highly with that of Washington State not far behind.

It is important to emphasize that the subjects interviewed did not limit the range of inland northern speech to the inland northern area, but tended instead to generalize it to a larger western geographic area. It should come as no surprise that the popular perception organizes speech characteristics in such a way. Take for instance the extra-southern perception of "southern" speech. In this case, very different pronunciations are relegated to a large geographical area because of the social, cultural, and ethnic perception of that area. This occurs in spite of the fact that the linguistic evidence points toward geographical and even cultural difference. A similar argument may be made for the perception of uniformity in "western" or "midwestern" speech. The lines that form the isoglosses of inland northern speech dissolve and flow into a large and loosely demarcated area in the popular perceptions of linguistic cultural geography.

In the appropriately titled recent article "The names of US English: valley girl, cowboy, Yankee, normal, nasal and ignorant," Hartley and Preston investigate further the folkish attitudes toward accents, both proper and improper. They found that respondents in Oregon rated the speech of their own state and of that of Washington State as the most correct in the United States. These subjects also rated the speech of the south, New York, and Massachusetts as incorrect. They also rated New York and Massachusetts, along with the south, the lowest on a scale of pleasantness (Hartley and Preston 1999: 212). Respondents from Indiana perceived the speech of the entire west and midwest as similar to their own speech patterns. They also perceived the patterns of the entire south and east coast from Maine to Georgia as most different from their own way of speaking. Florida, however, was seen as an exception and was classified as similar. The same results were produced by Michigan respondents, with the exception that they also saw the speech of Pennsylvania as different (217).

These results indicate the alien status of coastal and southern speech patterns as seen from the folkish viewpoint of western and midwestern speech, which clearly share common features. The fact that Florida is excepted from these generalizations reflects the popular notion that the population of Florida is largely comprised of people who are not native to that state. It is odd that Indiana residents should see southern speech as different from their own, however, as the southern half of Indiana is comprised largely of southern mountain speakers.

The authors offer the following summation:

> The qualitative labels support, then, our claim that incorrectness and salience go hand in hand in the perception of US English varieties and that the South and the Northeast (as represented by NYC, NY and NJ) are the leading recipients of these classifications. Those familiar with the gross caricatures of US regions will not need to be told of the popular culture support for these views. Although "everyone knows better," the following (at least) are common. Gangsters and crooks, immigrants (who speak poor English) and other ethnic minorities, hoodlums and street people live in NYC (and, by association, in NY and NJ). A disproportionately large African-American population along with redneck, barefoot, poorly educated, intermarried, moonshiner KKK members reside in the South. (233)

Thus the impressions reported to Hartley and Preston confirm the urban legend: New York is associated with crime, undesirable ethnicity and immigration, and unappealing accents. Also, the south is stigmatized by associations with the presence of blacks as well as Appalachian whites. It is important, as well to note the grouping together of Massachusetts and New York in the Oregon survey. This reveals the perception of similarity in the accents of Boston and New York, which, as has been described earlier, share many common salient features, the most important of which being the dropped /r/ and back vowel /ɑ/, as in the pronunciation of "rather."

In the related study by Hartley, "A view from the west: perceptions of U.S. dialects by Oregon residents" (Hartley 1999), the author found that Oregonians perceive New York City, New York State, and New Jersey to be one monolithic and undesirable dialect area and consider it to be as alien to them as southern speech. Most respondents used the survey choice "people there sound so different from me I can't understand them" to describe the south, New York State, New York City, and New Jersey. The fact that there is no perceived difference between the speech of the state of New York and the city of New York is very interesting. As has been already indicated, the speech of New York State is not only a type of, but also the source of inland northern speech, which is markedly different from northern coastal speech patterns, and which shares many features with the speech of Oregon. Indeed, many residents of New York State who travel to the south, west, and midwest are often told that they do not sound like they are from New York at all. The overgeneralizations present in the Oregon survey show that the prejudices against the speech, behavior, and ethnicity of New York City are so strong that states of New York and New Jersey have been brought to suffer from them as well. This is an example of the metonymic process that Milroy characterizes as "guilt by association" (L. Milroy 1999: 175).

In her recent work *English with an Accent: Language, Ideology, and Discrimination in the United States,* Rosina Lippi-Green studies the work of Preston and others and offers the following characterization of "the standard language myth," or the ideology of standard US English as held by non-linguists:

> Standard US English is the language spoken and written by persons
> –with no regional accent;
> –who reside in the midwest, far west, or perhaps some parts of the northeast (but never in the south);
> –with more than average or superior education;
> –who are themselves educators or broadcasters;
> –who pay attention to speech, and are not sloppy in terms of pronunciation or grammar;
> –who are easily understood by all;
> –who enter into a consensus of other individuals like themselves about what is proper in language. (Lippi-Green 1997: 58)

While Lippi-Green's study is focused on the mechanisms of language subordination and discrimination, especially as they apply to minorities, her outline helps illustrate the connections among geography (here largely a midwestern/western location), class, and broadcast speech.

Other studies in Frazer's anthology attempt to explore the socio-cultural and ideological causes for the rise of inland northern speech. They are Thomas S. Donahue, "On Inland Northern and the factors for dialect spread and shift," and the more ambitious undertaking by Frazer himself, "The language of Yankee cultural imperialism: pioneer ideology and 'General American.'"

Donahue begins by broaching the issue of an official language in the United States and discusses the "particular American paradox in which governmental regulation is despised, but secular authority and various 'self-help' sources are viewed as informal, yet binding, social legislation" (Donahue 1993: 50). This paradox provided some of the circumstances necessary for a rise of the speech area in question to a de facto standard: "Americans in several regions are coming to accept the idea that the structural character of Inland Northern is 'basic' and 'correct'" (50). Although "Inland Northern began as a geographical and regional dialect … it has gradually become known as the 'General American' dialect" (51).

Donahue considers the salient characteristics of inland northern to be clear diphthongs in /ay/ and /aw/, as in *hide* and *house,* articulation of postvocalic /r/, and a merger of the /a/ and the /ɔ/ phonemes, so that the vowel in *hot* is similar to the first vowel in *father.* These sounds spread due to the powerful descriptions, if not prescriptions, of *Webster's Second International Dictionary* under the guidance of John Kenyon, and also of Bender's *NBC Handbook of Pronunciation,* which was based on *Webster's Second.*

It should be emphasized that there are other very salient features of inland northern that are not included by Donahue, nor by Kenyon, nor by Bender. These would most certainly include the raising of the low front vowel /æ/, as in *bad,* which is pronounced so as to sound like a combination of *be* and *add.* They would also include the nasalized vowel /ã/ in e.g. *hot,* and most certainly the centralizing of the diphthong /ay/ before voiceless sounds and before /r/, as in *write, bite, rice, fire, wire, desire,* etc. Clearly, we are dealing here with a selection of speech characteristics of the inland northern area. While Kenyon endeavored to describe the cultivated speech of the Ohio Western Reserve, it seems unlikely that the allophones described above would not have been pronounced by the cultivated speakers of that area in the twenties. Moreover, these allophones are general characteristics of inland northern or Great Lakes speech from Upstate New York to Minnesota. It should also be emphasized that these allophones tend to wane as one approaches the western plains states and the northwest. While this type of speech is represented as inland northern, its characteristics seem to correspond to the pronunciation patterns of the western and northwestern states as well.

John Kenyon clearly was, as Donahue says, one of the major influences on the standardization of American pronunciation. His seminal work was *American Pronunciation,* which first appeared in 1924. Kenyon taught at Hiram College in Ohio's Western Reserve and was the pronunciation editor of the second edition of *Webster's New International Dictionary of the English Language* (1934), where he says that the "open o" was disappearing and the "whole country" was preferring low central /a/. In the preface to *American Pronunciation,* Kenyon refers to himself in saying, "the author has based his observations on the cultivated pronunciation of his own locality–the Western Reserve of Ohio. It is his belief, however, that this is fairly representative of what will here be called the speech of the North" (vi). Kenyon, however, really prefers and uses the term "General American."

Clearly, common sense would indicate that the recommendations of a liberal arts college professor in Ohio would not be sufficient to propel the speech of a single area to the status of a national standard. There must have been larger cultural and social factors at work here, and it is these factors that Donahue tries to isolate. He sees the "growth of industrialization around the Great Lakes in post-Civil War America" as the nuclear motivating force and says, "Inland Northern was carried to many other areas of the country with the basic social and economic influence of the growing wealth of the industrial Great Lakes region providing a motivating class, political, and cultural force behind it" (52). The number of regional speakers swelled as "Inland Northern became the dialect model for generations of eastern and southern European immigrants who came to the Great Lakes cities for jobs in the plants and mills during this era" (53).

Donahue seeks to locate the energy for the propulsion of this dialect to national status within the economy of the region itself, most notably in the influence of the itinerant managerial class. He invokes the larger sociological observations that "the professional, semi-professional, and business-elite classes prove to be more mobile geographically than any others," and that "migrant professionals ordinarily tend to be more successful than the average" (53). In addition, the "members of this group tend to be influential in the communities to which they move" (53).

Donahue proceeds from the work of Warner and Abegglen (1955) on the mobility of the business elite in America between 1928 and 1952. He sees the fact that about 11% of the national business elite consisted of migratory inland northern speakers, i.e. those who left the inland northern region, and concludes that "the mobility of the managerial elite is a basic cause of the spread of Inland Northern" (53). Thus cultivated speakers migrated out of the region and brought their dialect with them. He also sees Kenyon as indispensable in this alliance of management and language: "Kenyon was thus establishing as a de facto standard the cultivated speech found near him in Ohio's Western Reserve, and of course the speech of the managerial class in Cleveland as well: Inland Northern" (55)

One might be tempted to describe this as the managerial conquest of proto-General American speakers, as it seems to resemble the model for the spread of Indo-European, which is viewed, in some circles, to have been due to the power and influence of the conquering migrants. In the case of the rise of inland northern, it would seem probable that forces external to that region helped boost its status, and that it could not have risen to power without some form of major external sponsorship.

Donahue concludes that "SWINE [is a] Gesellschaft dialect which has spread through the influence of the industrial economy, the mobility of the managerial class, and the impact of mass entertainment media on the American populace" (57). While the characterization of inland northern as a Gesellschaft dialect is well taken, and the attribution of its spread to the influence of mass media and entertainment well observed, it must be emphasized that the national discourses of the industrial, media, and entertainment economies adopted the regional dialect for reasons that were largely external to the region itself.

The attempt to locate the causality for the spread of inland northern within the region itself leaves the realm of economy and escalates to religious, moral, and social proportions in Frazer's study "The language of Yankee cultural imperialism: pioneer ideology and 'general American.'" Frazer begins by rightly observing that "the Inland Northern dialect, through a consensus of educators, scholars, and media people, seems to have emerged as a de facto standard without any government action" (Frazer 1993: 59). Referring to Kenyon, Krapp, Kurath, and Bender, Frazer asks, "Why was the enthusiasm for 'General American' so out of proportion to the facts? Scholars greatly exaggerated the geographical delimitations of Inland Northern, and Kenyon wildly overestimated the number of 'General American speakers'" (60).

Frazer sees the causal factors as lying within a fundamentally puritan psychology: "The original Puritan theocracy of New England is widely remembered for the religious sanction it gave to intolerance and expansionism" (60). He also seems to be operating within the model discussed above that resembles the structure of the original Indo-European conquests: "The original Puritans saw themselves as conquerors, the conquest two centuries later of the Great Lakes area and the West beyond ... took place in the same spirit" (61).

Frazer also holds that the success of the "Inland Northern Yankees," was due to "their economic and social organization" (63). While the southerners who migrated to the west remained in rural communities and left behind "a loose social structure of rural neighborhoods based on kinship ... Yankees often moved entire congregations or even communities" and "tended to gravitate to the towns and cities rather than to the countryside" after the settlements had been established (63). Also, they "disproportionately gravitated to the professions and non-farm occupations" and became "the elite of frontier society" (64–65). He concludes thusly: "It is not hard to understand how a group who promoted their own culture and values so aggressively should have succeeded as well in promoting their own dialect of English as normative" (65).

While Frazer's description of the "victory" of the inland northern speech area in its rise to a de facto standard is indeed viable, the ascribing of causality in this process is more problematic. It assumes that the ethnic and cultural aggressiveness of the inland northern population itself created sufficient leverage so as to tilt the plane of language standardization in its direction. It almost seems as if Frazer wants to argue that the inland northern population was so persistent that it convinced the rest of the country to talk like they did. He does however, pose one last question: "It remains to explain how scholars in this century could have been sufficiently mesmerized by the Yankee mystique that they so exaggerated the Yankee dialect's territory and the number of its speakers" (65). In saying this, he seems to imply that the causal forces may have also to do with the reception and perception of the dialect in question by speakers external to that region.

In essence, the inland northern dialect became a desired linguistic commodity. We know that successful commodification is not always the result of the persuasiveness of the producer of the commodity, i.e. of the entrepreneurial skills of those who are marketing it. The success is often the result of the fashionable popularity of the commodity itself, which is determined by forces external to the producer. A viable example of this can be taken from the popularity of organic foods in the United States in the last quarter of the twentieth century. This was the result of a shift in taste within the upper bourgeoisie, a result of their economic and cultural power, and not a result of the economic and cultural power of organic food farmers. A similar argument can be made for the ascension of "midwestern" speech to the de facto norm; i.e. that it was the result of the currency of that linguistic commodity within the dominant areas that determine cultural capital. And the dominant cultural forces were certainly not those of "the managerial class in Cleveland" (Donahue 1993: 55).

During the decades that determined the direction and location of the desired pronunciation, national cultural and political power remained centered in the northeastern United States. It was the population of that region that chose to valorize the "midwestern" pronunciation as the norm. The problem with the approaches of Frazer and

Donahue is that they are unilaterally gravitational and magnetic. They see the national linguistic standard as gravitating toward the inland northern region because of the cultural, religious, and economic factors within that region. In other words, the region itself exerted a kind of magnetic attraction or pull upon other areas of the country. This model does not allow for antigravitational forces, that is, for the possibility that national consciousness was being repelled by factors in the northeast and south, and that it was this negative power that precipitated the movement toward the west.

In the introduction to the recent *Handbook of Perceptual Dialectology,* Preston offers an apology for the cause of perceptual dialectology: "There may be interaction as well as simply contrast between folk belief (and practice) on the one hand and scientific or specialist knowledge on the other. Folk medicines have been found in the laboratory to be extremely effective" (Preston 1999: xvii). He also emphasizes the fact that folklore and ethnography are viable subjects of social science inquiry. While Preston is clearly correct in noting the factors of contrast as well as interaction, it is precisely the interactive potentialities that must be emphasized here, for the basic argument of this study is that folk linguistic beliefs determined the national standard, and that it is imperative to study the social factors and catalysts thereof. Preston points in this direction when he says, "I believe that future work in the perception of variety might focus more specifically on the exact linguistic elements that give rise to perception" and exhorts scholarship to study "the triggering mechanisms of language regard among the folk and through such study the potential influence of such regard on the more general process of variation and change" (xxxviii). It is the task of this inquiry to illuminate the larger cultural factors that informed the folkish linguistic beliefs in question, for it was ultimately those cultural factors that precipitated the rise of standard American.

Chapter 2
Pronunciations of race

As stated in the introduction, it is the purpose of this study to illustrate a historical continuum in the United States that situates pronunciation and elocution within a perceptual differential of race and class. In order to properly demonstrate this, it is necessary to map out the general ideological terrain that encompasses the concerns of proper pronunciation. Such an investigation will, of necessity, depart from the realm of the purely linguistic, but it will ultimately return to illustrate how even the most ostensibly innocuous prescriptions on pronunciation often resonate against the backdrop of a perception of race and class. Some of the historical figures studied here were philologists and some were not, but they all acted as significant agents of folk linguistics, representative subjects in the perceptual dialectology of their respective eras.

1. Saxons and swarthy Swedes: race and alterity in Benjamin Franklin

One of the earliest examples of the emerging consciousness of race and language in America can be found in the papers of Benjamin Franklin (1706–1790). One of the "founding fathers" of the United States, Franklin was an extremely influential figure in American politics, history, and mythology. A self-educated publisher, journalist, inventor, statesman, and signer of the Declaration of Independence, Franklin's image is iconic with the popular ideologies of the origins of the United States. His writings on race and language are both symptomatic and influential: they represented as well as shaped the ideas of his era.

Writing within the colonial period, Franklin makes little or no mention of Americans as distinct from the English either ethnically, socially, or linguistically. Thus the anxiety of influence vis-à-vis the English that is characteristic of Webster or Mencken is not yet present. Franklin ascribes an English and Anglo-Saxon identity–both linguistic and cultural–to America and perceives a threatening alterity within the colonies themselves, a danger that is located in the presence of Germans and blacks. He was disquieted by the large numbers of German immigrants in Pennsylvania and also by the mere presence of blacks in the colonies, both of free and slave status.

In the letter to James Parker of March 20, 1751, Franklin complains of "the Importation of Germans in too great Numbers into Pennsylvania" (Franklin 1961: 120) and concludes that

> this will in a few Years become a German Colony: Instead of their Learning our Language, we must learn their's [sic] or live as in a foreign Country. Already the English begin to quit particular Neighborhoods surrounded by Dutch, being made uneasy by the Disagreeableness of dissonant Manners; and in Time, Numbers will probably quit the Province for the same Reason. Besides, the Dutch under-live, and are thereby enabled to under-work and under-sell the English. (120)

The appellations *Dutch* and *German* were coterminous in the eighteenth century. Germans are represented here first of all as a linguistic threat: they will remain monolingual, but the English will have to become bilingual. In the traditional dyad of dominance and subjugation, it is usually the subjugate class that is diglossic and the class in power that has the luxury of being understood in its own language. Franklin's representation of the Germans in this way assigns a position of possible dominance to them, one that threatens the integrity of the English language. In addition, there is another threat in the presence of inferior comportment, one that is to be avoided in an act of eighteenth century "white" flight to "safer" neighborhoods. Finally, this presence is seen as a source of economic destabilization: the other will appropriate the economic power of the English.

This threat to economic power is also visible in the letter to Peter Collinson of May 9, 1753, in which Franklin says that German immigrant laborers "retain the habitual Industry and Frugality they bring with them, and now receiving higher wages an accumulation arises that makes them all rich" (Franklin 1961: 479). (This is oddly reminiscent of the American attitudes toward Jews that were to emerge a century and a half later.) Franklin's prejudices against Germans are of necessity problematic and paradoxical for him, as they force him to make a distinction based on a consciousness of ethnicity that is ultimately schizoid. He is faced with the dilemma that this ethnic perception necessitates seeing a permutation of self as other: "When I consider, that the English are the Offspring of Germans, that the Climate they live in is much of the same Temperature; when I can see nothing in Nature that should create this Difference, I am apt to suspect it must arise from Institution" (479). Franklin then enters into a discussion of German structures of labor and economy as determinants of social behavior. The most important aspect of this gambit is that it finds a way to preserve a perception of consanguinity *a priori* and introduce a notion of behavioral difference *a posteriori*. Thus the German is represented as both self and other. This theme of Nordic consanguinity will continue on in the American discourse of race and language, from the ideas of Noah Webster to the antisemitism of the early twentieth century, and the presence of immigrants of greater difference, e.g. from Ireland and southern and eastern Europe, along with the escalating migration of southern American blacks, will act to reinforce this notion of Nordic consanguinity. The immigrants from northern Europe will no longer be seen as different, and the areas that they settle will be invested with notions of proper ethnicity, pronunciation, and comportment.

Because of this perception of consanguinity, Franklin can propose a mixing of German and English populations; this will eliminate the social difference and pose no threat of contamination: "Yet I am not for refusing entirely to admit them into our Colonies: all that seems to be necessary is to distribute them more equally, mix them with the English ... I am not against the admission of Germans in general, for they have their Virtues, their industry and frugality is exemplary; they are excellent husbandmen and contribute greatly to the improvement of a Country" (485).

Perhaps the most telling of Franklin's statements on affinity, difference, and ethnicity can be found in the "Observations Concerning the Increase of Mankind," which offers a very early example of the invention of racial and ethnic categories in order to justify gestures of segregation and exclusion. These categories are also invented in relation to language:

> Why should the Palatine Boors be suffered to swarm into our Settlements, and by herding together establish their Language and Manners to the Exclusion of ours? Why should Pennsylvania, founded by the English, become a colony of *Aliens,* who will shortly be so numerous as to Germanize us instead of our Anglifying them, and will never adopt our Language or Customs, any more than they can acquire our Complexion ... which leads me to one Remark: That the Number of purely white People in the World is proportionably very small. All Africa is black or tawny. Asia chiefly tawny. America (exclusive of the new Comers) wholly so. And in Europe, the Spaniards, Italians, French, Russians, and Swedes, are generally of what we call a swarthy Complexion; as are the Germans also, the Saxons only excepted, who with the English, make the principal Body of White People on the Face of the Earth. I could wish their Numbers were increased. (Franklin 1961: 234)

It is interesting to note that Franklin moves directly from language to complexion; the presence of the other will diminish both the language and the race of the dominant group. It is as if he had concepts of lightness and darkness *a priori* that he subsequently applies to populations that he wishes to include and marginalize respectively. The fact that he should see both Italians and Swedes as swarthy is not primarily a function of an objective perception; this would be difficult to justify empirically. It is rather one of organization and classification. Franklin's initial desire to marginalize the other, i.e. the non-English, creates a context that determines the visual observation, and that functions in the manner of a figure-ground perception.

One of the classic figure-ground problems is that of the image that can be seen either as a vase or two opposing faces, depending on the expectations of the viewer. Such is the case here; Franklin's observation of similarity in complexion is determined by the fact that all of those different peoples have a common utility for him as other. It is their status as other that elicits the visual reaction. This reaction then acts as a danger that unifies the constituents of that class in an associative narrative thread that proceeds improbably from Germans to Swedes to blacks. Of interest here is Franklin's surgical removal of the Saxons from his chain of associations. This reflects another instance of the solution to the problem mentioned above of a schizoid conception of the Germans, one that entails seeing self as other. Splitting the Saxons off from the rest of the Germans solves the problem by doubling the other into one group that is included and one that is rejected. Thus there are Germans who are related to Anglo-Saxons and Germans who are foreign.

It is also interesting to see how this is expressed in the metaphors common to the ideology of enlightenment in the eighteenth century. Franklin continues:

> And while we are, as I may call it, *Scouring* our Planet, by clearing America of Woods, and so making this Side of our Globe reflect a brighter Light to the Eyes of Inhabitants in Mars or Venus, why should we in the Sight of Superior Beings, darken its People? Why increase the Sons of Africa, by Planting them in America, where we have so fair an Opportunity, by excluding all Blacks and Tawneys, of increasing the lovely White and Red? But perhaps I am partial to the Complexion of my Country, for such Kind of Partiality is natural to Mankind. (Franklin 1961: 234)

This reflects the valorization of light characteristic of the eighteenth century enlightenment ideology. European colonization is making things brighter in an act of progress; in order to make room for civilization, there is a clearing of the woods, which is also a *clearing up* or enlightening. The white race is scouring the planet, brightening it to please superior beings, a statement that also has clear religious undertones that serve to justify Franklin's implicit recommendation, which is to restrict immigration so as to exclude all of the ethnic groups above perceived as other. This grand design is also rationalized by presenting it as a kind of obligation. It is as if the white race were on a mission to blanche the globe of difference.

Franklin's oddly subjective utterances are generated by the fact that he sees the mere presence of the other as threatening to the white population. In the letter to Richard Jackson of 11 February 1764, he says: "The Duty on Negroes I could wish large enough to obstruct their Importation, as they everywhere prevent the Increase of Whites" (Franklin 1967: 76). This statement, which is clearly statistically and demographically unjustifiable, reveals the paranoia that underlies Franklin's associations and categorizations.

It is most interesting to note that Franklin's ethnic slurs are almost exclusively directed against Germans and blacks, but not at all against the French, even during the period of the French and Indian War, when France was an enemy of Britain. In his papers, he makes numerous references to developments in the war and to the various victories of the French and British, but none of these references contains a disparaging statement on French ethnicity. This is especially surprising, since France was the real enemy of the time. Franklin's papers of that period, such as the letter to Mary Stevenson of September 14, 1767, attest only to the politeness and civility of the French (Franklin 1967: 250–255). The fact that they had no palpable presence in his quotidian realm exempted them from the attacks that he leveled against the Germans, with whose presence in Pennsylvania he was regularly confronted. Franklin also lived in Paris from 1776–1785 as the American commissioner to France.

Thus one sees in the writings of Franklin a very early example of the interplay of language and race in the discourse of immigration to America. A matrix that is at once linguistic and ethnic configures the other, who then presents a threat to the integrity of the language, ethnicity, behavior, and power–especially economic–of the dominant class. This is a threat that evokes a call for the limitation of immigration even before the formation of the United States.

The interconnection of language and race is also present to a lesser extent in the ideas of Thomas Jefferson, who employed the category of race rather gratuitously in his discussions of elocution. In the recent book *Jefferson, Natural Language, and the Culture of Performance,* Jay Fliegelman discusses the status of oratory in the eighteenth century. He holds that "the oratorical revolution had its own deeply racist dimension, especially because of its roots in physiognomy" (Fliegelman 1993: 192) and observes that "Jefferson argues for black inferiority in aesthetic terms" (192). In *Notes on the State of Virginia,* Jefferson says:

> The first difference that strikes us is of color–a difference fixed in nature ...
> and is this difference of no importance? Is it not the foundation of a greater
> or less share of beauty in the two races? Are not the fine mixtures of red

and white, the expressions of every passion by greater or less suffusions of color in the one, preferable to that eternal monotony, which reigns in the countenances, that immovable veil of black which covers all the emotions of the other race? (Jefferson 1972: 138)

Fliegelman offers the following comments on these ideas of Jefferson: "In contrast to the infinitely responsive interaction of white and red pigments ... the 'veil of black' permits no visible register of emotions, and hence no emotional communication ... blacks, in their blackness, violate the aesthetics of variety. Significantly, that variety is the touchstone of Jeffersonian liberalism" (Fliegelman 1993: 192–193).

These ideas of Jefferson are interesting, in that they contravene the prejudicial assessments of the behavior of blacks found in the nineteenth and twentieth centuries. Indeed, they reverse the common stereotypes of white and black behavior, which normally assign reservedness and understatement to whites, especially the English, and animation and overexpressivity to blacks. Jefferson, however, writing within the storm and stress ideas of his epoch, which valorize the expression of passion and emotion, is motivated to use these ideas in a differential and ultimately hierarchical fashion in order to elevate whites above blacks. This reversal of stereotypes is significant, in that it shows how the dominant class will be represented as possessing the proper modes of elocution and language, even if those modes become reversed.

2. From Noah to Noah: Webster's ideology of American race and language

Benjamin Franklin's words on the English language were written during the colonial period, before the birth of the United States as a separate country from Great Britain. The first major philologist to write as an American, however, was Noah Webster, and his ideas on the American language as distinct from British English contain the first instances of the conflation of language, ethnicity, and religion in the United States, a conflation that was to persist into the twentieth century.

In the preface to the 1828 edition of *An American Dictionary of the English Language,* Noah Webster couches the emergence of the American language in a complex of religion, culture, and politics: "The United States commenced their existence under circumstances wholly novel and unexampled in the history of nations. They commenced with civilization, with learning, with science, with constitutions of free government, and with that best gift of God to man, the Christian religion" (Webster 1828: iii). Webster sees an American essence that is always already Christian, and that is articulated through the medium of language as grace or divine gift. He says, in the following introduction to the dictionary, "It is therefore probable that *language* as well as the faculty of speech, was the *immediate gift of God*" (v). As the American language clearly originated in England, and as England's population was originally a mixture of Celtic and Teutonic, Webster is motivated to trace an origin for the American language through Celtic and Teutonic developments back to an original biblical point (see Bynack 1984).

He begins the narrative of language at the moment when God graced Adam with the faculty of speech. Then, Noah the philologist moves the narrative back to the separation of the three sons of Noah: Shem, Ham, and Japheth (v). He sees Europeans as the descendants of Japheth who migrated after the linguistic dispersion at Babel and "peopled the northern part of Asia, and all Europe" (vi). Their presence in Europe expressed itself in the linguistic primacy of the Teutonic and Celtic language families:

> The vernacular words in the Celtic and Teutonic languages of Modern Europe, which are evidently the same words as still exist in the Shemitic languages, are of the same antiquity; being a part of the common language which was used on the plain of Shinar, before the dispersion. (vi)

This primacy of Teutonic and Celtic, the function of which is to indicate England and English by implication, must be configured by Webster so as to appear foundational in the context of western civilization. The presence of Celtic is, however, but an unavoidable necessity mandated by the Celtic migration to Britain, which predates the Anglo-Saxon migrations. What Webster really seeks to foreground is the Germanic race. He says of ancient Greece and Rome:

> It is very evident that tribes of the Teutonic and Gothic races invaded those
> countries before they were civilized, and intermingled with the original in-
> habitants ... this is an inference which I draw from the affinities of the
> Greek and Latin languages with those of Teutonic origin. (vi)

Webster's speculations are but early forms of the waxing ideology of Germanic supremacy in the nineteenth century that sought to prove that a northern European essence was at the root of the dominant civilizations of Europe, Persia, and India. Webster believes in a profoundly Germanic infrastructure in the English language. He holds

> that the peculiar structure of our language is Saxon, and that its principles
> can be discovered only in its Teutonic original, it has been my business, as
> far as the materials in my possession would permit, to compare the English
> with the other branches of the same stock, particularly the German and the
> Danish. (38)

There is at work in Webster's ideology of language a notion of the essentially noble Teuton, a common man of more rural orientation, who is in possession of the language in itself and whose ownership must be discursively protected:

> It has been remarked that the common people, descendants of the Saxons,
> use principally words derived from the native language of their ancestors,
> with few derivatives from the foreign tongues, for which they have no oc-
> casion. This fact suggests the impropriety of writing sermons, or other dis-
> courses designed for general use, in the elevated English stile. To adapt a
> stile to common capacities, the language should consist, as much as possi-
> ble, of Saxon words ... (62).

Webster consistently seeks to situate English at a more primal and higher point than other European languages and cultures. It is a profound notion of anteriority, conservation, and purity that informs his philology, and that places American English in an antecedent status to the current state of English in Great Britain. Thus he says, in the preface, "The genuine English idiom is as well preserved by the unmired English of this country as it is by the best *English* writers" (ii).

The same ideology informs Webster's 1789 *Dissertations on the English Language,* in which he says:

> As an independent nation, our honor requires us to have a system of our own, in language as well as government. Great Britain, whose children we are, and whose language we speak, should no longer be *our* standard; for the taste of her writers is already corrupted, and her language on the decline. But if it were not so, she is at too great a distance to be our model, and to instruct us in the principles of our own tongue. (Webster 1789: 20)

Thus British English is in a state of decline, and Webster warns against linguistic association with the decadent and neologic Great Britain. He laments the presence of British expressions in American English that were "almost unknown in America till the commencement of the late war" (126). For Webster, the British invasion of North America was as much a linguistic danger as a political one and threatened the conservative authenticity of American English:

> Hence the surprising similarity between the idioms of the New England people and those of Chaucer, Shakespeare, Congreve, &c. who wrote in the true English stile. It is remarked by a certain author, that the inhabitants of islands best preserve their native tongue. New England has been in the situation of an island; during 160 years, the people except in a few commercial towns, have not been exposed to any of the causes which effect great change in language and manners. (108)

Webster's ideology of language sees systemic consistency and regularity in American English and manneristic deviation in British English, which is subject to "the caprice of fashion" (129) and "easily led astray by novelty" (130). In his idiom, the term analogy designates linguistic consistency, especially in the regular correspondence between pronunciation and morphology: "In many instances the Americans still adhere to the analogies of the language, where the English have infringed them. So far therefore as the regularity of construction is concerned, we ought to retain our own practice and be our own standards" (129).

Webster's ideology of American English sees the language as fundamentally Christian and Teutonic. It is purer and more authentic than other forms of English and, along with them, can trace its roots back to the Old Testament, before the confusion at Babel, all the way to the sons of Noah. It is the representative flower of the race that populated Europe and founded western civilization. It will be shown in this study that Webster's fundamental ideology persists into the twentieth century and forms the nucleus of debate on the standard American pronunciation. This debate consistently revolves around the American language as an expression of Teutonic supremacy and splits into various views on exactly which Americans are the best examples of this Teutonic essence and where they are located.

The chronological parameters in Webster's metanarrative proceed from Noah to Noah Webster, from the postdiluvian to the discourse of American independence. There was, however, a second deluge in the twentieth century that precipitated a psychic exodus to racial and linguistic high and dry ground. This study tells the story of that exodus.

3. Class and race in the nineteenth century

An ideological shift occurred in the discourse of pronunciation in the nineteenth century. The pivotal point in question is the onset of immigration to the eastern seaboard, and the ideological underpinnings of the works on pronunciation can be divided into two main groups: those of the antebellum period and those of the last decades of the century. A distinct anxiety of class and morality can be seen in the pronouncing manuals of the antebellum era, which progressively gives way to a nascent anxiety of race as the century draws to a close.

3.1. Sounding moral in the antebellum interlude

While the racial ideologies of Noah Webster laid the foundation for subsequent race-based understandings of American pronunciation, a racial-ideological linguistic continuum or tradition did not evolve until late in the nineteenth century. Indeed, Webster's theories re-

main largely anomalous for most of that century, and it was not until
the last decades that prescriptive statements on language began to be
articulated in the discourse of race. The end of the American Civil
War generated migration and mobility for American blacks, and, in
turn, a reconfiguration of their increased presence within white
American culture. A new anxiety of influence appeared that was no
longer simply an Oedipal reaction against the influence of British
culture upon the United States, as was the case with the ideas of
Webster. This new anxiety of influence became more complex as it
began to include a certain internal xenophobia, a profound perception and fear of alterity within American culture itself. And this idiom of anxiety also became articulated in a corporeal fashion, as one
of contamination, invasion, and corruption.

Until the end of the nineteenth century, and with the noted exception of the ideas of Thomas Jefferson, Benjamin Franklin, and Noah
Webster, the discourse of pronunciation and elocution in the United
States was often expressed in religious and moral terms and also
contained a certain consciousness of class. It is interesting to note
the class elements at work here, as one has been inclined, in the
main, to broadly differentiate the American and British discourses of
pronunciation along the lines of race consciousness and class consciousness respectively. The examples from the nineteenth century,
however, tend to problematize this distinction. There was certainly a
presence of class consciousness in the early works on pronunciation,
although class stratification was not structured in the United States
in the same way as it was structured in the United Kingdom. In the
United States, the consciousness of class was divided both between
the middle and lower classes, as well as within the middle class
among the subclasses of upper-middle, middle, and lower-middle
classes. In the United Kingdom, the division was clearly tripartite
during the nineteenth century among the upper, middle, and lower
classes. The early British works on pronunciation, however, themselves show little consciousness of class.

The most influential of the early English pronouncing dictionaries was John Walker's *A Critical Pronouncing Dictionary and Expositor of the English Language,* published in London in 1791 and
reprinted numerous times during the nineteenth century. It served as

the point of reference for many subsequent British and American pronunciation manuals. Walker's work is structured by the scholarly ideologies of the eighteenth century and may be seen to apply the enlightenment interest in regularity and systematicity to the configuration of language. Operating from a standpoint that eschews change, Walker holds that pronunciation is not as intrinsically fluid as it is believed to be: "The fluctuation of our language, with respect to its pronunciation, seems to have been greatly exaggerated. Except in a very few single words ... the pronunciation of the language is probably in the same state it was in a century ago; and had the same attention been then paid to it as now, it is not likely even that change would have happened" (Walker 1791: vi). Walker seeks to construct a non-dynamic ideal of language, in which the mutability of language is no given, and linguistic permissiveness has no place. Incorrect pronunciation and inconsistent pronunciation are practically coterminous for him, and the chief causes of error are "deviations from analogy" (vii).

Walker's idea of analogy is fairly straightforward: one should be able to predict the pronunciation of a given phoneme based on its environment, and one should be consistent in doing so, a few odd exceptions notwithstanding. Deviations should be then "corrected" out by comparison with the paradigm. Walker sees the logical principle of analogy as both the nature and the guardian of language: "If the analogies of the language were better understood ... many words, which are fixed by custom to an improper pronunciation, would by degrees grow regular and analogical" (vi). Here, Walker seems to be unaware that many "improper pronunciations" were themselves the product of a systemic leveling process that was regularizing in nature. For Walker, it is a certain "proper" pronunciation that needs to supply the governing paradigm. He sees analogy as a natural regulatory mechanism that needs to be maintained, and that will ultimately normalize and standardize the language. He wants to regularize pronunciation based on analogies; this will provide the language with "a fitness in one mode of speaking, which will give a firmness and security to our pronunciation, from a confidence that it is founded on reason" (vii). Here, pronunciation is a scientific construct that is also configured within enlightenment notions of democracy. In cases of disagreement on pronunciation, a tripartite consensus is to be arrived at by the court, the schools, and "a certain number of the general masses of speakers" (viii). This applies notions of proportional and representative government to the subject of language, and it does so in a mathematical manner: "The usage, which ought to direct us is ... a sort of compound ratio of all three" (vii).

One of the first calls for a standardization of pronunciation in the United States was made by Thomas Payson in his *Address delivered before the Associated Instructors of Boston and Its Vicinity, on their anniversary, Oct. 10, 1816.* Payson seems to share the nationalist feelings of Webster in saying, "It is a fact concluded by many of their [English] literary travelers through the United States, that, the English Language is, generally, spoken here with more correctness than in England; with the exception of foreigners resident among us" (Payson 1816: 26). He continues with the following recommendation: "Let there be a delegation chosen from all the universities, colleges, and publick schools of our country, to convene in some central situation. Let these delegates, when assembled, fix upon some one pronouncing dictionary" (28). Aside from these nationalist assertions, there is little ideology to be found in his exhortation.

The earliest examples of an ideological basis in the proscriptions on pronunciation in America are to be found in the manuals of pronunciation and elocution of the nineteenth century. These early American manuals tend to justify their projects by reference to the inculcation of morality and religion at the primary levels of education. The prescriptions do not claim a discrete or esoteric value for exercises in pronunciation, but instead buttress those exercises through the image of moral edification. Abner Alden's *The Reader,* published in Boston in 1802, teaches elocution and pronunciation through moralizing tales and psalms. Ralph Harrison's *Rudiments of English Grammar,* published in Philadelphia in 1804, uses excerpts from the gospels as pronunciation exercises. The anonymous and undated *New Pennsylvania Primer: being an approved selection of words, the most easy of pronunciation, adapted to the capacities of young children,* published in Harrisburg in the early nineteenth century, begins with a warning to pupils not to let learning lead to vanity and ends with a recitation of the Lord's Prayer. John Peirce's *The*

New, American Spelling Book, published in Philadelphia in 1808, is an interesting example, in that it has pronunciation tables that include accents and syllabification grouped according to similar sounds. The tables, however, are interspersed with Christian moralizing tales, biblical parables, and prayers, but these religious items have no particular organization, nor any visible connection to the linguistic materials being discussed and practiced. Thus the mere juxtaposition of pronunciation with moral instruction and advice against sinful behavior is, in itself, a transparent justification for the instruction of that pronunciation. This is a process that resembles somewhat the twentieth century techniques of advertising, which regularly juxtapose a marketed item with a desired phenomenon and create a perceptual liaison between the two, even though they may be categorically distinct.

Burgess Allison's *The American Standard of Orthography and Pronunciation, and Improved Dictionary of the English Language,* published in Burlington in 1815, presents pronunciation exercises in a context of morality as well as social level. The purpose of the undertaking is "to guard against every thing that might have a tendency to convey an impure idea, or to corrupt the morals" (Allison 1815: iii) and "to exclude every low or indelicate expression" (iv). A similar intent is visible in William Douglas's *A Key to Pronunciation, in which is shown the true pronunciation of a large number of English words as also, the erroneous manner in which they are most frequently pronounced by the illiterate.* Published in Philadelphia in 1809, this is a work in which the "true" pronunciation of the literate class is set off against the influence of the illiterate. B. D. Emerson's *The National Spelling Book and Pronouncing Tutor,* published in Boston in 1828, states that its purpose is to teach one "to pronounce the language with propriety" (Emerson 1828: 5) and uses as a vehicle tales of proper conduct, readings from the bible, and laudations of the supreme being.

Pronunciation is, in these early works, often connected to notions of good and evil. William Russell's *Lessons in Enunciation, Comprising a Statement of Common Errors in Articulation, and the Rules for Correct Usage in Pronouncing; with a Course of Elementary Exercises in these Branches of Elocution,* published in Boston in 1830, states that "the worst defects in reading and speaking ... extend through all classes of society ... [and] are all owing to the want of *a distinct and correct pronunciation"* (Russell 1830: iii). It decries "the degradation of the English language from its native force and dignity of utterance to a low and slovenly negligence of style, by which it is rendered unfit for the best offices of speech" (iii). Russell sees his work as "a means of remedying such evils" (iii). David B. Tower's *The Gradual Reader,* published in New York in 1851, also teaches pronunciation by using moralizing tales as a vehicle.

Often, the elongated title alone conveys the ideological bent of the work, as is evident in Seth T. Hurd's *A Grammatical Corrector; or, Vocabulary of the Common Errors of Speech: being a collection of nearly two thousand barbarisms, cant phrases, colloquialisms, quaint expressions, provincialisms, false pronunciations, perversions, misapplication of terms, and other kindred errors of the English language, peculiar to the different states of the union.* Published in Philadelphia in 1848, the work informs standardization with notions of proper deportment, refinement, and manners, and sets it off, in violent terms, against locutions of the lower and uneducated classes. For instance, the use of "dreadful" as an adverb is dismissed as "a gross perversion ... peculiar to New England and New York" (Hurd 1848: 32). Of the idiom "to let on," with the meaning of "convey" or "mention," as in "I never let on that I heard him" (53), it is said, "This horrid barbarism is heard chiefly in Pennsylvania and the southern part of Ohio, where, strange to say, it has obtained to a considerable extent even among the educated and polite" (53). Of the use of "then" as an adjective, as in "the then governor," it is said, "This is a most barbarous error" (119).

Alfred Ayers's *The Orthoepist,* published in New York in 1880, can also be viewed in the same vein. Elocution and pronunciation are represented as if barometers of social station: "The manner in which one speaks his mother tongue is looked upon as shoeing more clearly than any other one thing what his culture is, and what his associations are and have been ... it is the surest criterion by which to judge a stranger's social status, etc." (Ayers 1880: 1–2). They are also configured in a process of purification and moral edification.

Ayers sees his book as "a work tending to season the minds of children with piety and virtue, and to improve them in reading, language and sentiment" (vi). This indicates a kind of communion of language and morality, which is also visible in his statement of intent: "to imbue the tender mind with the love of virtue and goodness, is an especial object of the present work: and with this view the pieces have been scrupulously selected; and, where necessary, purified from every word and sentiment that could offend the most delicate mind" (vi). This approximates a notion of *language as morality.* In addition, the editor of the volume praises "the chastity of the language, the unity of the style, the grammatical precision and the correctness of moral sentiment" (v).

Albert Salisbury's *Phonology and Orthoepy: An Elementary Treatise on Pronunciation for the Use of Teachers and Schools,* published in Madison in 1879, also configures pronunciation as a sign of proper deportment, visible in the very first words of the preface: "An accurate and elegant pronunciation forms no small factor of a liberal culture. Careless and uncouth speech is the almost certain index of a general lack of cultivation and refinement" (Salisbury 1879: 5). Salisbury uses the inland northern speech of Wisconsin as a model of pronunciation:

> The palatal or uvular *r,* heard at the end of a syllable, or whenever not immediately followed by a vowel, as is *far, farm,* can be produced without the aid of the tip of the tongue, being formed farther back in the mouth. This is clearly a different sound from the lingual *r,* but the two are not discriminated by some ears. The common and disagreeable error of failing to sound the palatal *r*–giving *fahmah* for farmer, etc., is usually taken as an evidence of affectation. It is often, however, a matter of innocent, ignorant habit rather than affectation. (30)

The fact that he sees this as an affectation indicates a submerged perception of those phonemes as being of higher prestige value than the rhotic /r/ that he advocates. In an interesting reversal, however, he then lessens their status by ascribing ignorance to their cause.

Similarly, Lewis Sherman's *A Handbook of Pronunciation,* published in Milwaukee in 1885, presents itself as "a means of promoting correct and polished speech" (Sherman 1885: 3). Language is "the chief of those attainments which distinguish man from the lower animals" and "is justly regarded as an index of his culture and associations" (3). A physician, Sherman seems to construct an audience of status equal to the author, which he addresses in the opening paragraph: "Lawyers, physicians, preachers, artists and scientists may properly be held to strict account for the correct pronunciation of words which are peculiar to their several professions" (3). "Lower" speech forms are excluded a priori: "mere provincialisms have no place in cultivated speech" (4). His standard is "the custom of the best educated and the most careful speakers," and "the custom of the learned is always to be preferred" to that of "the uneducated, who are in the majority" (5).

The work *How Should I Pronounce?*, published by William Henry Phyfe in New York in 1885 is also class-based. He says of pronunciation, "that nothing marks more quickly a person's mental and social status" (Phyfe 1885: v). Phyfe vacillates between traditional American populist notions, which eschew any imposition of social regulation upon the people, and concepts that would actually recommend that imposition. It is within this moment of vacillation that his discourse begins to display a certain consciousness of race:

> The source of authority in pronunciation is the custom of the cultivated classes of the community, which it is the office of the dictionaries to reflect. Although language is an affair "of the people, by the people, and for the people," yet it is the intelligent few rather than the illiterate many whose opinions are of value in matters of this character ... (10)

> It is a well-known fact that, in the matter of distinguishing colors, the lower orders of humanity have a very limited range of appreciation. The rainbow, as it arches the sky, presents to the ignorant savage and to the cultivated artist very different objects for contemplation ... this is equally true of sounds. (16)

It would be difficult to account for this prejudicial generalization as exclusively determined by class consciousness. It seems codetermined, to a certain extent, by race-based ideologies as well, although these are not foregrounded to a very salient extent. In *The Standard of Pronunciation in English,* published in New York in 1904, Thomas R. Lounsbury, Professor of English at Yale, discusses the pronunciation of many sounds, but makes no mention at all of /r/. In general, Lounsbury observes the dynamics of class exclusion and inclusion in the status of pronunciation.

Within this complex elocutionary discourse of class, morality, and incipient race consciousness at the fin-de-siècle, there appears, occasionally, a certain hiatus of reason and scholarship. Edwin W. Bowen's "Authority in English pronunciation," published in *The Popular Science Monthly* in 1905, is a surprisingly descriptive and relativistic piece written at a time when such objective inquiry was uncommon, if not anomalous. Bowen problematizes the concept of authority and says that there never was and probably never will be an accepted standard of pronunciation. He recommends viewing the statements of contemporary orthoepists as observations rather than authoritative prescriptions. Of the phenomenon of the pronunciation guide *per se,* he says:

> The pronouncing dictionary, therefore, is a modern production; it was hardly known before the first quarter of the eighteenth century ... the pronouncing dictionary was called in to existence by the desire on the part of the imperfectly educated middle class to know what to say and how to say it. This desire became stronger and stronger as the members of that growing class of England's population rose by degrees into social prominence. Possessing little culture and few social advantages and lacking confidence in their meager training, such people were not willing to exercise the right of private judgment, and consequently they sought out an authority and guide. They were eager to learn the *jus et norma loquendi* of the nobility. It was natural therefore, since the occasion appeared to demand it, that self-appointed guides should come forward and offer to conduct the multitudes of social pariahs through the wilderness of orthoepical embarrassment in to the Canaan of polite usage. (Bowen 1905: 546)

Bowen's cogent observations on the bourgeois origins of the pronouncing dictionary merit some reflection. The European middle class was constructed in an act of separation from the upper and lower classes, most forcefully from the latter. While it sought to imitate aspects of the aristocracy, it was aware of the fact that it could not and should not be that class. As regards the lower class, however, the bourgeoisie painstakingly sought to continually separate out from itself all that smacked of the base and vulgar (Stallybrass and White, 1986). As the characteristics stigmatized as vulgar would certainly include the speech patterns of the lower class, it should be emphasized that it is in the very nature of the bourgeoisie to perceive the speech patterns of that "inferior" class as substandard. In other words, the pronunciation and elocution of the bourgeoisie must emerge in an act of substandardizing the speech patterns of the subordinate class. And it will perform this substandardization by using the components of the current value system as implements of separation.

On the whole, however, it is clearly evident that the examples cited seek to situate the instruction of pronunciation within a space that is social, moral, and religious. The proper pronunciation is supposed to indicate the presence *of* the speaker within an elevated social circle as well as the presence *within* the speaker of proper Christian moral values. The continual juxtaposition of pronunciation drills and moralizing tales effects, ultimately, a relationship of iconicity between the two fields. One can say that, in these cases, pronunciation becomes coded for class and Christianity.

3.2. Sounding ethnic at the century's end

A radical change takes place in the ideology of pronunciation in the latter part of the nineteenth century. The elocutionary discourse of class and Christianity becomes augmented by one of race, and this occurs to the degree that the discourse of race ultimately becomes the nuclear ideology of the standardization of pronunciation; the discourses of class and religion then become secondary or centripetal. Even when the racial elements are overwhelming, however, they always retain traces of the older social and moral ideologies.

An early instance of the inclusion of race within the discourse of pronunciation and elocution in the nineteenth century is found in Theodore Mead's *Our Mother Tongue,* published in New York in 1890. Mead opens his work with the following didactic and class-conscious words: "I once heard instruction in singing, of course very simple in kind, given to several hundred street boys in a reformatory ... that which is possible to a crowd of wild, ignorant boys, is possible to us all" (Mead 1890: 1). Thus pronunciation and elocution are couched in a socially stratified, ameliorative, and disciplinary context. This quickly changes to a race-conscious theme in the second paragraph of the work:

> Languages, like races, are far from being of equal beauty or value; and happy indeed are we of the Anglo-Saxon stock in the possession of our mother-tongue, for among the great languages of the world, whether dead or living, she undoubtedly stands in the front rank. Unfortunately, few there are who appreciate and honour her as they should, and especially here in America, under our rule of characteristic recklessness, this splendid part of our national inheritance, like our forests, our rivers, and our natural scenery, is steadily deteriorating, and day by day losing something of its strength, dignity and grace. (2)

Language and race are similarly configured here, and the use of organic metaphors to describe language also serves to emphasize its relation to the physical and biological. Like race, it is something to be bred, preserved, and nurtured. And just as the English "race" is seen as superior to all others, so too is the English language. In comparison with the British, Americans "have undoubtedly a different, and on the whole an inferior, manner of speaking" (3), and Mead's purpose is to ameliorate "the defects alleged against our way of speaking" (4).

Mead sees the British as having a structure that guards the language against deterioration, and that consists of the efforts of the aristocracy, the universities, and the parliament: "It is evident that these institutions form a triple barrier around the language entirely without equivalent in this country, where such safeguards are much more needed, owing to our constant absorption of foreign elements" (26). What is needed is "a wholesome check to the encroachments of the thoughtless and half-educated millions" (26). Mead's words are significant, in that they configure the American language as already being threatened by immigration in 1890, before the great migrations to the eastern seaboard. At that time, the two major groups forming an other to the older majority residents of the northeastern cities were the products of the northern migration of southern blacks or of Irish immigration. As Mead probably viewed the black population as sufficiently isolated from white culture to effect any influence upon the language, the blame then had to fall upon the Irish. He says of the decline of American English:

> First, that it is not universal, the most cultivated classes of our great cities having to a considerable extent held out against the innovation, as have also those rural districts, particularly in New England, which have had the least admixture of foreign elements; and secondly, that it is recent, coinciding with the great Irish immigration which has filled our households with Hibernian nurses and servants during the last half century. (31)

Here, one sees a confluence of class and race that threatens the English language; the other is configured as the Irish of a different race and of a different, servant class invading "our households." Mead illustrates this influence with the example of a family

> of pure Anglo-American blood, which has been established in this country for more than two hundred and fifty years, and during most of that time within fifty miles of New York; and yet in this family the change from the broad vowel, with its manly chest-tone, to the flat one which can hardly be other than nasal, has only been completed, or nearly so, within the last twenty years, though it had begun a generation earlier among those who had removed to the city of New York. (32)

Mead is speaking of the change from the "Italian sound of *a,* as is *far*" (31) to the front vowel /æ/ and gives, as an example, the speech of the father of this family, whom he heard "sounding the *a* in "command" so as to rhyme nearly with *respond*" (32). He is blaming this change on the Irish, who have introduced changes in pronunciation in New York that are having a wave effect upon the rural areas. It is difficult to understand what phonemes Mead is speaking of here: Irish English has more instances of the backing of /a/ than does American English: one need only think of the Irish pronunciation of "lad" /lad/ versus the American /læd/. What is significant, however, is not the accuracy of Mead's observations, but his ascriptions of causality and responsibility. It is clearly the immigrant who is affecting the "manliness" of "Anglo-American blood." Thus the immigrant is configured as a threat to the language, racial integrity, and social structure of the dominant class. Perhaps the most significant aspect of Mead's work is that it locates the source of the deterioration of pronunciation within a class of urban immigrants, most specifically those in New York City. This is at once a deterioration of language, race, station, and morality, and it is a very early example of the perception of New York as the harbor of such change.

Eugene H. Babbitt's *The English Pronunciation of the Lower Classes in New York and Vicinity,* which Babbitt published in 1896 while teaching at Columbia, is interesting in that it is a judgmental description of New York City speech that mixes linguistic scientific description with qualitative evaluations biased along the axis of class and race. Babbitt was the first trained phonetician to study the speech of New York, which adds a certain significance to his judgments, as they indicate a confusion of the categories of ethnicity and pronunciation in first professional reflection upon the speech of that area. A reprint of an article published in *Dialect Notes,* it is a very observant, if not very well researched study, whose major faults lie in its attempts to assign causality and class and ethnic location to the perceived speech patterns of New York City. Babbitt begins his study with the following justification:

> New York City and vicinity is, and always has been, something distinct, not only from the rest of the State but from the whole current of Anglo-Saxon traditions which has dominated the foundation and continuance of the American commonwealth ... the current saying is that New York was settled by the Dutch, is owned by the Jews, and governed by the Irish. (Babbitt 1896: 1)

Babbitt marginalizes New York *a priori* by representing it as alien to the Anglo-Saxon tradition. The major influences are Dutch, Irish and Jewish, a supposition that glosses over the large number of New Yorkers of English descent. His investigation of New York is first couched in ethnic terms, and it is quite startling to see, already in the last decade of the nineteenth century, the phrase "owned by the Jews," an affront consonant with the racial attitudes of the first half of the twentieth century. It is the "Anglo-Saxon traditions" that have laid a proper moral foundation for American culture and civilization, and it is the mercantile alien who threatens those traditions:

> The almighty dollar is by far the foremost object of all activity; whatever
> will bring the dollar, by fair means or foul, is regarded as legitimate enter-
> prise ... as in all such trade-centres, the Jew is very much in evidence; and
> all the conditions conspire to the end that he and the Yankee and the
> Dutchman turn toward one another and the community the worst sides of
> their commercial morality. (2)

In this passage, the Jew is placed on the forefront of moral decline;
it is as if he is exerting an influence upon the other ethnic groups.
The result is that "the average New Yorker is the outcome of all
these conditions" (2), but these conditions, in their worst form, are
not distributed equally throughout the population; instead, they in-
tensify as one descends through the class hierarchy:

> The upper classes live a life of their own, travel a great deal, and educate
> their children in private schools, in which most of the teachers are not New
> Yorkers. Their language is therefore independent of the environment to a
> large extent. The foreigners who learn English here, of course, learn the
> kind of English current there ... I think that no child under ten retains any
> trace of any other pronunciation after two years in the New York school
> and street life. The influence of the parents is almost infinitesimal, –quite
> otherwise than in rural districts. The children in most cases see very little
> of their fathers, and often hardly more of their mothers ... there is a distinct
> New York variety of English pronunciation, used by a large majority of the
> inhabitants, and extending over a considerable district. It is most marked in
> the lower classes, who do not travel or come under outside influences. (3)

The speech of New Yorkers is characterized by a "less vigorous use
of the front part of the tongue" (4) in comparison with the speech of
the rest of the country. Babbitt sees this as a decline in the quality of
expression, visible in the observations that the New Yorker "makes
the front vowels worse than the back ones," and that "in vociferous
pronunciation, such as that of the street Arabs shouting at play, or
crying wares, this tendency to retract the tongue is very noticeable"
(4). It is clear from Babbitt's discourse that the proper quality of
American pronunciation, which consists in a certain finesse with
consonants pronounced with the front part of the tongue, is being
engulfed by guttural threats. Another result of this tendency is that
"the interdentals are beginning to go" (4). He observes: "The most
striking and important peculiarity in consonants is the substitution of

t and *d* for *θ* and *ð*... It may perhaps fairly be ascribed to the influence of the large number of foreigners who have not the interdental in their own languages, and cannot pronounce it" (8). This is a rather unreflective assertion, in that it seemingly ignores the numerous historical and contemporary examples of the loss of interdentals in many dialects of English, both within the United States and the United Kingdom, that would be difficult, if not impossible, to attribute to foreign influence. Clearly, Babbitt wants to read the deviations from his desired norm as the product of the influence of the alien. One can thus conclude that the regularization and standardization of pronunciation originates, in Babbitt's discourse, from a moment of difference of race and ethnicity.

In 1911, Ellen Clark Henderson wrote a thesis at the University of Utah entitled "The Necessity for an Uniform Accurate Pronunciation of the English Language." Largely impressionistic and minimally scientific, her folkish descriptions, prescriptions, and etiology of American pronunciations are revealingly symptomatic of western perceptions of the cultural value of continuant and dropped /r/. Like Henry James, she constructs an idea of a dominant standard in France and Germany:

> There is but one best pronunciation of the French language; cultured Germans require an accurateness in speech which amounts almost to fastidiousness ... the tendency in London and in the south and east of the United States is to take the usage of the people for the standard of authority, while in the west and great middle west of the United States the tendency is to follow the standard of the dictionaries. (Henderson 1911: 2)

While her statements here are clearly impressionistic and unsupported, their value lies in their significance as cultural biopsies. She not only advocates standardization by referring to France and Germany, but also implicitly valorizes western pronunciation by associating it with dictionary recommendations. At the same time, she implicitly devalorizes the pronunciations of the south and the east by representing them as based on usage rather than principle.

Henderson's statements also indicate the perceived strength of the major speech areas. She holds that, in the United States, "even among the educated, there are three dialects, the New England, the

Southern and the Western; and unless public sentiment changes these three will continue to be spoken" (4). After setting out these large distinctions, she then uses the pronunciation of /r/ as an evaluative device:

> Among the educated who speak the New England dialect ... the misuse of the letter r is much more distinct than in any part of Great Britain, for in addition to giving it another sound they add it to many words. In the Southern dialect the difficulty is even more pronounced, final g's in ing endings are left off, and there is a decided drawl due mainly to a tendency to place the accent near the end of the word. In the Western dialect the wrong sounds are given to the a, o and u, of a great number of words and the final r is often over pronounced. (5)

In saying that the /r/ is misused, she means that it is dropped after vowels. While also criticizing the more constricted /r/ of her own area, the criticism is much less severe than that levied against the New England region. The attribution of lassitude to dropped postvocalic /r/ is magnified by its connection with black American English: "It is the r difficulty which is clung to most tenaciously and affected most assiduously ... it has been suggested that the r difficulty is a result of negro influence but this can not be proven" (12–13). The "difficulty" of which she speaks here is that of pronouncing the /r/ in all environments, as if it were a problem in need of correction.

She then begins a narrative of the etiology of non-rhotic /r/ that represents it as a recent uneducated deviation:

> It is supposed that the misuse of the letter r must have begun comparatively recently, for in the speech of the western people who only a century ago moved from the places where it is most prevalent, there is absolutely no trace of it. One hundred years ago the common ancestors of all must have spoken much alike ... when after many years of frontier life, the western people began to provide for education their teachers, realizing their lack of education, acquired the habit of consulting Webster's dictionary; and as a result the most accurate pronunciation of the English language is found in the Middle West. (14)

While correct in saying that rhotic /r/ precedes non-rhotic /r/, she does not seem to know that the initial bifurcation also preceded the colonization of English North America. For her, however, anteriority and dictionary presence are sufficient to justify a standardization based on western speech, and this is a process that is expressed combatively:

> The field of triumph is still open for the ambitious writer who may hope to strike the death knell of the prevalent r difficulty. So far it is spelled into the negro dialect and a very little into the speech of the typical southern gentleman ... in all serious literature there is not one proof that poets have sanctioned giving to the r any but the regular sound. Nowhere do we find such rhymes as "word" with "flood." (16)

Seemingly unaware of the rhymes of John Keats, or perhaps excluding them from the rubric of "serious literature," she contextualizes this struggle as a defense of the literate against the influence of the slave and the southerner. And it is interesting to note that this is to be a preservation of strength, race, and vitality: "We have lost those powerful Anglo-Saxon gutterals; at this time one half of our strong r's are in danger of being lost" (18). As with many prescriptivists, dropped /r/ is seen here as a sign of weakening:

> If we continue in our present course it will be a matter of only a short time until it will be necessary to have another reform which will change the appearance of the language as much as a complete change today would do. We would not easily get accustomed to seeing "lodge" rhymed with "large", "hot" with "heart" ... If this change ever comes the language will have lost much of its beauty, impressiveness and strength. (19)

Henderson's ideas reflect an early instance of the perception of the American west as not only a natural, but also a racial and linguistic preserve, a locus for an original ethnic and linguistic heritage that is also expressed within the discourse of standardization.

As indicated above, however, the presence of class consciousness also continues, in a parallel fashion, along with the consciousness of race. This can be seen in *Knowing and Using Words,* published in Boston in 1917 by William D. Lewis and Mabel Dodge Holmes, which defines language as a means of communication of social station: "Language is the clothing of one's thought. If it is spoken, the quality of the voice, the purity of the vowels, the distinctness of the consonants, all combine to indicate the social and intellectual rank of the speaker" (Lewis and Holmes 1917: iii). This proceeds right up through the period of great immigration to the United States and can be seen in Thorleif Larsen's *Pronunciation. A Practical Guide to American Standards,* published in 1931, which offers a similar class context for pronunciation. For him, speech is "a part of good manners, for the essence of good manners is to please" (Larsen 1931: vi).

A peculiar configuration of diction as an analog of morality, class, culture, and geography, but not of race, can be found in Helen Stockdell's *Speech Made Beautiful. Practical Lessons in English Diction,* published in 1930. Born in Virginia, Stockdell explicitly prefers the non-rhotic /r/ of Virginia coastal speech over inland continuant /r/ and devotes seven lessons and drills out of a total of twenty-three to the proper articulation of that phoneme, offering a panoramic account "from the rough-riding r of the West to the eliminated r of the rural South" (Stockdell 1930: 10). It is surprising to find dropped /r/ associated with the rural south, as it clearly would have been present in the cultivated speech of Richmond, Savannah, Charleston, Atlanta, and other coastal cities. Indeed, the western areas of the south would have been more rural and would have little instance of non-rhotic /r/. The phrase "the rough-riding r of the West" clearly associates the figure of Theodore Roosevelt with rhotic /r/ and shows its nascent iconic power. In her prescriptions, however, the unrefinement of that phoneme situates it on the margins of cultured speech, which is articulated in a moral and class context. The brief book jacket biography of Stockdell says that she was "born and reared in a family that cared for right speech" and was "taught to discern between good and evil in vital matters of accent, pronunciation, and voice tones." The literal connection of speech with the ethical concepts of good and evil underscores the notions of morality in her work. This is furthered in the introduction by W. Russell Bowie of Grace Church, New York City, who says, "there is need for a book on the right use of our English speech. We live in a world of hurry and noise. We shout against the bedlam of roaring traffic, of automobile horns, of iron subways, and of grinding wheels" (7). Here, again, proper speech is seen as a bulwark against the evils of the town, although rural speech is not yet held up as a proper alternative.

Stockdell advocates and praises "an aristocracy of speech ... that purity of letter sounds" (11), but indicts the irresponsibility of that class, who have become unvigilant. It is on "the careless, the indifference of the fortunate class, the educated, that blame should be laid–blame not only for lowering his own standard, but blame for failing to help the man below him in educational advantages by keeping clear before him right speech for his pattern and example" (13). This is clearly a distinction of class. There is a social hierarchy of speech here, and it is incumbent upon the upper class to didactically disseminate proper elocution.

She says that postvocalic /r/ is a semivowel, and that "the tongue lies passive in the mouth with its tip resting against the curve of the lower front teeth. The least motion of the tongue toward its consonant r position would be fatal to the fullness and clearness of the vowel preceding r" (48). The vowel sound should not be "tagged with that unlovely ur-sound that makes the accent called twang, burr, and other names" (48). Here, the loss of postvocalic /r/ is justified as a preserver of preceding vowel quality and thus the clarity of speech. This statement is made in disregard of the antithetical argument that the loss of /r/ increases the possibility of homophonic unclarity, as in, for example, the aural confusion of "god" and "guard." Thereafter, the justifications become ones of a personal aesthetic preference: "America has whole sections that might be called the Land of Ur ... there are thousands whose speech, and whose voices, are marred by this vowel twist. Under its blight lie scores of voices that might have found fame and beauty on the stage" (54). Thus the rhotic variant is seen as unaesthetic, while other non-rhotic variants are received more generously: "In other sections there are to be heard other variants. Thirty-third is thoity-thoid, thutty-thud, thetty-thed, or thurrrty-thurrrd, according to latitude and nationality" (98). The other allophones, such as the Brooklyn and Tidewater (oy), which, in many parts of the country, are considered to be even ludicrous, are presented here uncritically, in contrast to the triple /r/ of the "Land of Ur." Stockdell's work represents one of the last examples of a class-based understanding of pronunciation in the United

States that seeks to defend coastal speech, especially that of eastern Virginia, against the waxing influence of the west and midwest.

The advent of radio made Americans more conscious of their pronunciations and generated a new interest in the amelioration of speech. Courses such as *Practical English and Effective Speech* by the Better-English Institute of America, published in Chicago in 1930, are a good indication of the waxing national interest in pronunciation. This is a progressive comprehensive course in punctuation, phonetics, grammar, etc., aimed at adults and published in fifteen separate pamphlets that contain no specific phonetic exercises. Instead, they simply offer guides to the pronunciations of whole words. There are no specific recommendations for the pronunciation of /r/. Pragmatism and commercialism are used as justifications not only for speech improvement, but also for the assumption of the sign of culture that frames the presentation of proper discourse. The reader is told: "all of us want to be thought cultured ... to persuade others to our way of thinking ... in other words, we all want to be successful salesmen ... every time you talk to anyone a sale is made. Either you sell him your idea, or he sells you his" (3). Thus a cultivated diction is not ontologically justifiable but gains its validation via its association with a commercial imperative. This phenomenon is also present in the discourse of James F. Bender, discussed in section 2.7. below.

The manuals and guides on pronunciation and elocution of the eighteenth and early nineteenth centuries fall into two larger but not mutually exclusive groups. Those of the antebellum period tend to justify the amelioration of accent by reference to an ideology of Christian morality and of consciousness of social class. They are not, however, fully free of a consciousness of race. Those of the last decades of the century tend to be informed by a waxing ideology of race that initially complements, but then supersedes the concerns of class and morality.

4. Boston's last stand: the prescriptions of Henry James

Henry James (1843–1916) was a significant literary and cultural figure of his era and has a firm place in the canon of American writers. His brother William is considered to be America's first major philosopher. His novels, among them *The American* (1877), *Daisy Miller* (1878), *The Portrait of a Lady* (1881), *The Bostonians* (1886), *The Wings of the Dove* (1902), and *The Ambassadors* (1903), often deal with the dynamics of an American living in Europe or a European living in America and thus offer reflective insights into American culture and identity. One can say the same of his writings on language, which serve as telling barometric indications of the status of American pronunciation and elocution at the turn of the twentieth century, especially in the larger context of language, race, immigration, and national identity.

On June 8, 1905, having recently returned to the United States after living twenty years in England, James gave the commencement address to the graduating class of Bryn Mawr College. The title of the address was "The question of our speech," in which James lamented the degeneration of American English. The address is significant not only for its descriptions of American pronunciation, especially of continuant and dropped /r/, but also for its notions of standardization, race, class, and ethnicity.

James complains of "the unsettled character and the inferior quality of the colloquial *vox Americana*" and its "indifference to a speech standard" (James 1999a: 52). He holds that the idea of standard speech is taken very seriously by "the French, the Germans, the Italians, the English perhaps in particular," but in the case of the Americans, he says, "We alone flourish in undisturbed and ... in something like sublime unconsciousness of any such possibility" (45). He sees a standard academic language as foundational to the educative process: "Without that consensus, to every appearance, the educative process cannot be thought of as at all even beginning (43) ... we may not be said to be able to study–and *a fortiori* do any of the things we study *for*–unless we are able to speak" (45). As the address continues, it departs from its ostensible rationalization for a common speech standard, which is that such a standard should facilitate communication and learning, and engages in an associative discourse that connects language to social status and ethnicity. He says that substandard speech patterns "reduce articulation to an easy and ignoble minimum, and so keep it as little distinct as possible from the grunting, the squealing, the barking or the roaring of animals" (46). Proper articulation, however, is connected with "good breeding" (45), which he specifies in saying, "I mean speaking with consideration for the forms and shades of our language, a consideration so inbred that it has become instinctive ..." (47). The operative model here is that the speech of "noble" status should then become a national standard. This particular notion of status, however, is couched in metaphors of breeding that, in turn, evoke images of lineage and stock. It is, in effect, a notion of class difference that has developed into one of race or ethnicity. The implicit sequence would begin with a social practice that progresses to habit, and then to instinct, and ultimately assumes, in its instinctual manifestation, a bodily location. It is elevated speech educated into the body. Its opposite–substandard speech–shows, via the metaphors of squealing, barking, and roaring, that it is also associated with the body but has not evolved very far from the animal state.

For James, the endemic, if not epidemic problem is one of a national "limp, slack, passive tone" (50), and it is indeed a nebulous, undefined, and overarching notion of proper and improper "tone" that informs James's polemic. The degenerative state is one of vocal lassitude, a lack of conscious vigilance in speech, especially as regards "common" ways of speaking. In locating the etiology of this decline, James speaks within the xenophobic discourse of his period: "To the American common school ... and to the American Dutchman and Dago ... we have simply handed over our property ..." (53). The American language is seen here as the property of those of English descent who have negligently relinquished ownership to the masses of immigrants pouring into the eastern metropolises at the turn of the century. Of the common idiom, James says:

> It is prosperity, of a sort, that a hundred million people, a few years hence,
> will be unanimously, loudly–above all, loudly, I think!–speaking it, and
> that, moreover, many of these millions will have been artfully wooed and
> weaned from the Dutch, from the Spanish, from the German, from the Ital-

ian, from the Norse, from the Finnish, from the Yiddish even, strange to say, and (stranger still to say) even from the English, for the sweet sake ... of speaking, of talking, for the first time in their lives, *really* at their ease. (54)

It is the idea of talking at one's ease that characterizes American laxity, and that differentiates it from European languages, which James sees as maintaining a national standard. Clearly, James is constructing his own kind of Europe for his own ideological purposes, as neither the linguistic nor the political situation in, for instance, Germany or Italy in the nineteenth century would have remotely resembled any kind of unity at all. The immigrants in question are supposed to have spoken their native languages carefully and, after having relocated to the United States, run amok with the English language:

There are many things our now so profusely imported, and, as is claimed, quickly assimilated foreign brothers and sisters may do at their ease in this country, and at two minutes' notice, and without asking anyone else's leave or taking any circumstance whatever into account ... but the thing they may so best do is play, to their heart's content, with the English language, or, in other words, dump their mountain of promiscuous material into the foundations of the American. (54)

This passage seems to be introducing images of improper toilet training into the theater of language, which is being contaminated by immature and ill-mannered foreigners. This representation of foreigners as playful and permissive is quickly replaced, however, without a transition, by one of formidability and industry:

All the while we sleep the vast contingent of aliens whom we make welcome, and whose main contention, as I say, is that, from the moment of their arrival, they have just as much property in our speech as we have, and just as good a right to do what they choose with it ... all the while we sleep the innumerable aliens are sitting up (*they* don't sleep!) to work their will on their new inheritance. (55)

Here, it is the lack of vigilance of the "native" Americans that is causing the language to be corrupted by industrious foreigners. It is odd that the idea of inheritance is used, as this term implies a trans-

fer of ownership within generational family lines that would normally exclude "aliens." Once in possession of the language, the simultaneously playful and pragmatic immigrant uses it in a utilitarian
fashion, as if it were "oilcloth ... that they are preparing to lay down,
for convenience, on kitchen floor or kitchen staircase ... wonderfully
resisting 'wear' [it] strikes them as an excellent bargain; durable,
tough, cheap" (55).

James is constructing an associative conspiracy here to account
for his dissatisfaction with the American vernacular. It is the unfortunate result of a society with vague class distinctions. It is being
abused by a sort of American commoner, and the lack of an organized and elevated counterforce of cultivated speech allows the
abuses to spread unchecked. The commoner is also present in the
figure of the peasant immigrant, who is the product of a collage of
selective perceptions gleaned from myriad impressions of foreigners. The other is referred to metonymically as "Dutchman and
Dago," which could include Germany and Holland, as well as Italy,
as the designation Dutch was historically coterminous with German.
Thus, in James's discourse, there is no notion of a Nordic essence to
America either culturally, genetically, or linguistically, and it seems
that the other is constructed as simply non-English. It is interesting
to examine the roster of foreigners, who are all European, and who
all have equally exotic status, until one arrives at the phrase: "from
the Yiddish even, strange to say," which indicates a stronger alien
and resistant status for Jewish language and culture than for the others. Immediately thereafter follows the utterance: "and (stranger still
to say) even from the English," which indicates not only that the
presence of the immigrant will cause Americans to be estranged
from their own native English language, being the ultimate alienation, but also that it is the Jew who represents the instance of penul-
timate alienation. The subtextual communication is that if the Jews
depart from Yiddish, then America will eventually depart from English, i.e. the particular kind of English that James advocates. Thus
there is a dynamic present here that causes an alienation of self from
native language, e.g. Finn from Finnish, etc., but that also progresses
to the point where it effects a dispossession of English from the
English.

The other is represented here as loud and ludic, which evokes a stereotype of southern European behavioral characteristics that will eventually lead to linguistic promiscuity. The same immigrant is, however, industrious as well, and this generates a utilitarian, unaesthetic attitude toward language. The presence of oilcloth also links associatively to the pragmatic image of the (Jewish) mercantile class. James's particular idiom of anxiety is oddly reminiscent of that of Benjamin Franklin in this regard, in that the other also represents an economic threat to the class and race in power, and thus the danger of a multivalent disempowerment. As regards the linguistic danger, there is not only an alienation and dispossession of language, but also a deaestheticization thereof as well. One can well imagine how horrified James would be by the *valleyspeak* of our current generation.

Another important essay of linguistic complaint is "The speech of American women," which James published in parts in *Harper's Bazar* in 1906 and 1907. In contrast to their European counterparts, American women are motivated by a "dauntless confidence" and have the social freedom to express it: "They have, thanks to our particular social order, neither stages, probations, nor any form of discipline to pass through; they have none of the hierarchical complications of the older societies to reckon with" (James 1999b: 61). Consequently, they commit the same kind of linguistic promiscuity as do the other segments of American society that James marginalizes: the rural, the uneducated, and the immigrant. A lady has the option

> of speaking as she "likes," and still more from the state of being able to give no account, whatever, in such a matter, of any preference or any light. We might accept this labial and lingual and vocal independence as a high sign of the glorious courage of our women if it contained but a spark of the guiding reason that separates audacity from madness; but where do we find them prepared to answer the simplest of questions? (62)

Women are depicted here not only as mad, but also as not intelligent enough to formulate basic answers. Thus, according to James, they speak as they like without being able to account for their taste.

In addition, the speech of women is also lacking in regularity and pleasantness: "Even the cows in the field, the lambs on the moor, the asses on the green, low and bleat and bray with a certain consistency and harmony" (63). This passage also animalizes women by juxtaposing them with images of asses and cows and their speech with images of bleating and lowing. Moreover, he seems to imply that the speech of women is actually, in certain aspects, inferior to that of animals. In this vein, he adds that, regarding refined speech, "We take for granted an existing or a possible consciousness—we at least appeal to that; and we impute no such luxury either to Georgia crackers or to Dorsetshire hinds" (63–64). Thus there is, again, an unreflective aspect to nonstandard speech, both of men and of women, that is associated with the animalistic.

For James, emancipation is no real solution, as it has its linguistic disadvantages:

> Women, in societies where they do speak, have taken their cue in the first place from the men. Isn't it unmistakable in England, say, and in France, that the men have invented the standard and set the tone? ... Women, on our side of the world, actually enjoy and use the authority ... they are encamped on every inch of the social area that the stock-exchange and football-field leave free; the whole of the social initiative is in other words theirs. (66)

The image of encampment, with its military undertones, ascribes a formidability to this force while also emphasizing the theme of audacity. Woman, who would normally be receiver and guardian of eloquence, is, in America, the perpetrator of ineloquence. James recounts hearing the girls of the "most fashionable school in Boston" speak: "They ingenuously shrieked and bawled to each other across the street and from its top and bottom ... freely and happily at play ... they could scarce do other than hoot and howl. They romped, they conversed, at the top of their lungs ... they sat on doorsteps and partook of scraps of luncheon, they hunted each other to and fro ..." (69). Thus the supposedly elite woman articulates as does the immigrant and commoner, i.e. while playing, howling, eating scraps, and hunting, again in an animalistic manner.

While complaining of "the crudity of tone of my countrywomen in general" (70), James focuses on New England speech as a significant example of the recent decline of eloquence, which contrasts with a bygone era, for "the New England speech of other years had represented, indubitably, and from far back, the highest type of utterance implanted among us" (73). He contrasts it with the speech of his native New York, which appeared "poor and vain and abortive ... so much more positive, more seated and established ... more 'finished,' was that of the banks of the Charles" (74). And he invokes "the continued existence of two eminent ladies ... guarding the good idiom, and the good use and pleasant sound of it" (74). This cultivated speech was, however, vestigial, in a time when "Boston maidens slobbered unchecked" (74). James concludes the essay with a kind of Socratic dialog with such a young woman, whom he exhorts to improve her speech by imitating his, "by letting me just hover here at the gate and have speech of you when you can steal away. Only look out for the gleam of my lantern, and meet me by this low postern. I'll take care of the rest" (81).

With a prescriptive and didactic elitism that would make even Edwin Newman or William Safire blush, James advocates the standardizing of American pronunciation via an emulation of nineteenth century Boston Brahmin speech. Having returned to the United States after twenty years in England, and having acculturated himself to English class consciousness, social stratification, and received pronunciation, James seems to construct a memory of older New England speech that is filtered through his recent memories of England. In other words, this New England speech acts as a screen memory for the desired English speech and culture, which contrasts sharply with the populist and promiscuous American public mixture of worker, woman, and immigrant. Confronted with a most egregious example of such a situation in New York in 1906, James recollects a rustic New England antique, an unspoiled preserve of the elite and eloquent that exists apart from the metropolis in decline.

James locates a large part of the reasons for the "decline" of American English in a certain epidemic of permissiveness and laxity, an inability to clearly articulate phonetic difference that engenders homophony and consonantal elision. Consequently, he is vociferously opposed to the intrusive /r/ of the northeast coast:

You will perfectly hear persons supposedly "cultivated," the very instructors of youth sometimes themselves, talk of vanilla-r-ice cream, of Califor-
nia-r-oranges, of Cuba-r-and Porto Rico, of Atalanta-r- in Calydon, ... "Is
Popper-up stairs?" and "is Mommer in the parlor?" pass for excellent
household speech in millions of honest homes ... popper, with an "r," but
illustrates our loss, much to be regretted, alas, of the power to emulate the
clearness of the vowel-cutting, an art as delicate in its way as gem-cutting
... you will, again, perfectly hear a gentle hostess, solicitous for your com-
fort, tell you that if you wish to lie down there is a sofa-r-in your room.
(James 1999a: 49–50)

Acculturation to English speech and society also made another aspect of American pronunciation sound alien and dissonant to James:
the overarticulated /r/ of the west and midwest:

It is not always a question of an *r,* however–though the letter, I grant, gets
terribly little rest among those great masses of our population who strike
us, in the boundless West perhaps, especially, as, under some strange impulse received toward consonantal recovery of balance, making it present
even in words from which it is absent, bringing it in everywhere as with
the small vulgar effect of a sort of morose grinding of the back teeth. There
are, you see, sounds of a mysterious intrinsic meanness, and there are
sounds of a mysterious intrinsic frankness and sweetness; and I think the
recurrent note I have indicated–fatherr and motherr and otherr, waterr and
matterr and scatterr, harrd and barrd, parrt, starrt, and (dreadful to say) arrt
(the repetition it is that drives home the ugliness), are signal specimens of
what becomes of a custom of utterance out of which the principle of taste
has dropped. (50)

James's observations and characterizations seem oddly echoic of
those of Grandgent, especially in the irony of description. Having
been raised in New York, and having spent over twenty years in
England, James was clearly not very accustomed to the extensive
presence of rhotic /r/. This may, indeed, be the reason why he perceives it as alien to his particular ideology of American English.
Nonetheless, it also indicates that dropped /r/ still had high cultural
value in the early part of the twentieth century, and that the rhotic /r/
of the western regions had, to some extent, a lower cultural status,
although it was clearly seen as, and perhaps feared to be, a formidable opponent of the accent of Boston and New York.

5. Of tides and tongues: race, language, and immigration

One of the earliest examples of the confluence of race, language, and immigration can be found in the policies of the United States government that were directed against the native American population in the second half of the nineteenth century. In these policies, one sees the use of language for purposes of behavior modification in a racial context. The massive postbellum westward movement engendered hostilities between expansionist European and native Americans, and the solutions sought by the government were seldom bilateral. Oddly, some came to view the antagonism as a linguistic phenomenon, a perspective that, on the surface, seems to be surprisingly progressive. Unfortunately, the government's solution to the problem of the incompatibility of heterogeneous discourses was simply to eradicate the language of the other. Language was seen as the paradigm for behavior; thus instruction in English was presumed to produce, in effect, behavior in English, and the proper time to start was thought to be in childhood.

There was a "Peace Commission" organized to look into the conditions of Indian Tribes that consisted of the famous Civil War figure General William Sherman, three other army generals, and the commissioner of Indian affairs and his associates. The commission's report, issued in 1868, recommended teaching English to Indians as a panacea for the hostilities between native and European Americans, saying that "by educating the children of these tribes in the English language, these differences would have disappeared, and civilization would have followed at once ... through sameness of language is produced sameness of sentiment, and thought ... in the difference of language today lies two-thirds of our trouble" (Crawford 1992: 48). The report advocated that "their barbarous dialects should be blotted out" and assumed that this would "fuse them into one homogenous mass" (Crawford 1992: 48).

Ten years later, the *Annual Report of the Commissioner of Indian Affairs to the Secretary of the Interior* of 1878 officially advised that Indian children be "removed from the examples of their parents and the influence of the camps and kept in boarding schools" (174). Since the ideology of race at that time was one of exclusivity, Indian children could not be educated along with whites. Thus the United States Army brought, also in 1878, forty-nine Indian children to the Hampton Institute, a private boarding school for black children in Hampton, Virginia, so that they would be educated in English. It was decided, however, that the large racial distinction between blacks and whites was insufficiently discriminate, and that further segregation was necessary. Thus twenty-five boarding schools solely for Indian children were built between 1879 and 1902, and these had a total enrollment of 9,736 in 1905 (Rehyner 1992: 42–43). At these boarding schools, the Indian pupils were forbidden to speak their native languages and were often whipped for doing so (Reyhner 1992: 43). The exclusivity of English was reinforced by a directive of the secretary of the interior in 1880 mandating that English alone be used, as some mission schools had begun to offer instruction in native American languages (Reyhner 1992: 44).

The 1887 report of the commissioner of Indian affairs emphasized that the English language, "which is good enough for a white man and a black man, ought to be good enough for a red man," and concluded that "the first step to be taken toward civilization, toward teaching the Indians the mischief and folly of continuing in their barbarous practices, is to teach them the English language. The impracticability, if not impossibility, of civilizing the Indians of this country in any other tongue than our own would seem to be obvious" (Crawford 1992: 51). The report emphasized that "only through the medium of the English tongue can they acquire a knowledge of the Constitution of the country and their rights and duties thereunder" (Crawford 1992: 49). Forced education in English for Indian children continued until 1933, when the practice was halted by the Bureau of Indian Affairs (Reyhner 1992: 45).

This unfortunate episode in American history is a clear example of the configuration of language not only as an instrument, if not a weapon, of power, but also as the very instantiation of proper race, behavior, culture, and morality. This was conceived as a kind of complete linguistic transfusion that could replace one composite of language, thought, and behavior with another.

Another early example of the suppression of a linguistic minority can be found in the treatment of the Hispanic population of the

American west in the nineteenth century. The 1848 Treaty of Guadalupe Hidalgo, which ended the Mexican-American war, ceded to the United States the territory now comprising the states of Arizona, California, western Colorado, Nevada, New Mexico, Texas, and Utah, and guaranteed the rights of the resident Spanish-speaking population. Thus when California's constitution was ratified in 1849, it decreed that all state publications be in English and Spanish. The Gold Rush, however, rapidly transformed the Hispanic population from a vast majority into a minority, and the revisions to the constitution in 1878 suppressed the publication of official documents in Spanish (Crawford 1992: 52–53). Similarly, New Mexico, which had a population of more than 60,000 Spanish speakers in 1850, published official documents in both English and Spanish and supplied classroom translators in primary and secondary schools. While the influx of English speakers into New Mexico increased steadily, half of its population was still speaking Spanish in1906. The prominence of Spanish caused New Mexico to be long perceived as other, and the state was effectively rejected by its neighbor Arizona in 1906, when Congress passed a bill providing joint statehood for both states. Arizona's population had become overwhelmingly English speaking and voted the bill down, while New Mexico approved it. The opposition to Spanish steadily increased and, in 1910, Congress mandated English-only instruction in New Mexico schools and required English fluency for elected officials (Crawford 1992: 58–60). Eventually, however, Hispanics succeeded in including constitutional provisions for maintaining Spanish as an official language.

The earliest instance of official government legislation directed against an alien population of perceived distinct ethnicity can be seen in the case of Asian immigrants to California. The California Gold Rush effected massive immigration to that state, not only by English speakers, but also by Chinese laborers, over 20,000 of whom had entered California by 1853. This precipitated an intensive competition for labor between English and Chinese speakers, which caused California to enact anti-Chinese legislation in 1853 that levied a foreign miners' tax on Chinese immigrants. The opposition to Chinese immigration eventually reached Congress, which, in 1870, amended the 1790 naturalization act to define Asian immigrants as "aliens ineligible for citizenship" (Shingawa and Jang 1998: 41) and passed a preliminary exclusion law against Chinese laborers in 1875. The official Chinese Exclusion Act that outlawed Chinese immigration for purposes of labor was enacted in 1882 (Bonacich 1984: 74). This law was repealed in 1943, an injunction precipitated by the alliances of World War II. Similarly, in 1907, the US convinced Japan to curtail immigration to the US. In 1917, congress established a "barred zone" and passed an immigration policy requiring English language literacy tests and other restrictions aimed at China and India (Bonacich 1984: 75). Despite these efforts to suppress the indigenous and immigrant populations in the American west that were perceived as other, that region did not suffer, in the national consciousness, a consequent devaluation. On the contrary, the American west retained its value as the image of a reserve of proper ethnicity, language, and culture. American race consciousness would come to fix the stigma of alterity upon the east.

The waxing anxiety of race that one sees in the later nineteenth century escalated to xenophobic proportions in the early twentieth century. Directed against immigration to the eastern seaboard and coupled with the fear of southern black migration to the northern industrial centers, this xenophobia acted to frame the general discussions of race, identity, and national language. An examination of representative and influential racial theorists of the period will help illuminate the dynamics of the discourse that seeks to conflate the categories of language and race. Three such representative racial theorists are Burton Hendrick, Madison Grant, and Stephen Graham.

Burton Jesse Hendrick (1871–1949) was born in Connecticut and received an M.A. from Yale in 1897. He became a prominent New York journalist and won three Pulitzer Prizes, most notably for the 1920 *Victory at Sea.* He wrote for the New York *Evening Post* and for *World's Work,* but first made his mark with the leading muckraking journal of the time, *McClure's Magazine,* in which he published many of his racial theories. His most influential work, *The Jews in America,* was published solidly between the Immigration Quota Acts of 1921 and 1924. Hendrick's work contributed to the stigmatization of eastern European Jews and of New York City as well. Hendrick differentiates, however, the German from the Polish Jew and locates the sources of contamination in the latter. He produces a four-column list of "rich New Yorkers" (Hendrick 1923: 88–89) and assures the reader not to be overly concerned, because the few Jewish names on the list are "Germanic" and of "the German branch of the race" (91). His classificatory system is interesting, in that it maintains the hierarchical superiority of Teutonic families by elevating the German Jews above the other Jewish "races." Polish Jews are inferior because they possess "Slavic and Tartar or Mongol blood" (94). He concludes that

> the blood of the Turkish or Mongol people flows in the veins of the Eastern Jew of to-day. A further large Slavic mixture makes the Eastern Jew racially alien to Jews from other parts of Europe. Thus the masses that comprise one fourth the present population of New York City trace their beginnings, in considerable degree, to certain tribes that roamed the steps of Russia in the Middle Ages and happened to accept the religion of Judah as their own. (96)

Hendrick's racial interpretation of the Khazars thus characterizes New York City as alien not only to Teutons, but also to "proper" Jews and even to the Judeo-Christian heritage. It is also the source of surreptitious and conspiratorial contamination:

> Not only did they flock almost as one man to the city slums; by far the greater proportion of them gravitated to one city. At present the Jewish population of the United States is something more than 3,000,000; of these at least one half live in New York City. According to the Jewish Communal Register, all meat which is slaughtered near New York, and for its consumption, is killed by Shohetim—official Jewish slaughterers commissioned by rabbis; Gentiles are therefore constantly eating Kosher meat. (105)

Here, Hendrick leaps suddenly from demographic description to images of poisoning. His estrangement of the Jew becomes progressively more exotic: "Just as Japanese women blacken their teeth and Chinese women bind their feet, so the orthodox Polish Jewesses, after marriage, shave their heads. These are merely the outward indications of an Orientalism that controls all phases of Jewish life" (98).

Hendrick reminds the reader that other, mostly midwestern cities are not as contaminated: "Whereas the Jewish population of New York amounts to nearly 30 per cent. of the whole, the Jewish population of Philadelphia is only 10 per cent. of the whole; of Chicago 10 per cent.; of Cleveland 12 per cent.; of Detroit 10 per cent.; of St. Louis and Baltimore 8 per cent." (106). He continues by transforming the threat into a political one, saying that the "Jewish press of New York is devoted to Socialism ... any one who attends a Socialistic meeting in New York is immediately impressed by the fact that the audience is composed of East Side Jews ... practically all the orators of discontent who occupy soap boxes in the New York streets are unmistakably Eastern Jews" (148–149). Hendrick's discourse constitutes a condensation of the elements that were to motivate a shift away from the centrality of New York: the city is seen as a nodal point of ethnic, corporeal, and political contamination.

This ideology is evident in the works of other American racial theorists of the early twentieth century, such as those of the highly influential Madison Grant. Grant was a prominent New York City attorney, the president of the New York Zoological Society, a trustee of the American Museum of Natural History, vice president of the Immigration Restriction League, and a member of the Eugenics Research Association. In *The Passing of the Great Race,* published in 1918, Grant says of the recent Ellis Island immigrants:

> The native American is too proud to mix socially with them and is gradually withdrawing from the scene, abandoning to these aliens the land which he conquered and developed. The man of the old stock ... is to-day being literally driven off the streets of New York City by the swarms of Polish Jews. These immigrants adopt the language of the native American, they wear his clothes, they steal his name and they are beginning to take his women, but they seldom adopt his religion or understand his ideals and while he is being elbowed out of his own home the American looks calmly abroad and urges on others the suicidal ethics which are exterminating his own race. (Grant 1918: 91)

In Grant's view, it is the Nordic race that is being exterminated, the same race that comprised the ancient Greeks. He sees "three main Nordic strains of Greece, the Dorian, the Aeolian, and the Ionian groups" (159). His view of early Greek history is one of Nordic conquest:

> In Greece the Mediterranean Pelasgians speaking a Non-Aryan tongue were conquered by the Nordic Achaeans, who entered from the northeast according to tradition prior to 1250 B. C. ... the same invasion ... brought a related Nordic people to the coast of Asia Minor, known as Phyrigians. Of this race were the Trojan leaders. Both the Trojans and the Greeks were commanded by huge, blond princes, the heroes of Homer—in fact, even the Gods were fair haired—while the bulk of the armies on both sides was composed of little brunet Pelasgians, imperfectly armed and remorselessly butchered by the leaders on either side. (158–159)

For Grant, the decline of Greece can be explained racially: "Later, in 339 B. C., when the original Nordic blood had been hopelessly diluted by mixture with the ancient Mediterranean elements, Hellas fell an easy prey to Macedon" (161). The most valiant resistance to decline was afforded by Nordic heritage: "It is interesting to note that the Greek states in which the Nordic element most predominated outlived the other states" (162). Grant then represents, by association, Anglo-Saxon Americans as among the true visible remaining heirs to this noble strain:

> It is scarcely possible to-day to find in purity the physical traits of the ancient race in the Greek-speaking lands and islands and it is chiefly among the pure Nordics of Anglo-Norman type that there occur those smooth and regular classic features, especially the brow and nose lines, that were the delight of the sculptors of Hellas. (162)

The use of the term "Anglo-Norman" invokes the Norman Conquest of England and thus, by association and derivation, the "race" that established the English language in North America. Grant manages to include the southerner in his racial typography. He says that "men of the Nordic race may not enjoy the fogs and snows of the North ... and they may seek the sunny southern isles, but under the former conditions they flourish, do their work and raise their families. In the south they grow listless and cease to breed. In the lower classes in the Southern States of America the increasing proportion of 'poor whites' and 'crackers' are symptoms of lack of climactic adjustment." He sees the "poor whites in Georgia" as "excellent examples of the deleterious effects of residence outside the natural habitat of the Nordic race" (39).

Grant is perplexed about the situation of the southern mountain dweller and concedes that "the poor whites of the Cumberland Mountains in Kentucky and Tennessee present a more difficult problem, because ... the climate of these mountains cannot be particularly unfavorable to men of Nordic breed." Not stating what the problem is, and assuming a reader with specific preconceptions of the southern mountain population, he proposes that "there are probably other hereditary forces at work there as yet little understood," along with "bad food and economic conditions, prolonged inbreeding, and the loss through emigration of the best elements" (39). Echoing the words of Toynbee and Mencken, he concludes that "the problem is too complex to be disposed of by reference to the hookworm, illiteracy or competition with the Negroes" (40).

In Grant, as in many discussions of national language, the issue of standardization is integrated into the discourse on race and contamination of the purity of the dominant class. Oddly prefiguring the language-based modes of social inquiry that have dominated in the last quarter of the twentieth century, Grant has a linguistic–but, in his case, also racial–view of political conflict. Indeed, he titles a section of *The Passing of the Great Race* "Race, Language, and Nationality," and holds that "the history of the last century in Europe has been the record of a long series of struggles to unite in one political unit all those speaking the same or closely allied dialects" (56). He holds that "states without a single national language are constantly exposed to disintegration" (56) and that "the unifying power of a common language works subtly and unceasingly. In the long run it forms a bond which draws peoples together" (57).

This bond, however, must, in the best cases, be based on racial and linguistic consanguinity. A nation may have linguistic unity, but this is degenerate, unless it is combined with racial unity: "As to the so-called 'Celtic race,' the fantastic inapplicability of the term is at once apparent ... to class together the Breton peasant with his round Alpine skull; the little, long skulled, brunet Welshman of Mediterranean race, and the tall, blond, light eyed Scottish Highlander of pure

Nordic blood, in a single group labeled Celtic is obviously impossible" (62). For Grant, there was an initial linguistic-racial unity of Celts: "There was once a people who used the original Celtic language and they formed the western vanguard of the Nordic race" (62), but this race was "diluted" by "miscegenation" (60), and now one "must regard as Celts all the Berbers and Egyptians, as well as many Persians and Hindus" (62–63).

Thus Grant has linguistic and racial evidence with which to taint, marginalize, and disempower the Celts; in doing so, he thus neutralizes an exterior threat to Anglo-Saxon and Nordic hegemony, which hegemony, however, is preserved by virtue of a nuclear linguistic-racial unity. He sees "in the Teutonic group a large majority of those who speak Teutonic languages, as the English, Flemings, Dutch, North Germans, and Scandinavians, are descendants of the Nordic race while the dominant class in Europe is everywhere of that blood" (61–62). By disempowering the Celts, he also, implicitly and by association, disempowers the inhabitants of the American southern mountain area, who are largely descendants of Celtic settlers.

Grant represents perhaps the most extreme embodiment of a racial paranoia constituted in and through language, whereby proper elocution and linguistic standardization are seen, quite literally, as the discursive instances of racial protection of a superior class under siege: "As in all wars since Roman times from a breeding point of view the little dark man is the final winner ... who from his safe stand on the gutter curb gave his applause to the fighting man and then stayed behind to perpetuate his own brunet type" (74). The valiant neo-Aryan conqueror, Nordic man is "the pioneer" who bravely chose to "migrate to new countries, until the ease of transportation and the desire to escape military service in the last forty years reversed the immigrant tide" (74). Thus the courageous pioneer is being opportunistically followed and displaced by the cowardly draft-dodger: "our immigrants now largely represent lowly refugees from 'persecution,' and other social discards" (74). In closing the chapter, Grant interestingly invokes the American west: "this was also true in the early days of our Western frontiersmen, who individually were a far finer type than the settlers who followed them. In fact, it is said that practically every one of the Forty-Niners in California was of

Nordic type" (75). Here, Grant is among the first to include, within the supremacist and xenophobic discourse on race, language, and immigration, the image of the American west, which represents an open frontier, unurbanized and consisting of a natural purity that mirrors and acts as a geographic double for the racial purity that Grant desires. While his discourse is basically nostalgic, in that he says that the new immigrants have even persisted as far as the western frontier, it still implies a lingering comparative purity and aids in the delineation of the west as a locus of the vestiges of the ideal man.

In 1914, the noted Russian historian Stephen Graham, born in Edinburgh in 1884, published *With Poor Immigrants to America,* which was a travelogue of his voyage, in 1913, to the United States. In this work, he made some influential predictions about the future of the English language in America. He entitles a chapter "The American Language," thus differentiating it from British English and granting it an autonomous status, as did Noah Webster in the eighteenth century: "Even Americans of the highest culture and of Boston families speak English differently from any people in the old country ... the American nation is different from the British ... therefore its expression should be different" (Graham 1914: 245). He believes that "the contemporary language of America ... is in the act of changing its skin" (248). The choice of the word "skin" here is hardly coincidental, as shall be seen below. The first two examples that he provides of this linguistic molting echo the concerns shared with others of the time who comment on the American language: "One, two, three, *cut it out* and work for Socialism ... *I should worry* and get thin as a lamp-post so that tramps should come and lean against me" (248). The presence of loan expressions from Yiddish is represented as linguistic as well as social and political corruption.

Thus it is no surprise that Graham summarizes his conclusions on the future of the American language as such:

America must necessarily develop away from us at an ever-increasing rate. Influenced as she is by Jews, Negroes, Germans, Slavs, more and more foreign constructions will creep into the language,–such things as "I should worry," derived from Russian-Jewish girl strikers. "She ast me for a nickel," said a Jew-girl to me of a passing beggar. *"I should give her a nickel,* let her work for it same as other people!" The *I shoulds* of the Jew can pass into the language of the Americans, and be understood from New York to San Francisco; but such expressions make no progress in Great Britain, though brought over there, just because we have not the big Jewish factor that the Americans have. To-day the influence that has come to most fruition is that of the negro. The negro's way of speaking has become the way of most ordinary Americans, but that influence is passing, and in ten or twenty years the Americans will be speaking very differently from what they are now. The foreigner will have modified much of the language and many of the rhythms of speech. America ... will be subject to a very powerful influence from the immigrants. (250–251)

It is interesting to note that Graham configures American English as historically subject to alien influence and sees this influence as the cause of the major distinction between the speech of the United States and the speech of Great Britain. Thus he attributes the differences in the American vernacular to "the negro's way of speaking," but this will be replaced by another alien influence: American English will change because of "the big Jewish factor," a factor that is, however, absent in England.

Graham's discourse also embodies the nascent American attitude toward the city and the country, loci, respectively, of decadent civilization and robust culture. He describes the cities of New York and Chicago in terms of physical disease and affliction that destroys nature: "The leaves of the trees and the grasses of the fields were wilted and yellowed by the airs and fumes ... a one-armed man followed me for about a mile, attracting a crowd of street Arabs by his foul language ... the heat increased ten degrees, and to move a limb was to perspire ... negroes and negresses sat in doorways. The odour of carcasses came to the nostrils from Packing-town" (274–275). Graham's reaction leaps associatively among natural decay, physical deformity, immigration, odor, heat, black Americans, and death. He concludes that

Chicago is not America, neither is New York or any other great city. If going to America meant going only to the great cities, then few but the Jews would emigrate from Europe ... the cities are places of death, of the destruction of national tissue ... the national health is on the farms of Pennsylvania and Indiana and Minnesota, Michigan, Iowa, the Dakotas, the Far

West. The men range big out there; the stand-by of the people will always be found in these places and not in the cities. (277–278)

It is interesting that he adds Jews to his construct only in summation and thus as the capstone of his paranoid and xenophobic edifice. And here, he most essentially captures the visceral momentum of the country, which rolls as a train farther and farther west, more and more distant from the urban decay that threatens the "national tissue." The latter is an interesting condensation of the physical and the cultural and combines both bodily tissue and the tissue of social fabric. This condensation implies that the presence of the urban eastern European immigrant is both a corporeal and a cultural danger.

The linear progress of his migration away from immigration moves to more and more sparsely populated areas, through the Dakotas, and ends with the sign of the "Far West," majuscule and majestic, where the men range big as mountain ranges in natural defiance of the urban immigrant. It is also very consonant that he should choose states that were settled by northern Europeans: Germans in Pennsylvania, Iowa, and northern Indiana, Swedes in Minnesota, Dutch in Michigan, and Icelanders in the Dakotas. These constitute the "stock" and locus of the nation, for "New York and Chicago, though necessary, are abnormal. They are not so much America as unassimilated Europe" (278). Also, in a collection of short stories or vignettes entitled *New York Nights,* Graham observes that, due to the massive immigration, "New York is not America, but it is New York" (Graham 1927: 35).

His image of the United States is basically New York (and its surrogate, Chicago) and non-New York: "when I escaped into the country I found that New York was not America, but only a great hostelry on the threshold of that country. I learned the great control power of the Anglo-Saxon and Dutch Americans ... and the Germans and Norwegians and Swedes and Danes, who swiftly change to a species of American hardly distinguishable from the old Anglo-Saxon and Dutch type" (Graham 1914: 291–292). It is not, however, any and all rural areas that contain the "national tissue:" his compass is bent by the loadstone of racial ideology, which pulls northward in avoidance of "the welter of negroes and Spaniards and half-castes in the South, in the black pale" (284). Thus with one half-sentence trope, he cuts a wide, exclusionary swath from Virginia to New Mexico. Graham concludes, assuringly, that the Nordic elements will dominate, and that "the coming American will be a very recognisable relation of the Teutonic peoples" (292).

These broad xenophobic theories of race and language formed the larger contextual frame for the discussion of more specific and technical treatments of pronunciation and elocution. An early example can be found in the discourse of Alexander Melville Bell (1819–1905), who was the father of Alexander Graham Bell. He was born in Scotland and was a lecturer in elocution at the University of Edinburgh from 1843–1865. In 1870, he took a post as lecturer in philology at Queen's College in Kingston, Ontario. In 1881, he relocated to Washington, D. C., where he pioneered in using his system of "visible speech," an early symbolic phonetic alphabet, to educate deaf-mutes. His *Elocutionary Manual,* published in 1878, supplies a list of "Anglicisms, Scotticisms, Hibernicisms and Americanisms," with no overt rationale for the ranking (and also no discussion of Canadian speech), and notes that

> the leading Americanism of Articulation is associated with the letter R. This element has none of the sharpness of the English R which, however softly, is struck from the *tip* of the tongue. The American R has a very slight vibration, with the tongue almost in the position for the French vowel *e mute.* The high convex position of the tongue for the American *r* final or before an articulation–when the sound is almost that of the English *y*–has been noticed. (Bell 1878: 66)

Bell is describing here the continuant /r/ as conventional. The final sound that he discusses, which is heard today as the diphthong sound of *bird* in the New York and Tidewater pronunciation (boyd), he represents as substandard. It is "a sound which is very peculiar, and cannot be represented by Roman letters ... the effect of R before and articulation is nearly that of Y; as is *spohyt* for sport" (50).

Bell is, however, much less generous in his description of the dropped /r/. In the short monograph *The Sounds of R* (1896), he states:

> In early English, R was always trilled, as it continues to be in Scotland, where most of the characteristics of early English are still prevalent. But in modern English the trills have been softened away, wherever R follows a vowel; until little is left of the R but its vowel quality. We are accustomed to the entire omission of R in negro speech–where *do* and *sto* are all that we hear for *door* and *store;* but in educated utterance there is some phonetic effect left in R, even where it is least manifest. (Bell 1896: 10–11)

Bell indicates here that /r/ should be audible in all positions, even when preconsonantal. The omission of final /r/ would be more salient to his ears than it would be to speakers from the American midwest, as he would be accustomed to the Scottish trilled /r/ and the Canadian retroflex /r/, which is more audibly retroflex than the standard American /r/. It is interesting that Bell uses southern black speech as an example of the complete omission of /r/, when, in fact, there were many white speakers from the east coast of the United States who also drop the /r/, and some of whom he would have surely encountered during his years in Washington. He finds the monophthong variant, which, after reducing /r/ to schwa, then combines the vowels into one, so that *door* rhymes with *doe* and *store* with *stow,* to be the most transgressive and ascribes it to "negro speech," even though it must perforce ultimately derive from white southern coastal speech. After having framed the transgression in racial terms, Bell then continues the racial classification in order to debase the dropping of final /r/ even further by juxtaposing it with "refined" pronunciation, thus now invoking class distinctions:

> Such delicate shades of sound are the distinguishing marks of refinement in pronunciation; and they should be carefully preserved by teachers, and by writers on the subject. Instead of this we find what may be called white "nigger speech"–so far as R is concerned,–actually prescribed by certain purveyors of instruction in national utterance. (11)

Here, Bell moves toward making an even closer association of the dropped /r/ with black speech and seems to contrast it with national interests:

> The vowelized R is a vestige of the stronger element which was undoubtedly prominent in our speech at an earlier stage; and–rather than eliminate this vestige,–we should conserve it and strengthen it, for the sake of its en-

ergetic influence on our national speech. In fact, we find, even now, that R refuses to be entirely vowelized in the current of fervid oratory. The tongue unwittingly rises from its passive condition, to take a firmer grip on the elusive sound of R. Give, then, no countenance to the "white nigger-speech" which would deprive us altogether of the valuable expressiveness of this element. The omission of the R sound ... is, at best, a vulgarism. (15–16)

Here, the presence of the black is related to a general cultural weakening of voice and oral power that acts to deprive white culture of its expressiveness. The dropped /r/ is described as a passive and weakened vestige of earlier strength that still preserves its nuclear essence despite the atrophic tendencies; it "refuses" to yield entirely and "rises" from its passivity, becomes "firmer" and gets a "grip" on itself. It is represented as a sign of inner strength, resolve, and character, a noble masculine phoneme persevering in the face of cultural decadence and contamination from the south via blacks as well as whites who are being corrupted by blacks. Bell concludes his monograph with the following admonition: "Above all, we must preserve those fine shades of difference which mark the cultivated speaker, and avoid such vulgar elisions as those which form the subject of the present animadversions" (22).

Bell's racist discourse did not seem to shock his contemporaries, as is evident in *The Technic of the Speaking Voice,* published in 1915 by John Rutledge Scott, who quotes Bell's comments on dropped /r/ and black English and laments this elision of postvocalic /r/, to which he refers as "soft r:"

Partly, perhaps principally, on account of its brief, faint, elusive character, it seems probable, however much to be regretted, that soft r will ere long be altogether lost as an element of spoken language. In southern England and in our own Southern, Middle, and Eastern states, it is habitually omitted, or nearly so, by the educated and the illiterate alike; and by the former the omission is regarded as a refinement! Why the "Southern accent" should be called "sweet," and why the New England pronunciation of 'Hahv'd', for Harvard, should be esteemed a sign of "culchu," are insoluble mysteries to me. In Scotland the tongue-tip trill is used for both initial and soft r. In our Western states the r that should be soft is often produced with the blade of the tongue more or less tense, and the sound is prolonged. (Scott 1915: 76)

Scott then goes on to invoke the image of the "white nigger" by quoting Bell. Scott is overgeneralizing here, as the "middle states," i.e. the mid-atlantic states of Pennsylvania, New Jersey, Delaware, and Maryland comprise an anomalous coastal pocket and do pronounce the /r/ postvocalically. His overgeneralization indicates an obsession with this sound as an indicator of the true, vital culture that pronounces the /r/ and the decadent "culchu" that does not. Scott seeks here to dismiss the southern influence and to emasculate New England power by counterpoising the stronger presence of the Gaelic trill and the rhotic /r/ of the American west. Thus, for him, the /r/ becomes a marker of strength and a pivot for a rotation away from northeastern toward western power, the latter having already emerged culturally as a signifier of potency.

The frequency of the conflation of white southern coastal speech with black English has been noted by H. P. Johnson, in the article "Who lost the southern r?", published in *American Speech* in 1928. Johnson begins:

> "Do you suppose that the South will ever get over the influence of the Negro on its speech?" The speaker was a young man from Utah who was studying law in the University of Chicago. "What influence have you in mind?" asked his companion, a South Carolinian, who was specializing in English.
> "The dropping the *r.*"
> "You have spent two years in England, haven't you?"
> "Yes."
> "How many Negroes did you see in England?" (H. Johnson 1928: 377)

This passage is interesting in that it indicates two important aspects of southern coastal speech. The first is the conflation mentioned above. The second is the indication of obvious difference between British and American southern coastal speech, even though both of those regions drop the postvocalic /r/. The Utah resident has been confronted with three examples of dropped postvocalic /r/: standard British, southern coastal American white, and southern black; yet he made connections of affinity and causality only between the last two regions; the relation of British never occurred to him.

Johnson goes on to say, "So often has it been said that Southern people talk like Negroes that at last a few of the people of the South are beginning to believe it. Can the origin of *any* of the tendencies of the speech of the South be attributed to the Negro? Surely he had nothing to do with the dropping of the *r"* (377). Johnson then embarks on a lengthy expedition to discuss some of the speech characteristics of the south–including the fronting of the final velar nasal, as in speakin' for speaking, and the assimilation of final stops, as in /kɛp/ for /kɛpt/–in order to demonstrate that the speech peculiarities of the south all originate with the English speech of the white colonial settlers to that region. He traces instances of these locutions back to a firm Anglo-Saxon basis in the works of John Gay, John Keats, and in Walker's *Critical Pronouncing Dictionary and Expositor of the English Language.* He concludes: "As those who have long resided in the South know, the Negroes are the imitative part of the population. They are likely to catch all the *nuances* of the speech of those among whom they live" (382).

Johnson's discourse is indicative of the effort to insulate the speech of the southern white from the southern black and to show that the lines of influence proceed from the former to the latter, and not vice versa. Thus his discourse displays the presence of a two-tiered attempt at the decontamination of American speech. The first tier involves the north disassociating itself from the speech of the south and stigmatizing it as corrupted by the influence of black speakers. On the second tier, the south represents itself as in complete control of its own discourse; the speech patterns of blacks are merely quaint vestiges of white southern history, obedient imitations of the master discourse that do not escape from a subaltern sphere. Oddly, if one removes the racist ideology in his discourse, Johnson's account of black English is consonant with recent progress in the field. Shana Poplack's aptly titled *The English History of African-American English* studies the African American diaspora and argues convincingly that black vernacular English is, at its core, a non-creolized form of English, and that the differences and divergences between standard white English and black vernacular, as well as differences among varieties of black English are both post facto and postbellum.

The conflation of southern coastal speech with black English persists into the second half of the twentieth century, as has been attested by the noted linguist Raven McDavid:

> In experiments in Chicago, middle-class Middle Westerners consistently
> identified the voice of an educated urban white Southerner as that of an un-
> educated rural Negro ... similar experiments in New York have yielded
> similar results. And many white Southerners can testify to personal diffi-
> culties arising from this confusion in the minds of Northerners. In Ithaca,
> New York, I could not get to see any apartment advertised as vacant until I
> paid a personal visit; I was always told that the apartments had just been
> rented. (McDavid 1966: 15–16)

Thus it may be concluded that the south was doubly stigmatized and
marginalized: first due to the antipathy between the northern and
southern states after the American Civil War, and second due to the
associative connection between the speech of white southerners and
black southerners. The latter also involves the subliminal perception
of southern culture as the container of black culture. These stigmati-
zations acted to guarantee the exclusion of the south in the process
of locating the standard American pronunciation.

Thus the marginalizing of racially associated speech patterns has
a longer history in the south than it does in the north. In the case of
the south, the other was a function of the indigenous black population. In the case of the north, the other was the twentieth century
immigrant, and it was the presence of this immigrant that acted as a
catalyst for the first movements in the United States to make English
the official national language.

Another example of this can be seen in Margaret Prendergast
McLean's *Good American Speech* (1928). The chapter "General
Speech Conditions in America" begins with the following assessment: "It is pretty universally acknowledged, both in America and
elsewhere, that the speech of the general public in America is very
far below the standard which is expected in a country where com-
pulsory general education, widely distributed wealth, and unlimited
opportunities for higher learning, prevail" (53). Among the three
"recognizable causes of America's poor speech," she lists "the influence of masses of uneducated foreigners who speak English with

many non-English sounds, with foreign stress, foreign choice and arrangement of words, and intonation" (53). This negative influence "presents one of the greatest speech problems in several of our largest and most important cities. A definite effort is being made in several cities to solve the problem, but it has only begun" (53). It is interesting to note that McLean sees the same location and influence threatening the national speech that other elocutionists see: it is the immigrant and the city that are to blame. Written in the twenties, the phrase "several of our largest and most important cities" would clearly include New York and Boston. While McLean identifies similar threats to national speech and identity, she advocates a different cure than most of the other elocutionists; she prescribes that continuant /r/, which she defines as a "voiced fricative continuant," is to be "used only before a vowel or a diphthong" (131). She says that it "is not pronounced in standard or cosmopolitan English before a consonant" (133). She also prescribes linking /r/ but not intrusive /r/ (131). Clearly, she is advocating the preservation of the standards and characteristics of New England and New York speech, but she is seeking to purify them from foreign influence. Thus the dynamics of her discourse are such that the movement away from contaminating influences is not geographic, but instead one of social elevation within the same geographic area.

Margaret E. DeWitt was a significant interlocutor in the discourse of race, ethnicity, and speech. The founder of the "EuphonEnglish" and "Euphonetics" movements, she authored *EuphonEnglish in America* (1924) and *Our Oral Word As Social and Economic Factor* (1928). An outspoken opponent of H. L. Mencken and of "western" speech patterns, DeWitt advocated the use of northeast coastal speech as a basis for the national standard.

She defines "euphonetics" in a circular fashion as "the form that is euphonious or that is internationally recognised as *Accepted Standard* or *Good*" (DeWitt 1924: xiv). This is clearly tautological; the best usage is such because it is the most aesthetically pleasing, which, in turn, makes it the best usage. It is the "paramount form of a language that has evolved, not from logic and rules, but from usage–*good usage*" (xiv). And clearly, her justifications for this type of speech also do not evolve from logic or rules. This is not a general, but a class-specific speech that is "spoken by at least one group of interested New World natives" (xiv).

This work was written in the midst of the national xenophobia that gave rise to drastic governmental legislation to limit immigration. This xenophobia was central to the national discourse of the time and exerted a gravitational field that was able to draw even the most tangential social phenomena into its orbit, even if those phenomena had been initially separate from the discourse of race. Consequently, and very early on in the work, DeWitt ushers the discussion of national social problems into the topic of the standardization of language. She begins the digression by saying that "the oral mother tongue" is "the bond that holds together the main problems of a nation's home and world life" and then moves wholly into a discussion of immigration: "Early nationhood often requires a bulk increase in population, but the kind of immigrants who come in pioneering days are not on the whole mere lazy or intriguing grafters, because there is hardly enough inducement for that class, therefore selective immigration is not always as important a factor at that time, although it is never safely ignored." She claims that it is "a national danger to follow an unrestricted and, above all, non-selective immigration policy" and holds that, for no reason, "can a nation afford to de-racialise its nucleal self" (35). One is tempted to ask how she got from point A to points B and beyond, i.e. what is the perceived connection among aesthetically pleasing speech, immigration, pioneers, and thievery? The answer is that the associative paranoia of the time caused elements that vaguely or remotely recalled the discourse of immigration to be grafted on to that discourse in a fashion that seemed seamless or transparent to the participators in that discourse.

DeWitt privileges the pioneer over other immigrants and, in doing so, invokes an opposition between older immigration to rural areas and recent immigration to urban centers. The image of the pioneer is coded for a northern European ethnicity as well as a certain self-sufficiency and independence. Moreover, it is also coded for the establishment of a northern European hegemony over a racially distinct indigenous people. This force is "nucleal" to American culture, and one must not "de-racialise" it. Consequently, she advocates "a moderate race-consciousness" (35–36) and claims that America now suffers from "the far too unlimited influx of those aliens who are in great part racially opposed to us, or those who are but the unlamented dregs of Europe" (36). Such aliens "will but cause biological disintegration of a nation" and "infuse into a Body Politic blood that destroys the racial blood of a nation" (36). Our nation has no "dyke to protect it from the seething inrush and under-tow of a devastating tidal wave composed of conflicting races and the reprobates of all races" (36). We should be "advancing those races and individuals which have already been generously and will-ingly grafted on to the national tree" (36).

DeWitt's discourse is replete with the xenophobic images of the time. The danger is expressed in corporeal and aqueous metaphors. The other, who will poison the American body, is represented both as blood and as water, as a tidal wave, an image that not only meto-nymically conveys the means of alien arrival on the shores of North America, but that also communicates the permeating invasiveness of the danger. The only defense is a barrier, a dyke that fully insulates the body against the incursion. There are, however, present immi-grants who are not really other to the national body; these have been "willingly grafted on to the national tree" and must, therefore, ex-hibit familial or phylogenetic similarity with the ethnic root that is to be propagated. True alterity, i.e. the presence of a racially different other, would preclude the use of the image of grafting.

DeWitt digresses so far from the issue of language and pronun-ciation that her arguments seem to lose all connection to the initial subject. Indeed, one may begin to wonder whether the discourse of race is being displaced onto the discourse of language, or whether the discourse of language is being displaced onto the discourse of race. The answer is that both seem to coexist in a matrix of transfer-ence and counter-transference; each can substitute for and justify the other. In *Our Oral Word As Social and Economic Factor,* she argues against racial and ethnic integration: "How broad, human, sanctified, how *anything* is it to play with creation as if it were an art supply shop of many coloured paints or many mediums? Whom do these hysterical unifiers help in their desire to commingle mix and inter-change all things within their sight and grasp?" (DeWitt 1928: 11).

It seems here that she is referring to racial intermarriage, when, in fact, she is discussing simple racial coexistence. One is forced to conclude that the mere presence of ethnic and racial alterity itself is of sufficient psychological strength to invoke an image of miscegination. It is at this point that the notion of language standardization finds its utility: "And we, of the English-speaking world, how can we keep our rainbow of race-varied millions kin? We cannot improve spiritually in taking away the physical best of our many integral parts by mixing the rightful differences away into one muddled smirch. With us it is the oral word that will bridge the gap of race ..." (12). She uses linguistic standardization as an excuse for racial and ethnic segregation. The initial appearance of prejudicial inequality is then mitigated by a linguistic detour, and it is the decoy of language standardization that produces ostensible equality, a sort of linguistic civil rights, the image of which reverberates with related images of freedom of and through speech. The American people should be linguistically unified, not ethnically or racially. Thus she challenges the "race sentimentalist" in saying that, "the general social workers can do far more through speechways than they have begun to realise" (xxi). Language standardization becomes thus a substitute for racial equality: "many social workers ... advocate various race mixtures as a means of greater unity." Instead, she recommends "extreme conservatism ... is it less sane than to jump headlong into wholesale experiments unguided by history?" (xx).

DeWitt refers to the type of speech that she advocates in both local and universal terms. On the one hand, she speaks of an "Ameri-Canadian cause" of linguistic unification (128) in the "New World" (127); on the other hand, she speaks of "our own World-Accepted Standard" (127) as if it were a universal standard for English. Her descriptions reveal, however, a form of American English that is abstracted from eastern coastal speech: "It is the form which may be called the Eastern or General in the New World, and is a composite of forms that were once more local in parts of New England and the South. It is the equivalent form of the composite that was once more local in Southern England" (127). It is interesting to note that she uses the term "general" to refer to eastern patterns as opposed to western ones, and she may well be the only voice to do so. While the type of speech that she advocates resembles RP to a certain extent, she takes pains to differentiate it from British speech. She says that RP "is practically the equivalent of ... our own World-Accepted Standard" (127), but that this world standard is maintained in part by "wisely avoiding the poor imitation of extreme British forms" (137). It is best described as an American northeastern coastal stage speech, for which she takes the advice of Charles Grandgent: "It is not unnatural that, when localising especially good speech in the New World, Professor C. H. Grandgent said that we might turn to the stage" (121). She does, however, rightly observe that this particular speech was neither artificial nor British:

> Many people within the acting profession itself began to look upon stage diction as artificial, unnecessary for success. They too failed to realise that their ideas of the artificial were more dependent upon points of difference between the General or Western and the equivalent Eastern form. They too were inclined to think that all New/World actors aped the English, just as Mr. Mencken is inclined to regard it little realising that the non-extreme stage diction of the New and Old worlds alike was really based upon the living world-wide English speech. (135)

She observes that its difference from western speech does not indicate its identity with British patterns; she is also among the few who see Mencken's misprisions for what they are, and it is Mencken who is her chief adversary. She refers to his opus as "The Amuricun Lankwitch" and to Krapp and Kenyon as linguists of "The School of the Curly Tongue" (128). She is opposed to the celebration and propagation of the (mid)western pronunciation of /r/, as it signifies to her a rustication and unsophistication that is at odds with her ideology of American speech and culture. DeWitt's words are the last attempt to elevate the cultivated upper-bourgeois speech of New York and New England to the national standard. The same xenophobia, however, that motivated the cathexis of the (mid)western accent also motivates DeWitt to support eastern speech patterns: it is a solution to the problems of immigration in the twenties. Consequently, she is a strong advocate of the dropped postvocalic /r/: "The half or even third of the vowel in every word in the written form of which the vowel is followed by *r* and a pause, or *r* and a consonant, that is a basic detriment to speech as an entirety" (165). Thus in her reference key for "Euphonetigraph Notes" (316), *fur* is transcribed as [fə:]. She also transcribes the first vowel in *father* as [ɑ:] and *hard* and *last* as [hɑ:d] and [lɑ:st], clear markers of cultivated New York and New England speech in the twenties. [ɹ] does exist in *very* [veɹɪ]. It is important to note that there is no alveolar flap here, which differentiates it markedly from British speech.

Thus DeWitt advocates a supraregional "General Eastern," which seems also to be her notion of stage pronunciation. While it is indeed closer to RP, its impetus is not class-based, but racial and ethnic, and it is representative of the discourse of prescriptivism in the age of immigration, a discourse that only thinly veils an agenda of racism and exclusion.

While there is no official language in the United States, there are, however, individual states that have adopted English as the official state language. At this writing, there are eighteen states with such a mandate (Tatalovich 1995: 22). The first official language laws in the United States were passed in Nebraska (1920) and Illinois (Tatalovich 1995: 23). Their appearance closely paralleled the national legislation enacted to severely restrict immigration, which culminated in the National Origins Act of 1924. The discourse of language restriction in this period tended to specifically recommend not simply English, but "American" as the official language, and there were bills to that effect introduced in congress. A representative example can be found in the rhetoric of Montana Congressman Washington J. McCormick, who introduced a bill in 1923 that "would supplement the political emancipation of '76 by the mental emancipation of '23." He reasoned as follows: "America has lost much in literature by not thinking its own thoughts and speaking them boldly in a language unadorned with gold braid. It was only when Cooper, Irving, Mark Twain, Whitman, and O. Henry dropped the Order of the Garter and began to write American that their wings of immortality sprouted ... let our writers drop their top-coats, spats, and swagger-sticks, and assume occasionally their buckskin, moccasins, and tomahawks" (Tatalovich 1995: 70).

McCormick's discourse sets up the oppositions of east and west, refinement and nativism, artificiality and authenticity and identifies the last element in each binary opposition as American. Here, the American language is envisioned as most authentic and most essential in its western form. It is also connected to phallic images of masculinity and hostility, which are opposed to the less masculine and less potent images of the east; the sign of the decorative swagger stick is replaced by the sign of the mighty tomahawk. The implications of his discourse were obvious to the *New York Times,* whose editorial "Language by law established" of February 7, 1923 replied sarcastically, "It is a great honor to Montana that this fertile and patriotic suggestion comes from one of her Representatives in Congress. Westward the star of empire over language takes its way. Main Street will have to look to its laurels." One can see here the waxing tension between east and west, most specifically between New York and the western states. "Main Street" is here a trope for the urban civilization of New York, which scoffs at the implications of McCormick's rhetoric. Ironically, the sardonic prediction of the *New York Times* that "the star of empire over language" would move westward was to prove to be an ominous utterance indeed.

It is precisely this antinomy of east and west that informs the debate on immigration and language. This can be seen in the reaction of individual states to the National Origins Act of 1924. This landmark legislation was intended to greatly reduce the immigration from southern and eastern Europe and to entirely halt immigration from Japan. Thus the law was also occasionally referred to as the Japanese Exclusion Act. The act was passed by overwhelming majorities in the Senate (62–6) and the House of Representatives (323–71) and displayed an interesting geographic distribution. Of the seventy-one opposing votes in the House of Representatives, twenty-four were cast by New York, nine by New Jersey, eight by Massachusetts, five by Connecticut, and three by Rhode Island (Tatalovich 1995: 74). Thus the combined votes of New York and New England comprised sixty-nine percent of the opposition. In all, only thirteen of the then forty-eight states registered any opposing votes, and the entire western area recorded only one single opposing vote, that being from Nebraska. There were also no opposing votes registered from the southern states.

The division of opinion on the restriction of immigration plays out geographically as an opposition between the urban immigrant culture of the coastal eastern states and the rural Anglo-Saxon culture of the western and southern states. A good example of this opposition can be seen in the 1924 congressional debate between two congressmen: John Robison of Kentucky and Fiorello La Guardia of New York. Robison's attacks on La Guardia can be seen as representative of western and southern attitudes in general. Robison proclaimed:

> There is about as much difference in my district and the gentleman's from New York City, according to my information, as there is between the Sahara Desert and the Atlantic Ocean ... all of our working people are 100 percent American ... they know that unless the hordes of immigrants are checked and America ceases to be the "garbage can and dumping ground for the world" their wages will be reduced and living standards greatly lowered ... the hope of the perpetuity of our institutions is in the highlands of West Virginia, Virginia, Kentucky, Tennessee, Georgia, North Carolina, and South Carolina. Here lives the purest strain of Anglo-Saxon blood ... there is nothing but Americanism in the mountains. In the great city of New York groups of foreigners in recent years marched under the red flag of anarchy. There is no room in the mountains of Kentucky for the red flag. (Tatalovich 1995: 78–79)

Robison's discourse represents New York as contaminated by garbage and communism. For him, the notions of American essence and Anglo-Saxon consanguinuity are practically coterminous. Their locus is in the rural area, which is depicted as pure and as geographically elevated; the highlands serve as a geographical correlate for cultural superiority that, in its elevated position, is untouched by the pollution below. In this period, the discourse of opposition to New York consistently involves notions of rural idyllic purity, racial purity, linguistic purity and authenticity, and also political freedom. Fiorello La Guardia eventually became the mayor of New York and an icon of the presence of immigrant power in that city.

In 1972, the linguist Einar Haugen, born in Sioux City, Iowa, to Norwegian parents, published *The Ecology of Language*. The inaugural chapter, "Language and immigration," begins with this paragraph:

America's profusion of tongues has made her a modern Babel, but a Babel in reverse. City and countryside have teemed with all the accents of Europe and the rest of the world, yet America has never swerved from the Anglo-Saxon course set by her founding fathers. In the course of a century and a half the United States has absorbed her millions and taught them her language more perfectly than Rome taught the Gauls and the Iberians in centuries of dominion. Oriental and African, Spaniard and Frenchman, Jew and Gentile have all been domesticated, and this without leaving any serious impression on American English. (Haugen 1972: 1)

Haugen's image of America is one of a linguistic idyll, a waxing romantic force of Old Testament proportions, a biblical de-babelizing that redirected language back toward its edenic roots and reintegrated religious, racial, ethnic, and social differences into a kind of linguistic monotheism. His cosmology is one of the law of the father tongue properly instructed by obedient daughters, and the language in question is initially represented obliquely in ethnic terms as "Anglo-Saxon;" only at the end of the paragraph is the term "American English" used, which supposedly has not been impressed upon by the immigrant, but instead inherited intact by the offspring, the next generation. Haugen himself was born under the auspicious sign of that heritage; of northern European descent, he is from the heartland of America, the rural midwest, the region that generated the preferred general American accent, a standard that was not affected, according to Haugen, by the presence of the non-English speaking immigrant.

This is a conclusion that one could come to if one were viewing linguistic influence within the narrow binary categories of either assimilation or accommodation, i.e. if one were asking if American English remained largely unchanged and assimilated the foreign elements into itself–aside from the processes of foreign vocabulary borrowings common to most of the world's languages–, or if American English changed itself structurally in order to accommodate the foreign element.

For Haugen, the process has been one of simple assimilation on the part of American English and accommodation on the part of the foreign element. America "has absorbed her millions" and has impressed its language upon them, with the result that the immigrant language of the non-English speaker becomes creolized in the process: "Each language has parted from the strict purity of its native form, and has taken over elements from American English. Each language has been forced to adapt itself to new conditions, and thereby gives us a vivid picture of the immigrant's struggle for a position within the new nation and his gradual accommodation to its demands" (2).

Ostensibly, immigrant languages have had only regional influence on pronunciation, which has become systemic most notably in the cases of Wisconsin and New York City. By systemic is meant that the particular instance of pronunciation has been adopted by most of the speakers in that region who are not of the immigrant population that initiated the pronunciation in the first place. In the cases of the immigration of German speakers to Wisconsin and Yiddish speakers to New York, both the speakers of German and Yiddish, which is a dialect of German, devoice final obstruents. The German and Yiddish speaking immigrants to these respective areas transferred this process of devoicing to the pronunciation of American English, where it became systemic. Thus, in Wisconsin, the word *bars* tends to be pronounced not as /barz/ but as /bars/; in New York, the final fricative in the word *because* is heard as /s/ instead of /z/; and the final affricate of the word *village* is heard as /tʃ/, so that the words Greenwich Village both end in the same sound.

These are but local instances of systemic change induced by a foreign substratum. There seem to be no other general, i.e. non-local influences on the pronunciation of American English that can be attributed to immigration. None, unless one adds another variable into the equation: that the presence of the immigrant had an effect on the *orientation of the standard American accent,* i.e. that the presence of immigration had an effect on the *selection and location* of accent that was to become the national standard.

Haugen goes on to say, "This approach to the immigrant is one that has received little attention from historians of immigration. The fact is not surprising when we see that even linguists have often regarded the dialects of the immigrant as beneath their dignity. Nevertheless, some studies have been made, and anyone interested in finding them can turn to the appendix of H. L. Mencken's *American Language,* where the material has been ably surveyed" (2). Haugen is correct in saying that the linguistic presence and influence of the immigrant have been understudied, and his own work on the subject was among the very best. His contention, however, that they have been "ably surveyed" by Mencken is quite interesting, as it ascribes to Mencken a position of authority, objectivity, and, implicitly, advocacy.

As a professional linguist, Haugen was clearly aware of the problematic aspects of the work of H. L. Mencken, but here, his words are quite generous and seem to represent Mencken as a proper authority on the linguistic presence of the immigrant in America. Indeed, Mencken is generally regarded in popular spheres as the *doyen* of American English, as its first major scholar who laid the vast and solid groundwork of its study. The problem is that the integrity of this foundation is taken for granted, and no archaeological examinations or even infrastructural inspections of Mencken's discourse have been undertaken. The following chapter of this study shows how Mencken and the uncritical reception of his work contributed to an ideology of standard American English that suppresses the true causal factors of standardization.

6. Teutonic struggles: Mencken and Matthews

Henry Louis Mencken (1880–1956) began his career as a journalist for the *Baltimore Herald* and the *Baltimore Sun*. He published books on Shaw and Nietzsche and quickly rose to national prominence as an American intellectual and man of letters. His lifelong work, however, for which he is most well known, was the multi-volume *The American Language,* which was published in 1919, revised and enlarged in 1921, 1923, and 1936, and supplemented in 1945 and 1946. The reaction to the book was quick and positive and resulted in the reception of Mencken as the dean of American English, an attribution of authority that persists into the present era. In August 1919, the journalist Frederic J. Haskins entitled a tributary article in the *Minneapolis Tribune* "Here at last is a professor of Americanese," in which he deemed Mencken "the Christopher Columbus of Americanese." Mencken founded the journal *American Speech* and was affectionately called "the pa of American speech" (Algeo 1970: 6).

It would be purely hyperbolic to characterize Mencken has the discoverer of "Americanese;" perhaps a more accurate trope would be the Paul Revere of the language, the alarmist with one monotonous reveille whose anti-British message was to set the tone for subsequent accounts of the etiology of standard American pronunciation.

The chief operative mechanism in Mencken's accounts of the genesis of the general American pronunciation is clearly the avoidance of England; he seeks to represent the development of American standardization in opposition to the received pronunciation of Great Britain and tends to read the actors who contributed to the standardization of American in precisely that way. In the last edition of *The American Language* that Mencken himself edited in 1948, he invokes, by implication, the American revolutionary war and the dissociation from England. He says, "the voice of the people, in the last analysis, must decide and determine the voice of the people" (Mencken 1948: 28).

Mencken begins this descriptive odyssey of American pronunciation with the late nineteenth century "amateur philologian" (22) Richard Grant White and his 1876 *Words and Their Uses,* which advocates the dropped /r/ and the broad /a/, both of which are characteristics of nineteenth century New York and New England speech. Mencken chooses to excerpt the following passage from White: "It is only in a comparatively small, although actually numerous, circle of people of high social culture in New England and New York, and in the latter place among those of New England birth, or very direct descent, that the true standard of English speech is found in this country" (22).

Mencken begins here the process of associating the speech of New York and New England with that of England, in spite of the fact that he had, before him, a wealth of information that indicated that no English speaker would ever confuse northern coastal speech with that of Great Britain. British speech is to become, however, Mencken's straw man, his constructed hostile interlocutor. He says that *Words and Their Uses* was the *Stammvater* of all the cocksure treatises on "correct" English which still appear in large numbers, and are accepted gravely by the innocent. The schoolma'am followed it dutifully for more than a generation, either at first hand or at second, third or fourth, and the super-gogues who trained and indoctrinated her seldom showed any doubt of its fundamental postulates. (23)

The image of the female teacher helps to situate this process outside of the structures of dominant male power and implies that a proper modification of this tradition would result in a form of re-empowerment and an escape from indoctrination into individual freedom. It is interesting to note that the female teacher is represented as a schoolmarm, an image coded for unreflective rigor, discipline, and restriction of freedom that also serves to infantilize the student and represent him in a state of maternal dependency.

In the preface to the third edition of *The American Language* (1923), Mencken outlines the opposition in his agonistic struggle. It includes the "Society for Pure English, organized in England in 1913," which "now has an American secretary," and whose "American collaborators are rather intent upon ... augmenting the authority of standard English in America ... they are simply Anglomaniacs." His adversary is the Columbia English literature scholar Brander Matthews and the publisher of the *New York Times,* Adolph Ochs. Mencken seeks to represent Matthews's conception of standard American as the same as standard British and claims that Matthews envisions "England as the lordly husband and the United States as the dutiful and obedient wife." Thus Mencken represents himself not only in an Oedipal struggle to free the United States from a linguistic form of English tyranny–a sort of second American revolution on the field of language–but also as a hero who seeks to deliver America from a form of feminized servitude, which would thus imply a masculinizing and empowering of the United States. He accuses Matthews of seeing "every effort to study the growing divergences, cultural, political and linguistic, between the two nations as no more than evidence of a sinister conspiracy of Bolsheviki, Germans, Irishmen and Jews" (Mencken 1923: viii). This accusation against Matthews is one of the most telling of Mencken's slips. It will be demonstrated below that Mencken's representation of Matthews can be seen as Mencken's own projections of a paranoia located in language and a profound Anglophobia that together construct the chimeric opponent of Anglomania.

Brander Matthews (1852–1929) taught at Columbia University from 1892–1924, during which time he became the first professor of dramatic literature in the United States. Lawrence J. Oliver deems him "one of the most prominent and influential American men of letters during the late nineteenth and early twentieth centuries" (Oliver 1992: xi). He endeavored to establish New York City as the literary capital of the United States by founding several literary clubs and promoting the writings of New York authors. He was also a very influential scholar of the English and American languages who sought to determine the standard of American English and its differences from British English. Like many scholars of his time, he felt that both the American identity and the American language were being threatened by the influx of foreigners into New York, Boston, and the other seaboard cities. In the essay "The American of the future," published in 1906, he echoes the concern elicited by the pouring of immigrants into New York: "more than fifty thousand in four days!" (Matthews 1906: 3). He foregrounds the presence of a "half-million Russian Jews" (7) whom he contrasts with and subordinates to the "German Hebrew" and "Hebrew of German birth" (11–12).

Matthews asks if these immigrants "are worthy to be welcomed within our commonwealth? Will they trample America as the thronging Goth and Vandal trampled Rome?" He advocates the closing of the borders to "Orientals" who "abhor assimilation and have no desire to be absorbed. They mean to remain aliens; they insist on being taken back when they are dead,–and we do well to keep them out while they are alive" (5). His criterion is chiefly one of assimilation. If the other can lose its alterity, be absorbed into the dominant culture, and not destabilize the existing order, if "the children and grandchildren of these ignorant immigrants learn to revere Washington and Lincoln, and they take swift pride in being Americans" (11), then they are admissible. As long as this is the case,

> we need not fear any weakening of the Teutonic framework of our social
> order. Beyond all question we shall preserve the common law of England
> and the English language,–for these are priceless possessions in which the

> welcome invaders are glad to be allowed to share. The good old timbers of
> the ship of state are still solid and the sturdy vessel is steered by the same
> compass. (22)

The invocation of England and of common law do not function to
situate America as an obedient cultural, legal, and linguistic dependent and derivative of England. What Matthews seeks is a form of
Anglo-Saxon commonality, a broad, umbrella-like understanding of
a generally shared phylogeny that would also contain individual differences. His concept of American culture and American language
pivot around a general Teutonic essence, which is the parent of the
Anglo-Saxon essence, which, in turn, is informed by a masculinist
discourse of virility, vigor, strength, and order. In the 1921 essay "Is
the English language degenerating?", he begins by stating that the
purpose of the 1917 meeting of the American Academy of Arts and
Letters was "to consider its duty towards the conservation of the
English language in its beauty and purity," and that the committee
members "were of opinion that the condition of our noble tongue
was alarming and that this condition was perhaps even more alarming in the United States than it was in Great Britain." This was due
to the fact "that English as spoken and as written here in the United
States had entered on a period of degeneracy not unlike that which
befell Greek in the days of its decadence" (Matthews 1921a: 3).

The comparison with classical Greece is highly ideologically
laden. It is another instance of the nineteenth century racial and cultural ideology, seen in the theories of Hendrick, Grant, and Graham,
that seeks to genetically derive classical Greek and northern European race and culture from an Aryan or Indo-European parent.
Within this ideology, Teutonic culture, which would include Germany, England, the Netherlands, and Scandinavia, is seen as conservative, noble, and resistant to the corruption and decadence that
spread northwards from Rome. Germany made particular use of
these concepts in the nineteenth century–most visibly expressed in
the racial theories of Houston Stewart Chamberlain–in order to distinguish its culture from that of France and to elevate itself above
French civilization. The latter was a decadent and urbanized civilization, while the northern cultures had remained pastoral, thus con-
serving the essence that the Aryan ancestors had brought to the

northern regions. This was seen as the same noble essence that the Aryans brought with them to Greece, and which developed into the nucleus of western civilization. Within this ideology, Rome is dismissed as not only an unoriginal derivative of Greek culture, but also as a decadent corrupter of the same. The intellectual structures of western civilization were established by Greece, became diluted and contaminated by Latin culture, but remained intact in the pastoral Aryan artifacts of Germanic/Teutonic culture.

Matthews sees both the United States and England as proper heirs of this cultural nobility. It is also their duty to protect it from decay and foreign incursion, which are embodied as a weakening or flaccidity of culture. The necessary counterforce is represented in the passage above as "sturdiness." He directly quotes the language of the American Academy of Arts and Letters, which employs the term "Hellenistic degradation" (3), defining this as "resembling or partaking of Greek character but not truly Hellenic" and as "combining Greek and foreign characteristics or elements" (3–4). This reflects a specific understanding of Hellenism as a period in the history of Greece, in which Greek culture was heavily influenced by other cultures. Matthews sees two causes for this "Hellenistic degradation:"

> In the first place, the change took place when the language was no longer young, with powers of expansion natural to youth, but was already mature and fixt … and in the second place, the change came when the language was no longer in the possession of the people alone who had created it, but was spoken and written over a vast territory among many peoples separated from the main stem by political and other traditions. (4)

This is a clever displacement of the rhetoric of anti-immigration onto the field of ancient history. The culprit in the process of the decline of language is the influence of foreigners who precipitate the intracultural loss of vitality. For Matthews, "the deterioration of the Greek language" is "due directly to the degeneracy of the peoples who spoke Greek. They had lost character as well as ability. They had become weaklings mentally and morally; the virtue had gone out of them; and as an inevitable consequence it had gone also out of the literature and out of the language." This would not have occurred "if the Greeks had kept their virility … so long as a people retains its vigor and its vital energy, its language never grows old; it preserves its health and its freshness; it has the secret of eternal youth. It will never suffer from creeping paralysis of style or from fatty degeneration of the vocabulary" (5).

Matthews's specious interpretation of Hellenism is both a rationalization and apology for the marginalization of the immigrant in America. By analogy, the presence of the immigrant in the American metropolis effects a degeneration of cultural character, strength, intelligence, morality, virtue, virility, and vitality in such a way as to affect not only the contemporary culture, but also the noble heritage and heredity of the culture itself, and this degradation is articulated in the very mode of cultural self-expression. Matthews concludes that "linguistic decay is inseparable from racial decadence" (6) and asks "if the condition which helped to bring about the degeneracy of Greek is not similar to that of English today ... in its immediate contact with a host of other and inferior tongues" (13). He holds that the solution to this problem lies

> in the centripetal force of a standard language chosen out of current speech, carefully selected, recognized as a standard, imposed by the school-teacher and spread abroad by the printing press. The Hellenistic decay of Greek was due mainly to the degeneration of the Greeks themselves; but it might have been arrested, more or less, if a knowledge of standard Greek had been carried by books and magazines and newspapers to all those who spoke the language and if there had been schools everywhere impressing upon the young the nobility of the tongue in which Homer had told the early legends of the race. (15)

Thus standardization should be implemented for purposes of maintaining linguistic and racial purity. In Matthews, one sees an early example of the presence of racial arguments within the ideology of language standardization. It is not for the purpose of facilitating communication; it is for the preservation of a race-based notion of cultural and natural identity. Language is thus a semiotic medium that pronounces the superiority and hegemony of the dominant culture. If the immigrant is to stay here, then this linguistic identity is to be worn by that immigrant as a sign of the uniformity of the assimilating culture.

Matthews is not as Mencken represents him; he does not recommend an adoption of British English as the standard: "There are indisputable differences between the Londoner and the New Yorker … yet when all is said the differences between British English and American English, however many they may be, are relatively few" (13–14). He adds that the English language "is no longer in the exclusive custody of the inhabitants of the island where it grew to maturity" (20). What Matthews advocates is a supra-national standard of stage English pronunciation that would act as a linguistic umbrella and encompass both the United States and Great Britain. In "A standard of spoken English," he claims to have found this in the pronunciation of traveling stage actors:

> These performers have succeeded in shedding whatever local peculiarities of pronunciation and of enunciation they may have originally possessed. No longer do they speak British-English or American-English; they speak English pure and simple, as did Lord Coleridge and Lowell. And this should be an ideal for all of us, whether native to the United States or to any part of the British Commonwealth. (Matthews 1921c: 222)

This umbrella language would act to purify English and to maintain its Teutonic essence as the premier language of that race. In "One World-Language or Two?", he says, "The supremacy of English among the Teutonic tongues will be more and more widely recognized" (Matthews 1921b: 280). Thus language standardization for Matthews is the vehicle for the maintenance of Teutonic superiority and integrity in the face of massive immigration.

A contemporary of Matthews, Barret H. Clark, who authored, in 1930, *Speak the Speech. Reflections on Good English and the Reformers,* says that Matthews spoke "a dialect as genuine and as pure, as delightful and as quintessentially local" as one might find in Appalachia. He says that Matthews "told stories in a language that I'm sorry never got into any of his books. If it had, his writings would not have been so dull. If we judged him by these alone, we would imagine him to have been a rather pompous old professor, which he emphatically was not" (Clark 1930: 22–23). He also observed that Matthews pronounced "thaw out" as "thor out" (22). Clark's observations on Matthews's speech contradict the characterization of

Matthews as an advocate of British pronunciation, as he was perceived by Clark as speaking with an unmistakable New York City accent. Clark did not, however, support Matthews's advocation of the standard English of the stage. He argues against standardization but supports the "Mid-Western R" (30).

It is interesting to note that Matthews's concept of standard English would perforce maintain the dropped postvocalic /r/ as a marker of stage pronunciation. In doing so, he effects another solution to the problem of the corruption of the American metropolis by the immigrant. He maintains elements of the Boston and New York pronunciation, but he seeks to sublimate them of their local color, i.e. he makes these pronunciations very white. Cleansed of the taintings of locality, this pronunciation embodies the essence of Teutonic purity. It does so not by subjugation to British pronunciation, as Mencken would have one believe of Matthews, but by a gesture of Anglo-Saxon commonality. Curiously, as shall be demonstrated below, the Nordic and Teutonic nature of English is also that which navigates and motivates Mencken in his rally for general American English. The approaches of Mencken and Matthews are but two halves of the same solution. They are both steered by the race-conscious compass that seeks the best form and locus of Teutonic essence within the United States.

In the 1948 edition of *The American Language,* Mencken characterizes the accent that he would have this ideal common man speak as "general American." He utilizes Charles Thomas's taxonomy of three varieties of American English: "Boston-New York, Southern, and the Western or General" (Mencken 1948: 28). He says that general American is spoken by at least 95 million of the 140 million Americans: "It is constantly spreading, and two of its salient traits, the flat *a* and the clearly sounded *r,* are making heavy inroads in the territories once faithful to the broad *a* and the silent *r*" (15).

While he is correct in saying that the use of non-rhotic /r/ is waning, he is motivated to ascribe it to an association with British speech. This causes him to misinterpret valuable data from experiments on the perception of American pronunciation. Mencken discusses the study made by Wilke and Snyder in 1942, which demonstrated that the "general American" pronunciation was most pleasing to the American ear, and that the New York pronunciation was among the least pleasing. This experiment is treated in more detail in section 3.3. below. It is important here to examine Mencken's reading of the study. He says that

> the result of the poll was overwhelmingly favorable to General American. Of the thirty-two samples the five at the top of the list all belonged to it, and it also got more votes than any other form further on. The runner-up was Southern American. The Eastern speech of the Boston area came out very badly, and that of New York City even worse. (31)

Of the thirty-two speakers used by Wilke and Snyder, none is identified as speaking the "Eastern speech of the Boston area," nor is any speaker identified as displaying coastal New England speech. Mencken then makes a characteristic inductive leap to the speech of Great Britain: "Of considerable significance is the fact that Southern American got more votes than the speech of the Boston-New York region. To most Americans of other sections the latter shows ... the somewhat pansy cast of Oxford English" (32). While New York speech was indeed found at the bottom of these ratings, none of the participants related it to the sound of British speech. It is quite doubtful that any American would confuse New York City speech with Oxford English.

Mencken continues to focus on the dropped postvocalic /r/ as a sign of British influence and discusses some aspects of early radio pronunciation in that light. There were some announcers in the early days of American radio who used some aspects of British pronunciation. Mencken was understandably opposed to this and refers the reader to others who objected to this as well, specifically to Combs's 1931 article "The Radio and pronunciation," which opposes the broadcast use of Briticisms. Mencken says that "Josiah Combs, of Texas Christian University, for long an astute and diligent student of American speechways, flung himself upon it in *American Speech,* and in 1931 he returned to the attack" (32).

The problem is that the dropping of postvocalic /r/ is not among the features of British speech to which Combs and others objected. In the article referred to by Mencken, Combs discusses only a few phonemes of British speech: the occasional use of the diphthong /ay/

instead of the American high front lax vowel in the pronunciation of *civilization,* and the use of the tense vowel /e/ instead of the American lax version in the pronunciation of *again.* He also briefly mentions the backing of /æ/ and is in all likelihood referring to the British pronunciation of *dance* and *rather.* He makes mention, as well, of the pronunciation of the initial vowel in *either* as /ay/ as opposed to /i/:

> A number of announcers and broadcasters, American by birth and training, affect the British pronunciation of *i,* especially in such words as *prohibition, civilization, organization;* that is, the *i* is made long. It appears also in such prefixes as *anti-, semi-,* etc. There is little justification for such pronunciation in America. But it sounds "different, you know," and is therefore elegant! As to *either* and *neither,* the pronunciation suggested by the Standard Dictionary and by Worcester's is overwhelmingly in favor in America. (Coombs 1931: 126)

Combs judges these phonemes as foreign to American English; he makes no such mention of dropped postvocalic /r/.

Mencken is very interested in marking the dropped postvocalic /r/ in two ways: as a sign of weakness and emasculation and as a sign of British presence; hence his reference to the "pansy cast of Oxford English." In representing the sound as a product of cultural weakening and emasculation, Mencken aligns himself with a longer explanatory tradition from Jespersen to Grandgent. In representing the sound as an indication of British pronunciation, however, he stands alone. For it was not the association with British English that caused non-rhotic /r/ to become rhotic, but, instead, it was its association with the American areas in which postvocalic /r/ was dropped that motivated the sound change. It is not because Americans should not sound British, but because they should not sound like they come from American regions where the /r/ is dropped: New York, Boston, and the southern coast.

In *Words and Ways of American English,* Pyles writes, "Yet many of us can remember a time, no longer than twenty-five years ago, when standard British English ... was commonly regarded in this country as somewhat affected ... now, however, we have become so accustomed to it in the talking films and on the radio ... that we take it very much in our stride" (Pyles 1952: 233–234). This indicates that the perception of British pronunciation in the early days of American radio was very distinctive and could not have been confused with any American speech. On the contrary, the broadcasting of British radio programs in America actually served to accustom the American ear to British pronunciation, making it sound less foreign than it had sounded.

Mencken's assertion that southern speech was a runner-up in the study conducted by Wilke and Snyder needs to be qualified and nuanced. Southern coastal speech did better than average in the study, but southern mountain speech was rated poorly, as has already been noted. Mencken says that the reason that southern speech fared well was due to the fact that "it is most familiar in North and West in the talk of Negroes, and is thus associated with suggestions of the amiable and the amusing" (32). He continues in a footnote on the same page:

> This attitude, unhappily, has been changing since certain imprudent Negro leaders, like certain imprudent Jewish leaders, began objecting to the presentation of their people as humorous characters. Whatever has been gained for dignity by this reform has been more than lost in good will. Such saviors of the downtrodden always forget that people laugh *with* a comedian rather than *at* him, and that the general feeling he leaves behind him is one of friendliness. Potash and Perlmutter probably did far more to allay anti-Semitism in the United States than all the Zionists and Communists. (32)

Again, Mencken is invoking the political along with the ethnic in such a fashion as to associatively stigmatize the ethnic as not only a cultural, but also a political threat to American stability. In addition, in using the idea of imprudence, he is indicating a preference that blacks and Jews remain quietly on the margins. This passage also strengthens the connection between the speech of the southerner and the speech of the black and helps demonstrate their perceptual connection in the mind of the ideal white listener. The association of the southern coastal accent with blacks helps insure its exclusion from canonical pronunciation. Again, the south here is understood in a very restricted scope that includes only the southern coastal culture, linguistically and culturally distinct from the southern mountain and south midland regions, the speech patterns of which could not be confused with black English.

Mencken's lack of generosity, tolerance, and latitude toward speakers of black English is evident in his analysis of the nasalization of consonants, i.e. their assimilation to other consonants that are nasalized. He offers, as an example, the pronunciation of "brannew" instead of "brand-new." In the 1919 edition of *The American Language,* he says:

> Here the speech is powerfully influenced by Southern dialectical variations, which in turn probably derive partly from the linguistic limitations of the negro. The latter, even after two hundred years, has great difficulties with our consonants, and often drops them. A familiar anecdote well illustrates his speech habit. On a train stopping at a small station in Georgia, a darkey threw up a window and yelled "Wah ee?" the reply from a black on the platform was "Wah oo?" A Northerner aboard the train, puzzled by this inarticulate dialogue, sought light from a Southern passenger, who promptly translated the first question as "Where is he?" and the second as "Where is who?" A recent reviewer with alarm argues that this conspiracy against the consonants is spreading. (Mencken 1919: 219–220)

The reviewer to whom he refers is Hugh Mearns, and the article in question is "Our own, our native speech," which Mearns published in *McClure's Magazine* in 1916. It is interesting to note that the title of this article corresponds quite literally to the properties of the discourse of language purism that have been identified in George Thomas's study: "Our native language is that form of speech which we recognise as 'ours'. That is why in some societies, where linguistic nationalism has developed only recently, it is not uncommon to use no more specific name for the language than 'ours'" (Mearns 1916: 43). Mearns's article, however, makes no mention of a conspiracy of any sort; on the contrary, he proudly celebrates the deletion and assimilation of consonants as a trademark of Yankee speech that identifies it as separate from British speech and recalls the American Revolution: "America has never taken kindly to the English 't.' In revolutionary times, we remember, America would not give a Continental 'd' for all the 't' in Britain. Consistently, enough, all our 'T's' are rapidly turning into 'd's' and our 'D's'–are disappearing rapidly." His article lists scores of such examples in primitive phonetic notation and concludes with the words "It's intoxicating! One's own, one's native speech!" (43). The speech that Mearns is celebrating is colloquial white male speech; he makes no mention of blacks at all.

It is interesting that Mencken, who clearly has an encyclopedic knowledge of English dialect forms and, thus, of numerous instances of consonantal elision in the speech of native white speakers of English, should focus here on consonantal elision as being of particularly black origin. Moreover, Mencken observes, in other places in his multi-volume work on American English, that black English (which term he did not use; he spoke of "the speech of the Negroes") is received pronunciation from slaveowners whose English is of southern British origin. It is thus more likely that the consonantal elision recounted here is also a regional peculiarity of British English. Instead of explaining it in this way, Mencken accuses the "darkey" of spreading a conspiracy to weaken "our consonants," thus estranging and disempowering the black speaker altogether.

It is important to note the presence of hierarchy in the use of upper and lower case writing above. He writes "negro," "black," and "darkey," but "Southern passenger" and "Northerner." Thus the white, whether northerner or southerner, is elevated above the black. The dynamics of upper and lower case writing can be seen as a condensation of Mencken's most comfortable stance vis-à-vis blacks.

As editor of the literary magazine *The American Mercury,* Mencken was more generous to black writers than any other of his contemporary editors and published, in the 1920's, such figures as W. E. B. Du Bois and Langston Hughes. Yet his position on race is quite problematic, as has been noted in the most recent biography of Mencken, which characterizes it as "a mixture of enlightenment, paternalism, and racial stereotyping" (Hobson 1994: 247). It is basically a stance of "*noblesse oblige* ... with blacks, and decidedly not with Jews, he always felt himself in charge–never threatened, never challenged" (457). A position of comfortable superiority does seem to capture his orientation to a large degree. We see, however, that, when it comes to the matter of his desired American language, he does feel that this possession is indeed threatened by the presence of black English.

Mencken's ideal American speaker has his own colloquial and substandard speech, for which Mencken seems to feel no need to apologize. He represents his ideal speaker as rural, rustic, and race conscious. This can be seen in the 1923 edition of *The American Language,* in which Mencken attempts a folkish "translation" of the *Declaration of Independence* into the "American vulgate," because "the original is now quite unintelligible to the average American" (Mencken 1923: 398):

> People ought to choose the kind of government they want themselves, and nobody else ought to have no say in the matter. That whenever any government don't do this, then the people have got a right to can it and put in one that will take care of their interests. Of course, that don't mean having a revolution every day like them South American coons and yellow-bellies and Bolsheviki ... it's better to stand a little graft, etc., than to have revolutions all the time, like them coons and Bolsheviki ... (399)

He also "translates" Lincoln's *Gettysburg Address:* "Well, now we have got a war on our hands, and them crooks from the South are trying to do to us what they done to the poor coons" (403). The discourse of these "translations" constructs a certain kind of speaker: male, rural and rustic, individualist, white, less educated, and clearly race conscious. He is the embodiment of a general American essence, both in location and ideology. The use of the racist epithet "coon" is applied to black Americans as well as Latin Americans and equates racial with political threats: the black is invoked within the phrasing of anarchy and is thus represented as a threat to white stability. This threat is specifically to northern stability, as the rendition of the *Gettysburg Address* implies that the southern states seek to enslave the northern ones. In addition, the invoking of Bolsheviks serves to strengthen the implication of political instability while also broaching the images of the Slav, specifically the Slavic immigrant to the United States. It is also plausible that the semantic field of this image also includes the Jewish leftist. Thus the discourse of these reinscriptions synthesizes several threats to general white American male autonomy and marginalizes them: the black, the southerner, the communist, and the Slav.

When Mencken criticized "certain impudent Jewish leaders," he implied that they should be more circumspect. This contrasts with his linguistic celebration of the speech of the rustic white in the folkish renditions of the *Declaration of Independence* and the *Gettysburg Address*, in which imprudence is affectionately represented as the stuff of proper revolution and demonstration of civil rights for a certain class of privileged males.

Among the various gambits involved in the seeking of a locus for the ideal uncontaminated speaker, one that is particularly salient is the avoidance and suppression of the southern mountain, or Appalachian area. This suppression is especially interesting, as the Appalachian /r/ is more constricted, retroflex, and audible than the (mid)western /r/ and could have been a stronger counterpoint to the coastal non-rhotic /r/. The omission of the southern mountain area is the result of the negative ethnic and class connotations of that area. Mencken displays the race-conscious avoidance of this region, when he decides, in the 1948 edition of *The American Language,* to invoke Toynbee, from his 1935 *A Study of History:*

> The Appalachian has relapsed into illiteracy and into all the superstitions for which illiteracy opens the door. His agricultural calendar is governed by the phases of the moon; his personal life is darkened by fear, and by the practice of witchcraft ... he is a victim of hook-worm, a scourge which lowers the general level of vitality in Appalachia just as it does in India ... The Appalachian mountain people are the American counterparts of the latter-day white barbarians of the Old World ... [their] nearest social analogues ... are certain "fossils" of extinct civilizations ... such "fossils" as the Jewish "wild highlanders" of Abyssinia and the Caucasus. (Toynbee 1935, 2:311–312; Mencken 1948: 116)

This remarkable passage suggests that the Appalachian dwellers were once literate and thus enlightened, but that they then regressed into illiteracy and the preferred consequential condition of superstition. They are anomalous among the population of European descent, in that they have degenerated into a state that a Eurocentric perspective would characterize as precivilized and savage. Mencken then adds his own observations on Appalachian dwellers to Toynbee's characterizations:

They produce, at somewhat longish intervals, individuals of marked ability–whether by chance adulteries or by some fortuitous collocation and ef-
fervescence of Mendelian characters is not certain. But such individuals
usually escape from their native alps at the first chance, so that their genes
do not improve the remaining population, which continues to go downhill,
with excessive inbreeding to help it along. (117)

Mencken then includes the remarks of Vance Randolph: "The people in these isolated hill-regions intermarry excessively, and feeble-
mindedness is very common; it is not unusual to find whole families
and clans of people who ... pronounce words in some grotesque or
ludicrous fashion" (Randolph 1929: 203–204; Mencken 1948: 119–
120). Thus the Appalachian area, which could be a contender for the
national standard of pronunciation, as it not only retains, but overar-
ticulates the final /r/, and which offers the only national rival for the
(mid)western pronunciation, is marginalized and marked as dis-
eased, incestuous, genetically inferior and capable of poisoning the
gene-pool, imbecilic, and it is also analogized to an undesirable
other–the "Jewish Wild-Highlander." The rejection of Appalachia is
not due to its ruralness: the marginalization of the southern mountain dweller is an instance of the wholesale avoidance of southern
culture by the northern postbellum hierarchy.

Mencken's attempts to marginalize the Jewish influence on
American speech occur in a more oblique fashion. In the 1923 edition of *The American Language,* he says, "The Italians, Slavs, and
above all, the Russian Jews, make steady contributions to the
American vocabulary and idiom ... *I should worry,* in its way, is correct English." His characterization of the influence of Jews upon
American English, however, becomes less neutral when he adds that
the immigrant has "a very ponderable influence upon the general
speech," and is not "socially worthy of the suavity of circumlocu-
tion." He "throws his influence upon the side of the underlying
speech habit when he gets on in the vulgate. Many characteristic
Americanisms of the sort to stagger lexicographers ... have come
from the Jews, whose progress in business is a good deal faster than
their progress in English" (Mencken 1923: 212). Clearly, Mencken
is depicting the Jewish influence upon American English as one that
lessens the finesse of the language and acts to blunt its eloquence,

substituting instead a more crass and less polished form of communication. Again, the presence of the other is seen as destabilizing, as it "stagger[s] the lexicographer."

In a further discussion of the vocabulary used by Yiddish speakers of English, Mencken studies the preference of Yiddish terms over English ones and observes that the "East Side Jews" (416) regularly say *Tisch,* preferring the Yiddish/German term, but *window* and *chair.* He claims that, instead of *Stuhl,* "*chair* is always used, probably because few of the Jews had chairs in the old country" (417). He leaves the presence of window unaccounted for; it would be hardly feasible to offer the absence of windows in the old country as an explanation. The gratuitous interpretation of *chair,* which borders on wild speculation, serves to represent Jewish immigrants in a state of destitution, underscore a certain stereotype, and effect further marginalization.

His views on Jews demonstrate a more pronounced paranoia in the thirties, when he claimed that the Newspaper Guild had been "gobbled" by "the New York Jews," whom he also called "Franklin's Jews." He also wrote that "the great majority of American Jews in 1933 ... were violent partisans of the Bolsheviks" (Hobson 1994: 413). In the forties, he claimed that *Esquire* was run by "a gang of kikes" (Hobson 1994: 454). Here we see, foregrounded again, the conflation of the ethnic, the political, and the economic. White stability is threatened by the ethnic alterity of the Jew, which overlaps with the political alterity of communism; on the outskirts, usually safely away from the guarded center, lies also the alterity of the black.

These are, however, additional threats that augment the dominant danger represented by British language and culture. Mencken's Anglophobia was so strong that he actually supported Germany over England in the First World War, defended the sinking of the *Lusitania* in 1915 (Hobson 1994: 136–138), and even supported Hitler's Germany over England in the early years of World War II (Hobson 1994: 434–436). His Anglophobia also extended to American Anglo-Saxons, the American southern states, and puritanism, all of which contrasted sharply with his own German ancestry (Hobson 1994: 189). Focusing part of his paranoid conspiracy upon England enabled Mencken to situate his 1919 edition of *The American Language* in opposition to British English and to celebrate therein that opposition. While Mencken was correct in observing that some upper-class Americans of his era wanted to sound British, this observation gets lost in the discourse of his massive overgeneralizations.

While Mencken's scholarship in the multi-volume work *The American Language* and its supplements is thorough and exhaustive and clearly indicates a labor of love, it is oriented in large by his own ideological gyroscope, and he is unaware, in this work, of his navigational directions. This is evident in the passages already discussed above that locate general American in a space independent of and fortified against the undesirable influences of southern language and culture and of immigration. It is, however, most telling in his readings of the reasons for the emergence of rhotic /r/ as the national standard, and one is inclined to conclude that Mencken's description of this emergence actually resulted in a very influential prescription for American pronunciation.

In 1976, the journal *American Speech* published an exhaustive bibliography of American pronunciation since 1945. In the lengthy introduction to that survey, Lee Pederson represents Mencken's status as a linguist by saying, "More than any other single person, Mencken laid the foundation for the studies of North American English pronunciation that have appeared since" (Pederson 263). He praises "Mencken's exhaustive bibliographical descriptions" and says, "Although Mencken shrugged off paternal responsibility for American Speech, a strong case can be made today for his having fathered both the journal and the serious study of pronunciation it pursues" (263). Pederson's *Forschungsbericht* acknowledges only minor modifications of Mencken's research:

> The presentation was weakened by the perpetuation of the "general American" designation, the state-by-state coverage that resulted in a disjointed discussion of regional speech, Mencken's uncritical acceptance of some dubious sources, and an inadequate reflection of the developments in descriptive linguistics. All of these problems were resolved by McDavid's revision edited from the scholarly perspective of a professional linguist who was, at once, sympathetic to Mencken, able to preserve the style and substance of a great book, and sensitive to the advances in linguistic science. (288–289)

Here, Pederson restates the qualifications and general criticisms of Mencken that were expressed by Raven McDavid in his preface to the 1963 edition of *The American Language*. More apologies than substantial critiques, the assessments of both Pederson and McDavid overlook the major flaws of ideological origin in Mencken's discourse. By virtue of their status as bona fide linguists, these two scholars, in their support and minimal critique of Mencken, contributed to the persistence of important misconceptions in the etiology of American pronunciation, as well as to the continued suppression of awareness of the major determining factors thereof (see also McDavid 1981).

Thomas Pyles's *Words and Ways of American English* begins in full deference to Mencken and ranks him with the linguist George Philip Krapp: "In *The American Language* and the two supplements to that marvelously stimulating work, Mencken has dealt so fully and so well with the word stock of American English that any later writer must of necessity employ a good deal of his illustrative material. Indeed, there would seem to be little point in seeking out recherché examples simply because Mencken has used all the good ones" (Pyles 1952: vi).

The canonization of Mencken as the patriarch of the American language is partly responsible for the suppression of awareness of some very important factors that contributed to the standardization of American pronunciation. The xenophobic dynamics in Mencken's discourse cause him to read the emergence of standard American English pronunciation in a certain way and to contribute to that standardization by virtue of his power as a cultural icon of his era. It can be said that his race conscious statements do not need to make extensive use of the censoring mechanisms of repression and displacement; on the contrary, they appear at times to be unabashed. The function of this race consciousness in determining the ideology of his discourse is important, for race consciousness itself prohibits the use of the category of race as an objective analytic tool. Discourse thus becomes itself the tool of race consciousness and xenophobia, which, in and through discourse, construct the particular ideological ethic. Writing within this paradigm not only occludes the perception of categories of race as conceptual determiners of one's own discourse, it also blinds one to the perception of those categories in the discourse of others whom one is invoking or analyzing. These processes characterize Mencken's account of the rise of general American and his description and evaluation of the principal actors who contributed to that rise.

Thus many misprisions of the standardization of American pronunciation can be traced to Mencken's Anglophobic agenda. Mencken also contributed, however, to a misreading of the role of radio broadcasting in the standardization process. The following section concerns the presence of the radio voice in the post-immigration period.

7. Vizetelly and the birth of network standard

Francis Horace Vizetelly (1864–1938) was born in London, emigrated to the United States in 1891, and became a citizen in 1926. He was employed by the Funk and Wagnall's Company as an associate editor and, in 1914, became managing editor of the *Funk and Wagnall's New Standard Dictionary of the English Language.* He was also employed by the Columbia Broadcasting Company as a consultant on pronunciation and was dean of the Columbia Announcer's School of Pronunciation. Employed to train radio announcers, he was one of the greatest influences on network standard pronunciation in the United States. His discourse on elocution and pronunciation displays itself increasingly as a function of foreign immigration to the United States and is most profoundly informed by that immigration. It is also informed by an ideology of gender.

Vizetelly's contribution to the standardization of American radio pronunciation has been largely taken for granted and not subject to analysis. There are two culprits in this process: the general ideological metanarrative of American populism and the ideological explanations of H. L. Mencken, whose account of Vizetelly's influence has gone unexamined. In "The Pronunciation of American," from the 1948 edition of *The American Language,* Mencken situates Vizetelly at the receiving end of his lengthy treatise on the anxiety of influence that American English (i.e. Mencken's concept thereof) displays toward the "parent" form of British English. Indeed, Mencken sets up his entire narrative as a kind of Oedipal struggle against the father tongue.

After Mencken's misreading of Josiah Combs, discussed above, whom he allies to himself in his quixotic agon, Mencken then moves on to discuss Vizetelly:

> The early radio announcers, a generally uncultured and even barbaric class of men, recruited largely from the ranks of bad newspaper reporters, were not altogether to blame for their unhappy tendency to imitate English speech, for they were under pressure from various prophets of refinement ... but public opinion turned out to be strongly against any movement to extend this artificial polish to the speech of the current announcers, commentators, and crooners ... on February 4, 1931 the Columbia Broadcasting System sought to allay the uproar by setting up a school for announcers, and appointing the late Dr. Frank H. Vizetelly as its head ... he was no advocate of Oxford English and at once announced to his students that he was eager to "help in spreading the best traditions of American speech" ... the effects of Vizetelly's pedagogy were soon visible, and in a little while the effort to talk like English actors was only a memory in the CBS studios. (Mencken 1948: 33–34)

This passage begins with folkish images of simple American men who are oppressed by an allegiance to England. Their savior is Vizetelly, who liberated radio pronunciation from a mimetic bond to British speech. In doing so, he supposedly launched a national tidal wave that swept away the foreign colonist:

> So late as April 26, 1931, the Chicago *Radio Weekly* was still denouncing both the CBS and the NBC for attempting to "oust the American language from the American home ... and supplant it with English as she is spoken in England, or in the 'better' social centers of America, which is practically the same thing," but this was before Vizetelly really got under way. (34)

Vizetelly is represented here as the kingpin in this struggle for liberation from British speech. A close reading of Vizetelly, however, reveals no such agenda in his discourse.

In *Mend Your Speech* (1920), which is largely a prescriptive guide to semantic usage, Vizetelly's concept of language is not yet visibly affected by the presence of immigration, but it is, however, constructed by the presence of gender. The introduction to the work represents woman as the most errant violator of proper speech. While "the business man" tends to prefer simpler and more colloquial locutions that hamper his social mobility, "the woman of the 'awfully nice' class ... might pass for a woman of refinement if she could keep her mouth shut until she had learned to say correctly what she has to say" (Vizetelly 1920: 3). Men are represented as more modest and circumspect in their use of language and underestimate their linguistic facility, whereas women will overestimate their expertise and transgress the educated semantic boundaries of the terms that they are using.

How to Use English: A Guide to Correct Speech and Writing (1932) is similarly concerned with semantic prescription and also makes as yet no mention of the immigrant. It does, however, introduce the association of city, class, contamination, and decay into the discourse of language. Vizetelly justifies the necessity of speech training, for without it, "the child, contaminated by the illiteracies of the street and the vagaries of colloquial conversation, will quickly lapse into slovenly ways" (Vizetelly 1932: viii).

His most significant and influential work, however, was the 1933 *How to Speak English Effectively*, which was specifically aimed at "the announcing staff of the Columbia Broadcasting System" (Vizetelly 1933: xxviii). The work is framed as an urgent call to arms to protect and preserve the purity of American English and opens with the following words:

> At no other period in the history of the United States has there been so great a need for active steps to establish and maintain the purity of our language as at the present time. The tide of immigration of past years poured thousands of prospective citizens of alien birth and speech on our shores, and societies have been formed for the purpose of establishing and promulgating the languages of many of the foreign countries represented here. It is curious that the foreign-born, coming to a country where American speech dominates, should offer opposition to the speech of the land of their adoption, and aim to supplant it by their own–a foreign tongue. It was the realization of the danger that lay dormant in such a condition of things that inspired Theodore Roosevelt, when President of the Untied States, to declare that–"We have room but for one language here, and that is the English language; for we intend to see that the crucible turns our people out as

Americans of American nationality and not as dwellers in a polyglot boarding-house." The spirit embodied in this thought led the writer to compile this book. (ix)

The linguistic threat is stated here very clearly: immigration is contaminating our language and threatening its "purity." Thus the work at hand stands in direct opposition to the influence of immigration and introduces pronunciation as a weapon in that struggle. The invocation of the figure of Theodore Roosevelt as a patron inspiration is here far from gratuitous. Roosevelt was not only an opponent of immigration, an advocate of the "purity" of the northern European American heritage, and an antisemite, but he was also an icon of masculinity and embodied, more than any other American president, the image of presidential male authority. The virility of his image was constructed by several factors: he was a decorated hero of the Spanish-American War and the organizer of the First United States Volunteer Cavalry, The Rough Riders; as a lieutenant colonel, he led the cavalry charge up Kettle Hill in San Juan. The event, however, that is the most significant condensation of his heroic image took place on October 14, 1912, in Milwaukee, while he was campaigning for reelection on the "Bull Moose" party ticket. Shortly before a scheduled speaking engagement, he was shot in the chest by a would-be assassin. The bullet fractured a rib and settled close to his right lung. Undaunted, he mounted the podium and spoke for almost an hour with the bullet lodged in his chest. He showed the audience where the bullet had entered and said, "I have just been shot, but it takes more than that to kill a Bull Moose" (Harbaugh 1975: 421). In invoking the image of Roosevelt, Vizetelly is also conjuring a powerful sign of masculinity and vitality into the discourse of proper pronunciation.

Vizetelly sympathizes "with a New York *Times* correspondent who recently suggested that our vernacular is a patois 'perhaps due to the mongrel population in our midst'" (xv); he does not document this source. He goes on to say: "Most authorities feel that our native speech is a thing to be cherished along with other American traditions, and that every endeavor should be made to maintain its present purity in essentials ... there are several agencies that may be of great aid in keeping American speech standardized. The theater, the moving pictures and radio" (xvi).

He represents the need for and process of standardization as a weapon against the contaminating influence of immigration, which is set off in opposition to American traditions and purity of language. There is also an element of nativism in his conception of American speech. It is interesting to note that he configures the contemporary media as a bulwark in the struggle against those influences.

Vizetelly continues to invoke images of nativism and purity while gradually adding a geographical focus to his agonistic appeal. He begins by general references to the large cities of the east:

> During the last decade, speech improvement has received increased attention from American educators. The need for such training was felt particularly in the eastern populated cities and towns. Some observers and students of language have come to fear for the future of our native tongue, and to plead for an organized effort to preserve its purity. (xvi-xvii)

> Foreign accent and foreign idiom are particularly persistent in American speech. A dozen different languages may be spoken in the homes of a cosmopolitan city ... the problem is to keep ... American language in conformity with accepted usage. (xvii)

Clearly, it is the northeast that is spoken of here, as there was much less immigration to the southeast in the early twentieth century. The image of the eastern metropolis then becomes more and more clear: it is New York that is meant here, and it is configured within a matrix of city, immigration, and pronunciation:

> As a people, we should cultivate the speech of our homeland, and not the hybrid tongue that smacks of the subway, and is uttered with a washed-out pronunciation characteristic of spent vitality, or indolence ... plain American speech should be cultivated by everybody here. It may not be a pleasant fact to contemplate, but we New Yorkers are pitifully behind the times. Once, and not so many years ago, we "stepped lively" and spoke quickly. The world at large "sat up" and "took notice." Wherever a New Yorker went he was welcomed for his briskness of manner, keenness of intellect, and rapidity of negotiation in closing business deals. But we have fallen on evil times, and go about our business in a lackadaisical, semisomnolent

way, even to the extent of puling our speech, drawling or whining it out in affected tones, utterly devoid of spirit and virility. (xxiii-xxiv)

In this passage, he opposes the speech of the homeland to the speech of the subway, which are metonyms for the rural parts of America and for the New York urban area respectively. The figure of "plain American speech" is thus a more rural, simpler, and authentic speech that stands in contradistinction to the decadent city, which has "fallen on evil times." Thus the distinction becomes an ethical one as well, with the "homeland" and the "subway" standing for good and evil respectively; the latter is a product of the presence of the immigrant. The discourse here is clearly a nostalgic one that longs for the past greatness of New York. It is thus a very early indication of a change in the national image of New York, which no longer commands the respect that it once did. It is most important for the present discussion that this reflection of a change in status for New York takes place within the context of language and, most significantly, of proper pronunciation. The decline of New York is represented here as related to a general laziness and lack of virility. The image of virility, from the Latin *vir* 'man,' situates speech as an embodiment of robust masculine locution and recalls the incipient heroic figure of Theodore Roosevelt.

The sapping of this virility and its expression in and through language situate the problem in a corporeal location. This is not only bodily, but also genetic; for Vizetelly, the language about him in New York is "the lamentable moaning of an anemic and enfeebled race" (xxvi). This discourse displays the persistence of nineteenth century ideologies of race, class, and consanguinity. Using the idea of race here, especially in its singular form, functions as a divisive technique. It defines a group in terms of physical appearance and cultural behavior and thus grounds culture in the body. It is a particular racial group that is being threatened and "enfeebled" here by the presence of other racial groups, and the waning of the power of that race is situated in blood and language.

If the dominant race has become anemic, then it has lost its red-bloodedness, its robustness, and its power. Vizetelly envisions a kind of talking cure or speech therapy that will revitalize the race, and this type of speech therapy concerns the proper pronunciation of /r/:

> It is well known that races which habitually pronounce their *r's* are easily heard, while races that habitually do not pronounce their *r's* are inaudible. For clearness of tone production, the enunciation of the Glasgow Orpheus Choir has proved as great a revelation to the majority of English actors and actresses as that of the Mormon Tabernacle in Salt Lake City has to the people of the United States. Why? Because its members never fail to pronounce their *r's*. (31)

Rhotic /r/ is framed here in a context of proper race and religion. He recommends that the /r/ be fully audible, as it is "spoken by a vir-r-ile race" (31). Thus pronouncing the /r/ is not only a sign of virility but also a bodily infusion thereof, i.e. its use will refortify the organism. By hyphenating "vir-r-ile" in the manner that he does, he foregrounds and underscores the fully audible continuant /r/ as the nucleus of virility in itself, and thus of refortification. Indeed, Vizetelly seems to valorize the Celtic trilled /r/ most highly when he says, "In standard [British] English the trilled or vibrated *r* is almost absent; but this is not so when words containing that letter are spoken by the Irish or the Scots, or by the people of Tyneside" (30). Rhotic /r/ is, in short, to become the linguistic symbol of a proud America: "Our radio announcers are the torchbearers in a work which can succeed only as long as they exercise that vigilance which is not only the price of liberty, but the tribute they must pay to culture that generations yet unborn may call them blessed" (33). The triadic image of torchbearer, liberty, and vigilance allude to the Statue of Liberty. The pronunciation of the radio announcer is represented here as the proper expression of the American myth of individual liberty. He (the virile radio announcer is necessarily masculine) also protects that liberty in and through his language, which is used as a kind of linguistic customs official processing and assimilating the waves of immigrants who are granted admission under the sign of the Statue of Liberty.

Vizetelly's discourse displays prejudices and avoidances that are similar to those of others who have recommended "general American" as the proper national pronunciation. Not only does he shun the contaminated city, here clearly New York, but he also dismisses the speech of the south and the presence of black English as well. In dismissing the speech of the south, he, like many others of his day, does not differentiate between southern mountain and southern coastal speech:

> Nothing is more absurd than the prevailing popular belief that a drawl puts the cachet of distinction on the one that uses it. There was a time when Reuben and Rebecca were picturesque figures outside of New York; that is, in their native mountain regions. On the street, one meets, now and again, some man or woman who imitates Reuben and Rebecca, and this type is served up as an attraction on the air. Red-blooded, virile men and women have little or no use for the drooling drawls of effete sensuality or its simulation. Atonic debility, mental depression—actual or induced by copious libations of juniper juice—or amorous dreaminess are not indispensable attributes of healthful entertainment. (60)

One can only speculate as to which type of southern pronunciation Vizetelly has in mind here. By virtue of its attractive radio presence and connotations of effeteness, sensuality, ease, and its reveric quality, it seems to evoke images of gracious southern coastal speech rather than southern mountain, even though he locates it in the mountains. In any event, it is also opposed to the red-blooded elocutionary virility that he desires. This passage is, above all, an oblique characterization of the south as a monolithic unit that should be generally dismissed, and that does not merit the attention of differentiating analysis.

In addition, he also tends to imply a causal relationship between black English and southern speech, and he ascribes a larger debilitating influence to black English as well, but he does so in an even more oblique and encoded way. He asks:

> Who brought this type of expression here? Certainly not the English, who are famous, the world over, for clipped and mumbled speech ... perhaps we owe the drawl to the Russians, with their heavy lethargy that can be roused to frenzy only by artificial aid. Or is it due to the invasion of the North by the people of the South? In our speech some of us still drawl almost to the point of spiritless utterance. Men and women alike seem to be suffering from that indolent affectation of indifference which has been alleged to be

characteristic of the South–of Alabama, Mississippi, Kentucky, or Tennessee. (61)

It is most likely that the invasion spoken of here is an allusion to the massive black migration from the rural south to the industrial north in the latter half of the nineteenth century. There were no substantial communities of southern whites in New York, but there were clearly such ghettoized communities of blacks in Harlem, for instance, who would have preserved the characteristics of southern coastal speech. In his indictment of indolence as an epidemic, it is quite plausible that Vizetelly is using the "people of the south" here as a displacement for blacks. He also seems to be relating this indolence to black culture metonymically when he says: "No one should expect to make over an adult who has devoted twenty years of his life to acquiring a slovenly enunciation, and associated correct speech with the inharmonious mingling of jazz-like sounds" (41). The presence of jazz music relates the problem that preoccupies the writer associatively to black American culture. It is also interesting that he invokes the presence of the Russian as a possible contributing factor. This invocation serves as a condensation of the influence of the millions of eastern European immigrants upon the culture and language of New York. He includes them within his general paranoid metanarrative of an epidemic of sloth. Thus the *lingua americana* is being destabilized by the presence of southerners, black Americans, and eastern Europeans. It is also interesting to note that he excuses England from the list of suspects; this indicates that he is not taking pains to differentiate American from British English, because the difference is already self-evident. The languages are sufficiently separate so that no danger is presented to American English by British speech.

Vizetelly's particular conception of speech pathology is concerned with other alien influences. He continues to ask, "To what are we to attribute this lackadaisical semisomnolent sickness from which the Empire State is suffering?" (61) and posits that the problem "that menaces us may have come from overseas" (62). This is clearly an allusion to the recent immigration to New York, and he seeks to liberate standard pronunciation from all of these influences.

He cites, but does not document, the New York educator Elizabeth D. McDowell, whose petition for scrutiny he advocates:

> Before we can go very far, we must, however, come to some agreement about what speech we should teach. Shall it be the dialect of the Irish-American kindergarten teacher; that of the Jewish American teacher in the first grade, or the drawling tones of the third-grade teacher who was born "way down South?" Definite care is necessary if we should have pleasing English spoken by children brought up in polyglot communities. (173)

This is a coded alert implying that, if the influence of "alien" teachers is not checked, then the result will not be "pleasing English." The passage also reiterates the linguistic threat posed by Jews from eastern Europe and by southerners and implicitly recommends that the standard language be cleansed of those influences. There is one interesting point of veracity in the passage, however: the observation that radio and movies have made America speech conscious. This had a considerable impact in New York, as it confronted New Yorkers with a mirror of their own discourse, and a fragmented one at that.

One very important aspect of Vizetelly's recommendations on pronunciation is his attitude toward standard British English. While Mencken and others claimed that he was seeking to rid American pronunciation of British characteristics, close examination of Vizetelly's texts reveals that he had no such agenda. He did not ascribe the dropping of postvocalic /r/ in New York and Boston to British influence; on the contrary, he saw the dropping of /r/ in London and New York as independent phenomena that were, however, pathological and both in need of correction:

> Mispronunciations abroad are due partly to the influence exerted by the people who ape the so-called Oxford accent, and partly to the wider-spread use of shopkeeper's English. The first have steadily debased English speech with exaggerated idiosyncracies. They cannot ask you to dinner; they ask you to "dinnah." They do not come to a lecture; they come to a "lectchah." (32)

Both instances of dropped /r/ are symptomatic of an emasculation of civilization, and it is clear from Vizetelly's discourse that he sees different causes for the disease in America. It is due to alien influences: Russian, American black, southern American, etc., and not to the presence of British pronunciation in the United States.

Mencken's misrepresentation of Vizetelly was taken at face value by subsequent accounts of the history of radio pronunciation. In *The Early Days of Radio Broadcasting*, George Douglas discusses Vizetelly and the standardization of radio pronunciation and lifts data and quotations wholesale from Mencken:

> By the early 1930s, CBS took the lead in formalizing procedures of this sort by setting up its own schools for announcers, and it appointed Professor Frank H. Vizetelly to head it. Vizetelly had been born in London and lived there until he was a young adult, but after coming to the United States had come to respect the virtues of a uniform American pronunciation, and he was determined to set down standards of purely Americanized English for radio announcers ... in his work for CBS, Vizetelly made it clear that attempts to import a stilted form of English had no place on American radio ... Vizetelly condemned this tendency in favor of a pure and natural style of American English, a style, it should be added, already spoken by the best of the early announcers. In various lectures on the virtues of American speech, Vizetelly made it clear that he was no admirer of "Oxford English," but instead was bent on "spreading the best traditions of American speech, which does not suppress its consonants nor squeeze the life out of its vowels." (G. Douglas 1987: 64)

Douglas makes no apparent effort to examine Vizetelly's discourse first-hand. Such an investigation would have revealed that Vizetelly had a very different agenda than that represented by Mencken. The American instantiation of postvocalic /r/ was the product of an ideology that had little to do with the presence of England in the United States. It was to be a remasculinization of American culture, making it virile again. Thus one of the effects of Vizetelly's training was the suppression of the female voice from the cast of announcers. Puzzled, but able to offer no account for this, Douglas observes: "One interesting difference between the twenties and thirties was the almost complete disappearance of women as announcers after 1930. In the 1920s a fair number of women announcers were working in radio, but during the golden age of the thirties and forties they almost completely disappeared from the scene" (65). The suppression of the female voice was but one of the steps toward constructing the ideal and ideological voice that was to be euphemized by the designation *standard.*

Douglas subscribes to the naive view of the rise of network standard and quotes James F. Bender's *NBC Handbook of Pronunciation*, which will be discussed below, and which recommends that "the American broadcaster would be well advised to use a pronunciation widely known among phoneticians as General American, the standard presented in this book" (65). Douglas observes:

> And standard American it became ... no major metropolitan radio station would have hired to stand before a microphone the possessor of a Brooklyn accent, a hillbilly or Tidewater twang or a Boston broad A. Radio was a mass medium and it was the correct but warm and genial American pronunciation that was wanted. Thus American radio came to provide us with the sound of American English at its best, and it would be hard to think of any greater contribution of the radio medium in the first half-century of its existence. (65)

It is interesting to observe that Douglas's representation of general American displays the same gambits of avoidance that have characterized many of the prescriptions for proper pronunciation. To be avoided are New York, Boston, the southern mountain, and the southern coastal areas. The term *Brooklynese* was commonly used to refer to the speech of New York City in general; thus Brooklyn here is a metonym for New York. The term *hillbilly* clearly indicates the southern mountain area, and Tidewater the southern coast. In the typical gesture of generalization, southern mountain and southern coast are grouped together; ergo the phrase "hillbilly or Tidewater twang," even though the speech characteristics of those regions are as diverse as any two American regions can be. Moreover, one could well imagine the reaction in Norfolk proper to the implication that Tidewater speech does not sound "warm and genial," nor is it "English at its best." Yet this is indicative of the discourse of unexamined presumption: the sound impression is taken to be qualitative *a priori,* and one need not investigate the processes involved in the connection between prejudice and phonetic perception; one does not ask why the Nebraska farmer should sound "warm and genial" but not the Charlestonian. The process begins with the stigmatization of an ethnic group, is then followed by the stigmatization of the region associated with that ethnic group, and then, and only last, by the stigmatization of the pronunciation of that ethnic and regional unit. This process gets masked, however, by the *post hoc* reasoning that purports to seek the example "at its best." This type of reasoning also masks other racial moves in the selection process. For instance, the famous sportscaster Mel Allen, who was known for decades as "the voice of the New York Yankees," was born Melvin Israel. CBS persuaded him to change his name, as it might become a "hindrance to his career" (Halberstam 1989: 151).

While Vizetelly was busy establishing the guidelines for the proper pronunciation of American English at CBS radio, that network hired an announcer who would prove to be the archetype for subsequent radio broadcasters: Edward R. Murrow. In an early tribute to Murrow, the CBS announcer Eric Sevareid wrote, "It was not his perfect poise, his magnetic face, or even his compelling voice that made him the first great literary artist of the new medium of communication. No practice, training, or artifice made him the greatest broadcaster by far in the English tongue. He was simply born to the new art" (Sevareid 1946: 177). The last phrase of Sevareid's tribute forms the title of the major work on the development of radio news in the thirties, which is Jeffrey Cole's *Born to the New Art: CBS Correspondents and the Emergence of Broadcast News, 1930–1941*. Murrow is clearly the pivotal and seminal figure in Cole's account of the formation of the medium.

Murrow was born in North Carolina in 1908. In 1913, his family relocated to Washington State, where his speech patterns were formed, and where he was educated, as well. (It is important to recall that the data reported to Preston and Hartley in their experiments on perceptual dialectology locate the most neutral American speech in the Pacific northwest.) He graduated from Washington State University in 1930 with a bachelor's degree in speech and went to work for CBS News in 1935. In 1937, he was put in charge of all European broadcasting for CBS. He rose to fame as a war correspondent narrating, from London, the events of World War II to the American public. His reception in the United States was absolutely staggering. His nightly radio audience was estimated to be

15,000,000 listeners (Cole 1985: 193), and he was repeatedly lauded by journalists and heads of state alike as the foremost American foreign correspondent of that era. When he returned to the United States for a three-month stay in 1941, he received a hero's welcome and a testimonial at the Waldorf-Astoria in New York. Murrow's broadcasts during the early years of World War II are generally viewed as a decisive factor in the transformation of American sentiment from isolationism to interventionism. Indeed, Morrow's connection to the decisive events of World War II has a certain providential tone: he and his wife were invited to dine with Franklin and Eleanor Roosevelt on December 7, 1941, the day that Japan attacked the United States.

It would be beneficial here to reflect on the cultural dynamics at work in the creation of the image of Edward R. Murrow. His speech patterns clearly reflected and embodied the nascent ideologies of proper ethnicity, gender, and geography that were operant in the thirties and forties. The presence and power of those speech patters would have been massively strengthened by their juxtaposition with the cultural signs of World War II. The drama, pathos, and unequivocal morality of that war could only have empowered that accent by association. The fact that Murrow narrated to Americans such dramatic events as the Battle of Britain, which he reported live from the rooftops of London (182), and the Allied Invasion of Normandy would have overdetermined that accent as, literally, the pronunciation of male power and concretized its status for generations to come. And this is clearly what took place. Murrow hired and trained Eric Sevareid, Charles Collingwood, and Howard K. Smith, all of whom spoke in the Murrow tradition, shared the speech patterns that that epoch called "general American," and eventually became prominent CBS television reporters in their own right. In a 1965 CBS television broadcast, Eric Sevareid characterized Murrow as "the man who invented me" (171). In his last appearance on the CBS Evening News on November 30, 1977, Sevareid said that Murrow "was a shooting star and we will live in his afterglow a very long time." (234). The modes of articulation established by Murrow were to determine the selection of successive announcers at CBS. Those who were hired and trained by Murrow in turn hired and trained Walter Cronkite, Mike Wallace, Harry Reasoner, Roger Mudd, Dan Rather, and Chet Huntley (230). Walter Cronkite, who was often characterized as the most trusted man in America, characterized himself as "a direct descendent of the Murrow tradition" (232).

By the forties, the ideology of network standard American had generated its operative discursive superstructures. NBC had hired James F. Bender, director of the speech and hearing clinic at Queens College, to train its announcers. In 1943, he published the *NBC Handbook of Pronunciation,* in which he represents the nature of standard American in interesting ways. He begins by invoking the lack of a superimposed standard:

> Americans have always resented superimposition in matters dealing with standards of pronunciation. Government *académies,* designated to indicate "correct" pronunciation, have not been tolerated. Although other countries have attempted to exact "pure" standards for many centuries, America had not chosen to do so ... the British Broadcasting Corporation, a government controlled and subsidized agency, does have a rather rigid standard of pronunciation for its announcers ... named "Oxford English" or "Received Standard Pronunciation." It is the kind of pronunciation attributed to the influence of the great public schools and universities of England. But it is not the dialect spoken by most Englishmen. Rather, it is the pronunciation that is employed by the upper middle classes and nobility who receive their education in the old, endowed institutions of learning. (Bender 1943: ix)

Employing the conventions of the discourse of the particularly American brand of capitalism, Bender begins by presenting the traditional adversaries of Americanism: big government, aristocracy– especially the traditional aristocracy of England–, and their hierarchic imposition of power upon the populace. The phrase "government controlled and subsidized" indicates that this oppressive power is a product of the large bureaucracy supported by taxes, ergo taxes upon the people. Bender emphasizes that the pronunciation recommended by the government-aristocracy complex is not the one that is spoken by the populace at large. It is forced unwillingly upon the people, as if shouted down to them. This frames and introduces his discussion of standard American as an entity of liberation and as a product of democratic and deregulated populism. It is, literally, the sound of representative government. In addition, there is an oblique reference to French culture in the term *académies,* which suggests images of elitism. This serves to supplement the negative representation of the adversary as also elitist and to supplement, as well, the representation of American populism as relatively free from class consciousness. It is plain and straightforward:

> From a realistic point of view, that pronunciation is best that is most read-ily understood, and that pronunciation is most readily understood that is used by most people. Thus a standard of pronunciation for the American broadcaster is reasonably based upon the speech heard and used by the ra-dio audience that the broadcaster reaches ... when a broadcaster speaks over a powerful station or nation-wide hook-up, he desires to use a pro-nunciation that is most readily understood by the majority of his listeners. In such an event, the broadcaster would be well advised to use a pronuncia-tion widely known among phoneticians as "General American," the stan-dard presented in this book. (ix)

Thus the decision to employ "General American" is produced by traditional American virtues. It is realistic, based on simple common sense, used by reasonable men, and understood by the most people. Thus its superstructure displays no ostensible ideology; on the con-trary, it is a neutral, objective, and disinterested decision, generated by a preponderance of data.

Bender provides a short list of broadcasters–Lowell Thomas, Art Baker, Frank Singsier, Ben Grauer, George Putnam, and Charles Lyon (x)–and says that they "may be cited as exemplary speakers whose phonetic patterns resemble General American more closely than either New England or Southern dialects" (x). It must be reiter-ated that the desired accent is that of a male speaking voice. Bender's use of masculine pronouns in referring to the broadcaster–he uses five of them in one paragraph–is indicative of this, and it is indicative, as well, of the lack of awareness of one's own discourse. Bender does not simply recommend the male voice, it is assumed *a priori* in his discourse and belies his ostensible agenda of populist representation. He states, "The names of women speakers are not included, simply because professional announcers are overwhelm-ingly men and because male voices are generally used for purposes of standardization" (x). This tautology masks the exclusionary and marginalizing moves involved in the process of standardization and purports to simply reflect the status quo as is. The result is that the ideology of the male voice becomes transparent, and thus its possession of positive personality characteristics remains unmarked. Bender holds that the

> three main dialects used in the United States and Canada are frequently referred to as (*a*) New England or Eastern, (*b*) Southern, (*c*) Western, Middle Western, or General American ... ten or eleven million Americans and Canadians speak the New England or Eastern dialect, twenty-six million the Southern variety, and at least ninety million speak General American. (ix)

Bender seems to be unaware that his syntax states that some Canadians speak "southern." Additionally, it has been already demonstrated that the use of the umbrella term "southern" is exclusionary by virtue of its function as a generalization. Here, the strength of numbers, represented as if popular votes, is clearly on the side of "General American." It is interesting to note here the synonymic relationship among "Western," "Middle Western," and "General American" and the implication that the terms are interchangeable. Beginning the category with the term "Western," this discourse implicitly represents a certain American essence as western in nature and thus connects the newly established radio standard with the American west and its massive network of cultural associations.

This connection had already become iconic in the popular perception of the pronunciation of the American plains states. That pronunciation acquired its cultural prestige by virtue of its connections with the ideology of the American frontier and its unambiguous disassociations from characteristic New York and "southern" speech. Thus it came to "sound better," to appear "warm and genial," and to evoke the associations indicated in Tucker and Lambert's 1972 study, which will be discussed in greater detail below. The authors found that speakers of network standard were rated higher on a list of character attributes that reads like a litany of proper Christian virtues: "upbringing, intelligent, friendly, educated, disposition, speech, trustworthy, ambitious, faith in God, talented, character, determination, honest, personality, considerate" (Tucker and Lambert 1972: 179–181).

The ideological aspects of Bender's conceptions of language are reflected in the development of his publications and interests. He was initially trained as a speech pathologist and received his PhD from Columbia University in speech pathology and psychology. His first independent publication was *The Personality Structure of Stuttering* (1939), which was based on the research done in his dissertation. In this study, he restricts the field of investigation to stuttering by college males alone. Earlier, he had co-authored, with Victor Kleinfeld, several technical manuals on speech correction, such as *Speech Correction Manual* (1936) and *Principles and Practices of Speech Correction* (1938). These works tend to be limited to instances of the pathology of speech and not the sociology thereof. In the forties, however, Bender left the field of speech pathology and turned his interests to the social issues involved in pronunciation, and the *NBC Handbook of Pronunciation,* first published in 1943, falls into that category. Yet, there is still a thematic connection maintained between these two phases of Bender's career. His interest in amelioration is far from gender neutral; it is clear from the onset that he is concerned exclusively with the improvement of male speech.

At the middle of the twentieth century, Bender focused his interests in the amelioration of male speech upon the field of career development and advancement, most specifically salesmanship, and published, in 1945, the pronunciation manual *Salesman's Mispronunciations.* The introduction to the volume justifies the undertaking by saying, "Good speech is one of the three or four outstanding personality traits of the successful salesman ... the salesman's speech reflects not only his personality but the company he represents as well" (Bender 1945: 1). Again, the standard that he recommends is that of the *NBC Handbook of Pronunciation.* Writing at that time as the director of the National Institute for Human Relations, Bender reports on studies of the "selling personality" and claims, "The evidence indicates that those whose earnings are greater than the average of their group are superior in pronunciation to their less productive colleagues ... an exact knowledge of the meaning and pronunciation of words used in American speech seems to be an accompaniment of selling success in this country" (1).

Bender's volume fits well into the larger genre of the pronunciation manual, but its self-justification is articulated in a manner quite different from that of the examples found in the nineteenth century. While the latter configured pronunciation in a moralizing context, Bender frames it as an issue of entrepreneurial pragmatism. Just as the earlier manuals included reading passages that reflected the Christian values associated with proper pronunciation, so does Bender include passages that reflect the ideology of his enterprise. The practice reading passage that Bender constructs narrates the concerns of the "harassed salesman" desiring to be at the "zenith" of his "economic prowess" (51), while "Penelope, his beloved spouse, was ... blithely planning on what she would do with the increased allowance her uxorious hero would donate" (52). In addition, precious, high-register vocabulary, containing some foreign loan words, is interspersed into the reading passage and reflects the class interests of status and upward mobility of the implied reader. Pronunciation is configured here as a socioeconomic instrument for commercial purposes that also empowers a certain class of privileged white men whose compliant wives wait at home with the patience of Penelope in anticipation of their "allowance."

In 1949, Bender published *How to Talk Well*. His introductory paragraph states that "clear speech is just about the best tool to influence others the way you want to influence them" (Bender 1949: vii). The book arose from an evening course that he was teaching called "Speech Training for Executives" (viii). It contains repeated justifications of the crucial importance of proper speech by many of the contemporary captains of industry. As always, Bender recommends "General American" as the proper mode of pronunciation and exaggerates its scope and influence, claiming that it is "killing off the less vigorous dialects" (108). He says that it will continue to do so and predicts that by 1996, "all educated Americans will speak General American" (109). He also claims that "more than fifty percent of all Oscars have gone to actors and actresses who speak General American" (109) and uses that statement as a rationalization for adopting it as a mode of pronunciation. He supports his recommendation by saying that the broadcast networks prefer general American, and that the American Speech and Hearing Association and the

Speech Association of America teach it as a model (109). He also urges men to imitate Fred McMurray and women to imitate Shirley Temple, respectively, as models of pronunciation (110). In 1961, he published *How to Sell Well: The Art and Science of Professional Salesmanship*. The similarity in titles between *How to Talk Well* and *How to Sell Well* are not coincidental; they indicate a fundamental conception of language as an instrument of male persuasive power and influence. *How to Sell Well* refers the reader to the earlier *How to Talk Well* for purposes of proper elocutionary presentation.

The last work that Bender published on language was *Salesman's Errors of Grammar* (1946). He then distanced himself more and more from the issues of speech improvement and turned instead to the study of the social and psychological development of the salesman. This period includes *Do's and Don'ts of the Sales Interview* (1945), *Courtesy Hints for Salesmen* (1946), *Victory over Fear* (1952), and the wonderfully titled *The Salesman Takes a Wife: A Message to the Wives of our Salesmen* (1954). For Bender, locutionary power is configured as masculine *a priori,* and an overview of his works reveals a dominant interest in the facilitation of male self-presentation. First, he is interested in the obstacles produced by the pathology of speech, then in those involved in the sociology of speech, and finally in those present in the symbolic aspects of speech acts. This development has its teleology, which is the use of speech and speech acts for the purposes of commercial persuasion by men.

Chapter three of this study explores further the processes by which the virtues reported to Tucker and Lambert came to be disassociated from the speech and image of the urban east and associated with the speech and image of the (mid)west. It does so by taking cultural biopsies, explorations of some major shifts in American consciousness that are representative and symptomatic of the construction of the myth of the west and the investiture of that region with cultural and linguistic capital, so that it became a space for the performance of "proper" American language, race, and morality.

Chapter 3
Occident, orient, and alien

1. Harvard looks west

The ideology of proper pronunciation is inextricably bound to education, class consciousness, and upward mobility. Elevated and cultivated registers of pronunciation are also indications of social standing and of level of education. This is evident in comparisons of the speech patterns of the lower middle and upper middle classes, especially as these are related to the prestige markers of education. The pronunciations of the American college-educated population tend to show fewer regionalisms than the pronunciations of the non-college-educated population. Similarly, the pronunciations of college students at select private colleges and universities tend to show fewer regionalisms in comparison with the pronunciations of college students at less selective colleges and universities. The former tend toward network standard pronunciation more than the latter. This is well reflected in the artifacts of popular culture, especially in film. In the 1997 film *Good Will Hunting,* which takes place in Boston, the pronunciation of Harvard students is clearly marked by continuant postvocalic /r/, while the speech of the working class residents of South Boston, also of college age, shows the dropping of /r/ postvocalically. Also, the 1997 film *I Know What You Did Last Summer,* which takes place in North Carolina, displays a similar class division in pronunciation within the same age group. The speech of the college-bound high school seniors tends toward network standard, while the speech of the residents of comparable age, who are not pursuing higher education, shows strong regionalisms.

Since educational institutions incorporate the ideologies, value systems, and class sensibilities of a culture, they will also reflect the discursive and rhetorical ideologies of that culture as well. Ideological changes in culture are reflected in university life and policy, and, to some extent, university life and policy can have a shaping influence on the values of a given culture. American universities and colleges were not immune to the national hysterical reaction to eastern immigration in the twenties. On the contrary, their policies and discourses were symbiotically related to the anti-immigration movement; i.e. they were influenced by and also themselves influenced that movement and its prejudices against eastern European immigrants, especially Jews.

In 1922, the president of Harvard University, Abbot Lawrence Lowell, stated that the university had a "Jewish problem" and recommended restricting the number of Jewish students admitted to the university. He was disturbed by the fact that Harvard's Jewish enrollment had been only six percent in 1908, but had increased to twenty-two percent by 1922 (Dinnerstein 1994: 84; Yeomans 1948: 209). In addressing the class of 1922, Lowell said:

> During the earlier period of our country, and indeed to some extent so long as there was a broad area of frontier life to the westward, newcomers from other lands were easily assimilated ... now that our population has become vastly more dense, and huge numbers of strangers newly come from overseas are massed together in industrial centers, the problem of assimilation has become more difficult. This is a cause of the recent efforts of Americanization. (Pollak 1983: 117)

One might be persuaded to conclude that Lowell cribbed parts of his commencement speech from the nostalgic post-frontier laments of the historian Frederick Jackson Turner, for whom the closing of the frontier had similar effects upon his own ideology of immigration. On September 25, 1901, Turner wrote, in the *Chicago Record-Herald,* the following characterization of immigration in the post-frontier state:

> The immigrant of the preceding period was assimilated with comparative ease, and it can hardly be doubted that valuable contributions to American character have come from this infusion of non-English stock into the American people. But the free lands that made the process of absorption easy have gone. The immigration is becoming increasingly more difficult of assimilation. Its competition with American labor under existing conditions may give increased power to the producer, but the effects upon American social well-being are dangerous in the extreme. (Turner 1901b)

This passage from Turner will be reexamined in section 3.2. below in the discussion of the closing of the frontier. His idea, however, seems to have undergone some refinement on its way to Lowell's commencement address. Lowell's discourse reflects the phenomenon of a waxing national consciousness of claustrophobia. The closing of the frontier in 1890 signified, on a subliminal level, not only the bridling of American expansiveness, but also a sense of a lack of space for ventilation, for aerobic cleansing of undesirable elements. Since the cleansing could not take place organically, i.e. in and of itself, this, in turn, engendered a necessity for inspection and control. Foreign elements had to be measured and weighed in proportion to the whole. There is also present here a general consciousness of western openness and eastern urban confinement, even though the western area is no longer perceived as infinite. Precisely for this reason, the west, as a national symbol, needs to be protected from the strangers massed together in industrial centers. It is also a source of proper cultural and ethnic vitality.

In *The American College and the Culture of Aspiration, 1915–1940,* David Levine observes that

> the adoption of regional quotas by Dartmouth, Harvard, and other New England colleges was intended to make each school competitive in the hard-fought battle for upper-middle-class suburban WASPs from the Midwest and West ... national scholarship contests established in the 1920s and 1930s at the major eastern colleges were designed in large part to substitute lower-middle-class WASPs from the Midwest and West for the poor ethnic students in their own backyards. (Levine 1983: 145–146)

The Ivy-League schools of the northeast, especially Harvard, Yale, Princeton, Columbia, and Dartmouth, were especially nervous about the presence of urban Russian Jews on their campuses (Levine 1983: 147). This caused a turning away from the city and a turning toward the areas called, either in part or whole, "west." The dean of admissions at Yale referred to the undesirable situation of the City College of New York, whose Jewish enrollment had risen to eighty percent, when he said that Yale would become "a different place when and if the proportion of Jews passes an as yet unknown limit" (Levine 1983: 149). The antisemitic hysteria reached Dartmouth in the early thirties, when the average Jewish enrollment increased by two hundred and fifty percent between 1933 and 1935. Dartmouth decided to require a photograph on its application form for the first time; this was rationalized in a letter from the dean to the president, which said that the Jewish student is "of a physical type that is unattractive to the average Dartmouth student" (Levine 1983: 152). A letter from the dean of Columbia to Yale's dean of admissions represented the use of the College Board examinations and Scholastic Aptitude Test as a way to maintain cultural homogeny on campus: "most Jews, especially those of the more objectionable type, have not had the home experiences which enable them to pass these tests as successfully as the average native American boy" (Levine 1983: 152). In 1932, the *Yale Daily News* warned that if Yale did not institute "an Ellis Island with immigration laws more prohibitive than those of the United States government," Yale would be overrun by Jews (Levine 1983: 156).

The pioneer in this development was, however, Harvard, echoing the apocryphal adage that "as Harvard goes, so goes the country." On June 5, 1922, Harvard's Board of Overseers recommended a "more effective sifting of candidates for admission" and called for the formation of an *ad hoc* faculty committee to address the problem (Pollak 1983: 115). Ominously, the committee was chaired by the noted philologist Charles H. Grandgent, whose words in 1920 on the future of American pronunciation, especially of the phoneme /r/, proved to be quite prophetic indeed. In April, 1923, there appeared the "Report of the committee appointed to 'consider and report to the governing boards principles and methods for more effective sifting of candidates for admission to the university.'" The document deflected the "question of racial proportion in the student body" (Harvard University 1923: 1) and said that "the question should be approached not from the standpoint of race, but in an effort to accomplish a proper selection of individuals," so that "the student body will be properly representative of all groups in our national life" (1). The committee pursued "the building up of a new group of men from the West and South, from good high schools in towns and small cities" (3), and noted that "for years our graduates in the Central States and the West have urged us to establish contact, ere it be too late, with the educational systems of their regions" (3). It sought to "appeal particularly to rural schools and to those situated outside the regular Harvard recruiting ground" and to "raise the proportion of country boys and students from the interior" (4). Thus the committee denied the criterion of race and instead displaced the focus of recruitment onto geography. In doing so, it invoked traditional American images of populism, broad democratic appeal, and representative government. In other words, it used traditional American populist discourse in order to mask an underlying ideology of race. Instead of explicitly focusing on race, the committee focused on a metonym of race, i.e. on geographical location that was coded for proper racial content: the west, the central states, the towns and small cities, the country boys from the interior, and even the south. Of special note is the phrase "country boys from the interior," which indicates a protected internal area, a heartland insulated from the influence of coastal degeneration, where one would find, in the words of Columbia's dean, "the average native American boy."

In his treatise on the sound of /r/, Grandgent offered the following ominous and ingenuous speculation:

> America has, in the main, followed about the same paths as the parent lands; but our enterprising Middle West, unwilling to abandon the *r* tradition, has developed and cherished an *r*-substitute, homely, to be sure, but vigorous and aggressive. What has the future in store? Will decay pursue its course; or will a reaction set in, restoring to the English-speaking world a real *r* of some kind, or a tolerable substitute? (Grandgent 1920: 56)

It is an interesting coincidence that, three years later, he himself was to issue a Harvard committee report that would shift the gyroscope of elite private college recruitment in a rural westward direction. This was a Copernican revolution in the recruiting orbit of the northeast educational power elite that overcame the massive gravitational force of the cultural capitals of New York and Boston and bequeathed to the western regions the proper mark of racial and cultural status.

In his well-received work *Antisemitism in America,* Leonard Dinnerstein says of this turn of events at Harvard:

Never before had any secular American university openly acknowledged
that it wished to limit the number of its Jewish students ... in the same fashion the elevated number of Jews at many other American universities was
perceived as an invasion that would ultimately undermine both Christian
traditions and the social prestige of schools that housed too many of them
(Dinnerstein 1994: 85).

While Dinnerstein's reading is quite correct, this event also signified
a much more profound revolution in the conception of American
identity. In this small committee report, Harvard University, arguably the nation's most influential educational institution, constructed
an ideal male student who embodied the university's concept of
proper race, culture, and ethnicity. In constructing this identity, Harvard, for the first time, looked *away from itself* for the appropriate
source of such an ideal student. That is, it looked away from its traditional recruiting grounds of the New York, Boston, and general
northeastern urban power elite and defined a location *elsewhere* for
the sustenance and protection of its identity. It constructed the Nordic Christian (mid)western country boy as the savior of its heritage,
and, in doing so, radically changed the geographical location of the
then operative ideology of the native American. This brief committee report signified the academic sanctioning of the newly nascent
occidental consciousness. Popular culture had been looking westward, and now this movement was sanctioned at the highest educational level. It signified, literally, a rearticulation of the discourse of
identity.

It must also be reiterated that this particular embodiment of western migration, which originated negatively as an avoidance of eastern immigration, was an essentially racial reaction of segregation
that, at its point of emergence, articulated itself as a gesture of democracy and pluralism, as an act of greater inclusion, especially of
the common man. Thus the discourse of segregation was inverted so
as to appear to be a form of greater geographic accommodation, and
the discourse of race was displaced onto the discourse of populism.
The matrix of race and exclusion was thus remapped onto the matrix
of populism and inclusion. This transformation of matrices would
prove to be the operative discursive mode in the understanding of
the nostalgia for the west and of the standardization of American

English. Decades later, these transformations were to generate James Bender's recommendations on the most reasonable and representative male broadcast voice.

2. Resonances of the post-frontier

The historian Frederick Jackson Turner begins his famous essay "The significance of the frontier in American history," which was originally a conference paper for the American Historical Association convention of 1893, with the following quote from the 1890 census report, one which is of major significance for Turner:

> Up to and including 1880 the country had a frontier of settlement, but at present the unsettled area has been so broken into by isolated bodies of settlement that there can hardly be said to be a frontier line. In the discussion of its extent, its westward movement, etc., it can not, therefore, any longer have a place in the census reports. (Turner 1967a: 1)

> This brief official statement marks the closing of a great historic movement. Up to our own day American history has been in a large degree the history of the colonization of the Great West. The existence of an area of free land, in continuous recession, and the advance of American settlement westward, explain American development. (1)

This event is commonly referred to as the closing of the frontier. Characterizing it as such seems, at first, to be an overreaction, as the absence of an unbroken frontier line and the presence of some lacunae in that line are equated wholly with closure. Nevertheless, Turner's words convey the profound change in American consciousness that resulted from this event. The continuous presence of the image of infinite open and free space to the west had come to an end. This generated a waxing sense of claustrophobia in American consciousness. For Turner, the presence of this frontier is the very instantiation of American notions of democracy, populism, and individualism:

> But the most important effect of the frontier has been in the promotion of democracy here and in Europe. As has been indicated, the frontier is pro-

ductive of individualism. Complex society is precipitated by the wilderness
into a kind of primitive organization based on the family. The tendency is
anti-social. It produces antipathy to control, and particularly to any direct
control. The tax-gatherer is viewed as a representative of oppression ... the
frontier conditions prevalent in the colonies are important factors in the
explanation of the American Revolution, where individual liberty was
sometimes confused with absence of all effective government. The same
conditions aid in explaining the difficulty of instituting a strong government in the period of the confederacy. The frontier individualism has from
the beginning promoted democracy. (30)

Turner configures here the west as a cradle of democracy that also
influenced European politics. In doing so, he invokes traditional
American images of antiauthoritarianism, individualism, and family
values. Operating within a classically liberal understanding of democracy, he holds that the western side of the frontier acted to liber-
alize the eastern side: "It was *western* New York that forced an ex-
tension of suffrage in the constitutional convention of that State in
1821; and it was *western* Virginia that compelled the tide-water region to put a more liberal suffrage provision in the constitution
framed in 1830" (30–31). Thus the very impulse of American individualism is seen as emanating from the west, and it does so in and
of itself. It needs no protection; on the contrary, it is the raw and vital source of democratic balancing and correcting influences upon
the illiberal tendencies of the east. Westward expansion meant, simultaneously, the eastward expansion of the democratic balance of
nature. The specter of the closing of the frontier indicated a distur-
bance in this natural balance.

Turner was among the first to juxtapose the closing of the frontier
with the presence of eastern immigration. In the essay "Social forces
in American history," he laments the recent

evidences of the invasion of the old pioneer democratic order. Obvious
among them is the effect of unprecedented immigration to supply the mobile army of cheap labor for the centers of industrial life ... beginning with
1900, over eight million immigrants have arrived. The newcomers of the
eight years since 1900 would ... repopulate all the five older New England
States as they stand today ... In 1907 there were one and one-quarter million arrivals. This number would entirely populate both New Hampshire
and Maine. (Turner 1967b: 316)

The choice of New England as a point of comparison is multivalent. It indicates the massive presence of immigration on the east coast and the danger that it presents to American traditions. His comparative statements on repopulation bear the connotation that the original populace is being replaced by immigrants. It also serves to divide east from west and to mark the former as negatively transformed and the latter as a kind of preserve. Turner observes that this immigration

> has come in increasing measure from southern and eastern Europe ... one-quarter of them were from the Mediterranean race, one-quarter of the Slavic race, one-eighth Jewish, and only one-sixth of the Alpine, and one-sixth of the Teutonic. In 1882 Germans had come to the amount of 250,000; in 1907 they were replaced by 330,000 South Italians. Thus it is evident that the ethnic elements of the United States have undergone startling changes; and instead of spreading over the nation these immigrants have concentrated especially in the cities and great industrial centers in the past decade. (316)

Turner's words echo the national concern that the northern European American heritage is under threat from those of foreign race and religion. It is interesting that, instead of saying the German immigration was augmented by the southern Italian, he says it was replaced by it, as if the presence of the foreign race acted to remove the Nordic element altogether.

Turner's discourse also echoes the national perception of the metropolis as other, as an entity that is essentially un-American both in race and culture. He sees a triadic and conspiratorial revolution: "The familiar fact of the massing of population in the cities and the contemporaneous increase of urban power, and of the massing of capital and production in fewer and vastly greater industrial units, especially attest the revolution ... capital and labor entered upon a new era as the end of the free lands approached" (317). The repetition of the term "massing" reflects Turner's claustrophobic concern over the encroachment upon open spaces: "The passage of the arable public domain into private possession" (317) has altered the function of American individualism and threatened traditional American identity:

This is peculiarly the era when competitive individualism in the midst of
vast unappropriated opportunities changed into the monopoly of the fundamental industrial processes by huge aggregations of capital as the free
lands disappeared ... in New York City have been centered, as never before, the banking reserves of the nation, and here, by the financial management of capital and speculative promotion, there has grown up a unified
control over the nation's industrial life. Colossal private fortunes have
arisen. No longer is the per capita wealth of the nation a real index to the
prosperity of the average man ... in a word, the old pioneer individualism is
disappearing, while the forces of social combination are manifesting themselves as never before. The self-made man has become, in popular speech,
the coal baron, the steel king, the oil king, the cattle king, the railroad mag-
nate, the master of high finance, the monarch of trusts. (317–318)

Thus the vital force of American culture has been mutilated by the
closing of the frontier and the urbanization of the economy. Where
once there was individualism, there now stands monopoly, which
manifests itself as a reimposition of the horrifying figure of aristocracy onto the democratic and populist fabric of America. The heroes
are now "kings" and "barons." This transformation of the American
essence is the necessary result of closed spaces, and New York
looms here large and baronial as the symbol of metropolitan confinement, contamination, and greed. It is an insatiable behemoth on
the eastern rim alien to the western essence of America, which essence must be preserved:

On the other hand, we have the voice of the insurgent West, recently given
utterance in the New Nationalism of ex-President Roosevelt, demanding
increase of federal authority to curb the special interests, the powerful industrial organizations, and the monopolies, for the sake of the conservation
of our natural resources and the preservation of American democracy.
(319)

Turner differentiates between the individualist, who is represented in
the figure of the pioneer, and the monopolist, who is represented in
the figure of the urbanite. Both are at liberty to act in fully capitalis-
tic self-interest. The presence of an infinite frontier, however, pre-
vents the pioneer from gaining monopolistic control. No government
is needed to guarantee this; on the contrary, such intervention would
curb the individualist impulses of the pioneer. Thus the frontier,

combined with weak government, produce the American essence. The absence of that frontier then engenders the monopolist and, consequently, the necessity of government intervention. This intervention is, however, fundamentally un-American. Thus Turner's discourse displays quite contradictory notions of individualism and a fundamentally post-edenic resignation. The deregulated state of nature is forever past, and the very act of government intervention indicates the loss of the vitality and spontaneity necessary for ideal democracy to continue. The natural cooperation of free land and anarchy produced the democratic spirit, and, now that the free land has disappeared, government intervention is needed in order to reconstruct and preserve the absence of government intervention. Thus the present fallen post-frontier condition is in a permanent state of incommensurability, if not absurdity. Here, Roosevelt reappears as an icon of the west. He is the anarchist-as-president, a symbol of the post-frontier condition: i.e. the regulated maintenance of anarchy. This necessitates the construction of simulacra of pioneer democracy that must remain forever within a state of inauthenticity.

For Turner, the closing of the frontier also has subsequent effects upon the ideology of immigration. On September 25, 1901, he wrote, in the *Chicago Record-Herald,* the following characterization of immigration in the post-frontier state:

> The immigrant of the preceding period was assimilated with comparative ease, and it can hardly be doubted that valuable contributions to American character have come from this infusion of non-English stock into the American people. But the free lands that made the process of absorption easy have gone. The immigration is becoming increasingly more difficult of assimilation. Its competition with American labor under existing conditions may give increased power to the producer, but the effects upon American social well-being are dangerous in the extreme. (Turner 1901b)

Turner's rhetoric was to resurface in the 1922 Harvard commencement speech of Lawrence Abbott Lowell in the context of the restriction of Jewish enrollment and the necessity of recruiting in small western towns in order to maintain the proper student complexion at Harvard. Similarly, Turner's discourse represents the open frontier as capable of absorbing foreign elements without

changing the nature of the proper American "stock." Since, for
Turner, the frontier was, by definition, infinite, the presence of alterity would have to remain proportionately insignificant, i.e. in a state
of infinite regress. The making finite of the lands to the west thus
inverts the influence of immigration; it becomes an increasing threat
to finite space and to the "American social well-being." Here, the
sign of labor accesses the image of urban industry, which, for
Turner, is the nemesis of pioneer democracy.

It was happenstance that caused American identity at the onset of
the twentieth century to enter a period of crisis, as two contingent
determining phenomena coincided: the closing of the western frontier and the opening of eastern immigration. The latter was characterized as tide, wave, flood, deluge, etc.–aqueous metaphors that
would have ebbed away into the western infinity had the frontier
remained open. The closing of the frontier denoted a western wall in
the popular imagination, which meant that the eastern foreign tide
would rise nationwide. Thus Turner employs the image of immigration covering the older New England states. This flood was a threat
to the Teutonic American essence and expressed itself archetypally
in the discourse of immigration reform during the congressional debates of the twenties. For instance, the Michigan congressman Earl
C. Michener said, in a speech before the House in April, 1924:

> Water seeks its level, and without a dam at the border the overflow will in-
> undate us and the time will soon be when the salient features of our gov-
> ernment will be obliterated and when we will be more foreign than Ameri-
> can ... the early pioneers, who with the ax in the forest and the plow in the
> prairie transformed the great American wilderness into this modern Garden
> of Eden, were men from Northern Europe. (Wrobel 1993: 119–120)

Similar diluvian images were used by Turner. Writing in the Chicago *Herald Tribune* in 1901, he addressed the problem of "Jewish
immigration" and held that "Russian and Polish Jews ... Italians,
Slovaks ... and other immigrants of Eastern Europe" were disruptive
of American cultural continuity and "have made New York City a
great reservoir for the pipe lines that run to the great misery pools of
Europe" (Turner 1901). Here, immigration and industrialization are

condensed into an image of a direct plumbing connection to the contaminating influences of eastern Europe.

Such images are condensations of a problematic national consciousness. They can be viewed as figures of dream-work, of a national nightmare that expresses itself in the figure of the safety, purity, and openness of the high arid plain and the danger of suffocation and contamination by the tides of the eastern shore. Out of this dream-work arose the figure of a nostalgic hero: the American cowboy.

In the article "Frederick Jackson Turner and Buffalo Bill," Richard White observes that "Turner and Buffalo Bill shared a conviction that the experience that had produced them was no longer available: the Wild West, the frontier, was dead. And the icons of that frontier themselves became tinged with an aura of loss" (Richard White 1994: 45). The sign of the cowboy was itself an act of compensation, a construction made by a profound consciousness of loss: "Many, however, felt that the actual cowboy was vanishing even as the iconographic cowboy populated the American imagination. Ironically, the cowboy became an American symbol in the very era that announced the end of the West and the closing of the frontier that had created him" (46). The cowboy as a popular icon is *a priori* a nostalgic phenomenon, and one can trace the rise of the icon as the inverse of the decline of the real cowboy. Both cowboys and Indians had been part of the first Buffalo Bill's Wild West shows in 1882. As the frontier disappeared, more and more cowboys began to appear in the shows until, in the twentieth century, they clearly dominated the representation of the west in the post-frontier age (Richard White 1994: 45–46). Thus the fiction of the cowboy belies the true situation of decline. The historian William Savage deems one of the earliest cowboy heroes, Tom Mix, "the most fictitious man who ever lived" (Savage 1979: 115).

For Buffalo Bill and especially for Turner, the west had been won by Anglo-Saxon men, and the presence of Indians, Hispanics, Asians, women, blacks, and non-English speaking Europeans was not seen as infusional, but either as peripheral, or as an obstacle to be overcome in the process of colonization. The cowboy was a conservative symbol that was always already an adversary to the urban east: "The image of the future–a not altogether happy future–became the city ... progress had ceased to seem desirable" (Richard White 1994: 46). The cowboy image instantiated the ideology of American race and stood in opposition to eastern immigration. White observes:

> Many Americans began to think that only descent from "real" Americans could now produce Americans. Genealogy, which would become an obsession of native-born Americans, was tied to this growing conviction that what their parents had secured through experience, they secured as an inheritance; descent from true Americans had replaced the pioneers' consenting to undergo the quintessential American frontier experience. New immigrants, to whom this frontier experience was foreclosed, seemed like dangerous, exotic, and inassimilable aliens to many native-born Americans. (46)

The turning away from the eastern sources of immigration was also coupled with notions of cultural emasculation. White adds that Turner and Buffalo Bill "worried not only about assimilation but about manhood as well. Like most of their peers, they understood American space and American experience in gendered terms. The frontier was masculine; machines and cities were its antithesis. They emasculated men, robbed them of their true manhood. Thus cities and machines were defined as feminine" (49).

The historian Richard Slotkin, in *The Fatal Environment: The Myth of the Frontier in the Age of Industrialization, 1800–1890*, holds that the creation of the image of the frontier in the eastern industrial cities was a backdrop for eastern labor and immigration problems. Eastern newspapers often termed immigrants as "savages" or "redskins," and Theodore Roosevelt associated Indians with the class of whites that he termed "the cumberers of the earth" (Slotkin 1981: 618; see also Nemerov 1991: 297).

These anxieties found expression in the art works of the period. Of special significance are the numerous paintings of the "last stand" of George Custer, which Slotkin reads as indices of the conflicts between labor and management in the era of late capitalism (Slotkin 1986). These images, which underwent frequent repetition after the Battle of Little Bighorn in 1876, invariably depict a small band of pioneers surrounded by an enclosing circle of Indians. A radical condensation of the situation can be seen in Frederick Remington's *Fight for the Water Hole* (figure 2), which depicts five cowboys under attack distributed around the perimeter of a small crater-like depression, at the center of which is a small pool of water. Foregrounded in the center left of the painting is a vigilant, scrutinous cowboy. One can see the painting as a gesture of retrenchment and expression of anxiety. Water here is a polysemous image of waning natural resource, precious fluid, and cultural power, a power that is being threatened by the inrush of foreigners. Alex Nemerov has observed that the genre of last stand paintings and others that depict foreign frontier intrusions can be read as displacements of the anxiety of immigration. The geometry of the painting *Fight for the Water Hole* demarcates the porous lines of two perimeters: the shrinking western frontier and the border of eastern immigration (Nemerov 1991: 285–288).

The word *frontier* is a specific semantic adaptation of the French *frontière* 'border.' This derivational relationship enhances the correspondences between the American anxieties over the western frontier and the eastern border. Nemerov juxtaposes three paintings: Remington's *Dash for the Timber* (figure 3) Charles Schreyvogel's *Defending the Stockade* (not shown here), and Louis Dalrymple's *The High Tide of Immigration–A National Menace* (figure 4). He holds that these paintings reflect the concerns of "an Anglo-Saxon race in a world 'overrun' with immigrants" (301). The Indian and the immigrant are related by virtue of their common disrespect for borders. Nemerov sees this particular representation of the west as emerging "from a culture in which the idea of closing the door, of enacting anti-immigration legislation, was important. Faced with the challenge of showing an intrusion, Schreyvogel made his picture in the terms in which his culture understood the word: as a forceful violation of racial and national borders" (303). It is fruitful to view Dalrymple's *The High Tide of Immigration* alongside an example from the genre of the last stand painting, such as Charles Russell's *Caught in the Circle* (figure 5), for a similar spatial dynamic is evident. In both works, the threatened entities are seeking high ground in their flight from the alien.

Nemerov notes that "as such, the image of the frontier–that great space of right and wrong, of white and red–became a powerful tool

by which the eastern environment could be defined. The era's countless paintings of combat between cowboys and Indians or soldiers
and Indians may be understood in these terms" (297). Nemerov astutely observes the structural similarity between Remington's
Mounted Policemen Arresting Burglars Uptown in New York (figure
6) and Schreyvogel's *How Kola!* (figure 7), which depicts mounted
soldiers overcoming fallen Indians. Both paintings emphasize the
superiority of the mounted uniform and the inferiority of the Indian
and scoundrel. Nemerov notes that "when we consider that Schreyvogel made his painting in Hoboken, New Jersey, it becomes all the
more possible to read *How Kola!* in urban terms" (298).

One of the purposes of this study has been to demonstrate the
nodal point in the national xenophobia and paranoia of the early
twentieth century that attempts to find a common denominator
among the foreign elements expelled as other: the Jew, the Slav,
communism, the city, etc. Nemerov observes in the paintings of
Remington a similar associative paranoia:

> Remington, for his part, could see urban situations specifically in frontier
> terms. Like many who prided themselves on a supposedly pure Anglo-
> Saxon lineage, he was traumatized by the country's large-scale influx of
> foreign immigrants. Blaming them for the country's unprecedented labor
> problems, he advocated violence, a manifestly frontier approach, as a "so-
> lution." "You cant glorify a Jew–coin 'loving puds'–nasty humans," he
> wrote to his friend Poultney Bigelow, the editor of *Outing* magazine. "I've
> got some Winchesters and when the massacreing begins which you speak
> of, I can get my share of 'em and whats more I will." He continued by ex-
> coriating "Jews–inguns–chinamen–Italians–Huns, the rubbish of the earth I
> hate." (298)

Thus one sees a similar associative network at play both in the paranoid reaction to eastern immigration and in the construction of the
frontier and the American cowboy hero. Indeed, the Winchester-
armed cowboy is set in opposition to one amalgamation of others.

An excellent example of the fusion of urban and frontier anxieties
can be found in Remington's painting *The Emigrants* (figure 1),
which depicts white settlers in westward migration under attack by
Indians. The title of the painting is itself a condensation of the problems of both eastern immigration and western emigration, but these

are represented in inverted form; it is the whites who are migrating in a direct line across a border, and who are under siege by aliens. In the center is a white man standing up to his knees in water, which is here a multivalent image. It is water as the high tide of immigration, as waning resource, as precious fluid, as cultural power, and it is itself a border to be crossed. Indeed, one could view the tropes of repetition, inversion, and condensation in this painting as forms of dream-work.

A similar ideology and a similar associative network can be seen in the discourse of the presidential icon of the American west, Theodore Roosevelt. In *The Winning of the West,* Roosevelt traces these themes all the way back to the Germanic invasions of the fallen Roman empire (Slotkin 1981: 621). The first volume of the six-volume work is entitled *The Spread of English Speaking Peoples* and begins with these words: "During the past three centuries the spread of the English-speaking peoples over the world's waste spaces has been not only the most striking feature in the world's history, but also the event of all others most far-reaching in its effects and its importance" (Roosevelt 1905: 17). The work introduces itself as a study of race, language, and the most significant event in world history. The narrative begins with the *Herrmannschlacht,* Arminius's defeat of the Romans in 9 A.D. The expansion was thus begun as an act of war and spread as such:

> From the Volga to the Pillars of Hercules, from Sicily to Britain, every land in turn bowed to the warlike prowess of the stalwart sons of Odin ... as a result, the mixed races of the south–the Latin nations as they are sometimes called–strengthened by the infusion of northern blood, sprang anew into vigorous life, and became for the time being the leaders of the European world. (19–20)

America inherited this same tradition, but in a purer form: "In America, there was very little, instead of very much assimilation. The Germanic strain is dominant in the blood of the average Englishman, exactly as the English strain is dominant in the blood of the average American" (29). This is a result of the insular culture of England, in Roosevelt's view. Subsequent immigration has maintained the dominance of the preferred ethnicity: "It is to be noted that, of the new blood thus acquired, the greatest proportion has come from Dutch and German sources, and the next greatest from Irish, while the Scandinavian element comes third, and the only other of much consequence is French Huguenot. Thus it appears that no new element of importance has been added to the blood" (39). Roosevelt sees westward expansion as a continuation of an unbroken proto-Teutonic bellicose mission that is at once racial and political. He ends his introductory chapter with this summary:

> The warlike borderers who thronged across the Alleghanies, the restless and reckless hunters, the hard, dogged, frontier farmers, by dint of grim tenacity, overcame and displaced Indians, French, and Spaniards alike, exactly as, fourteen hundred years before, Saxon and Angle had overcome and displaced the Cymric and Gaelic Celts. They were led by no commander; they acted under orders from neither king nor congress; they were not carrying out the plans of any far-sighted leader. In obedience to the instincts working half-blindly within their breasts, spurred ever onwards by the fierce desires of their eager hearts, they made in the wilderness homes for their children, and by so doing wrought out the destinies of a continental nation. (45–46)

The American west is the proper destiny and telos of the Teutonic race, which should best operate in the absence of government, i.e. under classical American notions of economic liberalism, which are represented here as genetic. This is a purity of race and instinct; blood is not only the transmitter of race, but also the container of an instinctual and natural form of social order, which thrives within the non-intervention of government on the frontier and establishes firm family values in the end.

Nemerov summarizes pithily and aptly Roosevelt's ideology of the Anglo-Saxon hero: "Anglo-Saxon superiority could be explained in terms of a succession of frontiers, from the Black Forest to the Black Hills" (Nemerov 1991: 301). The image of the Anglo-Saxon cowboy was thus the current Darwinian flower of Germanic superiority over foreign elements. This can be clearly seen in N. C. Wyeth's remarkable painting *The First Cargo* (figure 8), which depicts a landing of massive, sword-bearing Vikings. In the background is a horizontally striped furled sail that tropes the American flag. This painting sets up an equivalency between cowboy and Viking.

The anxiety over the closing of the frontier soon generated a plethora of frontier novels, the premier author of which was a sometime New York dentist named Zane Grey, who topped the bestseller lists nearly every year between 1914 and 1928 (Etulain 1996: 27). His most successful western novel was *Riders of the Purple Sage* (1912), which sold an astounding two million copies during his lifetime and perhaps two million more since then. The more important media for the purposes of this study, however, are the subsequent ones of film and radio, for it was via visual and oral representations that the western figure was to rise to the status of American iconicity and to exercise the greatest mimetic influence, especially upon American speech.

Between 1920 and 1954, Hollywood produced more than three thousand low-budget B western movies. They starred such actors as Buck Jones, Ken Maynard, John Wayne, Gene Autrey, Roy Rogers, Eddie Dean, and Lash Larue. They were usually filmed in a week and cost only a few thousand dollars to make (Ray White 1996: 135–136). The heroes were almost exclusively white Anglo-Saxon males. Blacks were largely written out of the narratives; when they appeared, they were stereotyped as subservient to whites. There were only four B westerns made that cast blacks as heroes; they had all-black casts and were aimed at black audiences (150). The marginalization of blacks was a creation of the white anxiety of the twenties and thirties and did not reflect the actuality of black presence on the American frontier, which was considerable. For instance, it has been estimated that blacks comprised up to fifteen percent of the cowboys who drove cattle out of Texas after the Civil War (Durham and Jones 1965: 44–45).

Consequently, the complex of postlapsarian and diluvian anxieties, i.e., the anxiety over the passing of the frontier and the anxiety over the waves of immigration through the eastern cities, constructed the sentimental and nostalgic figure of the cowboy hero, a figure that became an icon of the American, and that identified that American as male, Nordic, and western. The process of iconization caused those phenomena that were syntagmatically associated with

that figure to become themselves fused with the icon. Most important among these are the discourse and pronunciation that were
loosely perceived as "western" and essential to the icon: an unem-
broidered and plain style of minimal affect, except in the case of
hostility, when the affect was allowed to become more expressive,
and a pronunciation clearly showing a fully audible postvocalic /r/,
along with the low front vowel /æ/. It is clearly well beyond the
scope of this essay to undertake an assessment of the panorama of
popular western icons. It is beneficial, however, to illustrate the present argument by performing some brief cultural biopsies, by analyzing some representative figures from popular culture whose presence has indicative value for larger generalizations on the dynamics
of the fusion of pronunciation, icon, and sign of America. Two such
figures are Will Rogers and John Wayne.

In the biography entitled *Imagemaker: Will Rogers and the
American Dream,* William R. Brown characterizes Rogers as "a
mythic national hero, believable because he is most symbolically
one with the national eidolon, the god with four faces: the American
Adam, the American democrat, the self-made man, and the American Prometheus" (Brown 1970: 9–10). These descriptors are also the
chapter headings of Brown's biography of Rogers, whose full name,
William Penn Adair Rogers, at once resonates historically and patri-
otically. Rogers may be viewed as a popular culture version of and
successor to Teddy Roosevelt. There was a groundswell of support
for his candidacy as the Democratic presidential nominee in 1928
(16). This native Oklahoman used a plain and straightforward style
of speech that evoked images of the western common man. This was
a style of speech that audiences heard on Rogers's radio broadcasts
of the twenties and thirties, as well as in his films of the thirties and
forties. Brown observes that "during the period of uncertainty and
big change in the twenties and thirties, audiences identified Will
Rogers with the dream of the dignity and worth of the individual, of
freedom, and equality, of success, and of progress. He would, therefore, be one with the dreamers of the dream in his audience–a steady
friend who could be trusted, believed, and taken seriously" (23). He
also adds, "More importantly, they found a voice of the American
dream when they heard him speak or read his columns" (62). In-

deed, Rogers is seen as a condensation of those phenomena associated with the American dream. For Brown, Rogers was successful "in bringing the light from the great American dream into one focus. In that sense, Rogers was comprehensive in joining himself to the vision of Paradise to be regained" (272).

The image of Rogers is informed by the sentimental idea of the recovery of a paradise lost. The trajectory of his meteoric rise in popularity was inscribed by several important phenomena: the closing of the frontier and the resultant nostalgia for an open western "paradise," the closing of the eastern gates of immigration and the related xenophobic fear of non-Nordic elements, and the rise of the media of radio and film. The image of Rogers was constructed as a new cultural gyroscope whose center of gravity now lay in the western plains, rotating counterclockwise to the eastern industrial cities and consolidating national identity in a new way. This was the plain-speaking plainsman with the heartland accent: male, Anglo-Saxon, individualist, Adamic, and Promethean. The erection of this cultural edifice necessitated the inscribing therein of principal cultural virtues: "by the transmission of his message through the mass media, he was a daily, trusted companion" (273). This was literally a rhetorical figure whose presence was largely aural and whose speech patterns themselves became invested with trustworthiness, reifying the already waxing phonetic iconicity of the western accent.

The linguistic presence of Will Rogers was not unknown to scholars writing in the mid-twentieth century. Pyles writes of Will Rogers:

In our own day many have found cause for amusement in the supposed cowboy lingo in which was couched the cracker-barrel philosophy of Will Rogers, the Oklahoma pundit, But despite the widespread adulation of Rogers as a "great American" and even a "typical American," it is very doubtful that any educated adult American ... ever tried to talk like him. The rip-snorting, hell-for-leather turgidity and hyperbole of our western frontier in the last century have frequently been supposed to mirror the boldness and admirable self-confidence which we are pleased to think of as typical of us. This sort of language is, however, no more typically American than the bombast and fustian and the "inkhorn terms" of Elizabethan English are typically English. Nevertheless, it continues to connote in the American imagination the virgin wilderness, the covered wagon, the great

open spaces, the manly fortitude of the pioneer–in all, a way of life which
most of us have never really known and which is certainly more interesting
when viewed through the shimmer of romance than ever it actually was.
(Pyles 1952: 289)

While trying to convince the reader that no one really speaks like
Will Rogers, and that no one really embodies the characteristics idealized in the folklorish western images of popular culture, Pyles actually winds up describing the ideology of those images quite well.
Through the tropes of metonymy, metaphor, and hyperbole, these
images served, respectively, as displacements, condensations, and
exaggerations of the ideal white male hero. The most important
missing trope here is irony, and Pyles is correct in saying that few or
no people match that ideal figure. The ironic space, however, between the ideal image and the real male is a force-field of centripetal
power that holds the fascination of the reader, listener, and viewer.
While no one really talks or acts exactly as does the image, that image still pulls the subject in its direction, here clearly a westward
one, and encourages the subject to act more like the image of this
hero than like the image of the Bostonian or the New Yorker. Also,
Pyles's comparison of the relationship between Elizabethan English
and British pronunciation is quite far from the mark; there is no
Elizabethan pronunciation left in England. Shakespeare's plays tend
to be performed in RP, which has taken as a standard the systemi-
cized dropped postvocalic /r/ of the nineteenth century, a sound that
would have been quite unlikely in the speech of Elizabethan actors.
At the present time, there is a similar discrepancy between the sign
of high RP and each instance of British English vernacular. This
discrepancy may be compared to the discrepancy between the idealized American pronunciation and the individual instances of vernacular, but the power of the image does serve to sway common
pronunciation in the direction of the ideal.

At the time of Will Rogers's death in 1935, the image of a more
powerful western folk hero was on the rise: John Wayne appeared in
seventy-two films in the thirties alone, and it was to him that the
iconic power of the western hero was to be transferred into the
postwar generation. Shortly before John Wayne's death, the actor
Maureen O'Hara testified before congress: "To the people of the

world, John Wayne is not just an actor and a very fine actor. John Wayne is the United States of America. He is what they believe it to be. He is what they hope it to be. And he is what they hope it will always be" (Roberts and Olson 1995: 647). O'Hara's words properly delineate the dynamics of iconicity. The icon and the signified are here inseparable; an identity has been achieved: John Wayne is the United States of America. The referential dynamic is, however, one of desire: it is based on belief and hope, projected into the future, which, by virtue of their expectant nature, problematize the icon and the meaning thereof. In other words, the presence of the icon is largely compensatory and indicates anxiety over the absence of that which it instantiates. The icon is, in this sense, largely totemic and indicates the cultural power of the figure who has passed.

The title of the most recent biography of John Wayne serves as a case in point. It is simply *John Wayne: American*. Largely eulogistic and minimally critical, the seven hundred page biography represents this cultural hero not as derivative of the political hero, but as a principal archetype who is anterior to certain major political figures. The authors Roberts and Olson open their study with a quotation from the noted theater critic Eric Bently: "Richard Nixon and Ronald Reagan are only camp followers of Wayne, supporting players in the biggest Western of them all, wagons hitched to Wayne's star. In the age when the image is the principal thing, Wayne is the principal image ..." (Roberts and Olson 1995: vii). There is an interesting reversal here in the notion of camp. Normally, one imagines camp figures to be lesser folkish images of major political or historical figures. Here, the process is inverted, and the political figure exists in derivative, insubstantial, and deferential relationship to the cultural myth. The authors end their biography with these words: "Somewhere, every day, he strides cross a television screen, seemingly too large for the medium. With a western landscape filling the background, he looks snake-eyed at a villain, goes for his gun, and restores order. He speaks American. He walks American. He is remembered" (648). The three-word sentence "He speaks American" is immediately intelligible, transparent, and self-evident. It indicates that the proper virtues of twentieth century America have become fused with a particular accent. In this case, the accent is not idiosyn-

204 Occident, orient, and alien

cratic, but generic. It instantiates the location of an ideology of race, morality, gender, and culture in a general national region. The three-word sentence also serves to marginalize other national speech areas and to exclude them from the rubric "American." It is also interesting to note the dynamics of the construction of this archetype. A man of Scotch-Irish descent with the sexually ambiguous name Marion Morrison was transformed into an icon of male Anglo-Saxon heterosexual (if not homophobic) and hegemonic power.

The consolidation of proper cultural values in the western region effected a transformation in the domestic customs of the white middle class. The twentieth century suburbanization of American culture and the related "white flight" from the cities can be seen in the context of the post-frontier and urban immigration. The ideal new suburban home is often on the frontier of middle class homesteading, and its borders are the lines between development and the undeveloped, between claimed and unclaimed nature. It is a new settlement to the west that anticipates further incursions into undeveloped land. In *The Lawn: A History of an American Obsession*, Virginia Scott Jenkins sees the origin of the suburban lawn as such:

> The intellectual legacy of the Judeo-Christian tradition shaped the way that Europeans approached the "wilderness" and left a lasting imprint in American thought. Morality and social order seemed to stop at the edge of the clearing. Safety, happiness, and progress depended on rising out of a wilderness situation. It became essential to gain control over nature. The concept of control may be a man's view of nature and the wilderness ... men's fantasies involved the massive exploitation, alteration, and control of the land ... the front lawn is an area to be controlled and mastered. A good lawn has sharp edges and strict boundaries. No weeds or animal life should mar the manicured and manufactured perfection of the grass. All intruders must be guarded against and, when found, killed. (Jenkins 1994: 118–119)

The suburban plot is architected out of domesticated and condensed images of the frontier (see also Jackson). It is located on the perimeter of development, but it is itself developed and controlled. Its continual maintenance is the very processing and control of nature. It exists as a polysemous clearing: a clearing of land, a clearing of broad space, and under a broad clearing of sky. It has fresh air, the aerobic freedom and purity that was felt to have been essential to the original frontier. It is far from the city and it is very white. It has been cleansed of urbanness and ethnicity. Those who migrated to the suburbs from defined urban ethnic neighborhoods jettisoned those environments in the process of migration. The suburb also continually pushes outward into nature. Its claiming of nature is itself the purification of contaminated urban sources. The only noises one hears are those of nature and of the machines that remind one that nature is being controlled, that nature is being consumed and processed as a purifying agent. As Turner, Lowell, and others noted, immigration was not a "problem" as long as there was an infinite frontier to assimilate and dilute the immigrant element. Nature was thus envisioned as an ecological preserver of race and culture. Similarly, the suburban subset of nature exercises the same dynamic; it assimilates the other in an ecological dialogue with the sign of nature. Consequently, the proper accent of the upper-middle class suburb is, of necessity, purged of perceptible regionalisms. It is the vocal sign of purity.

The deregionalizing of individual speech and the process of accession to the standard must always remain, however, an asymptotic one, i.e. in a state of ever increasing approximation. In his introduction to *Perspectives on American English,* Dillard holds that

there is no *geographical* locus of such accentless American English. ("Accentless" could only mean that all or most prominent, stereotypable features have been leveled out.) Some recent sociolinguists and psycholinguists ... have suggested, however, that there is a locus for such a neutral dialect in the media, especially in television broadcasting and specifically in the networks' nationwide newscasts. Thus the dominant newscasters of the 1960s and 1970s, Huntley and Brinkely and Walter Cronkite, among others, have given us a speech pattern for imitation in which non-prevocalic (as well as prevocalic: initial and medial) /r/ is articulated but where there is no "intrusive" /r/ (idear of it), where diphthongs like /ay/ and /aw/ have very low initial articulation points and full off-glides, and where the vowels of *Sam* and *cab* are neither lengthened ... nor raised. (Dillard 1980: 11)

Dillard is correct in asserting that there is no one area of the United States where accentless American English is spoken. Indeed, an analytic consciousness keen upon seeing only difference could demonstrate that there is no one single accentless speaker, network or otherwise, and that accent can even be variable within a given idiolect. It has been the goal of this study, however, to show that an ideology of "accentless" or standard speech was based upon generalization and extrapolation from a geographical area that was then instantiated as the network standard. The newscasters with that accent were thus invested with the same virtues that were attributed to western heroes; hence the household characterization of Walter Cronkite as "the most trusted man in America." Cronkite's discursive presence could have been invested with those virtues only after they had already acquired access to iconicity, after they had been fused with a the speech patterns of the proper white American male and his proper geographic origin.

It would also be productive to compare the representative western heroes, Will Rogers and John Wayne, with two heroes who typify aspects of the urban east, specifically of New York City. This involves taking cultural biopsies in the opposite direction and examining icons whose discourse and behavior are fused with the image of the post-immigration eastern metropolis. Two such figures are Humphrey Bogart and James Cagney. While the biographies of Will Rogers and John Wayne represent those heroes, in numerous repetitions and variations, as quintessentially American, the biographies of Humphrey Bogart and James Cagney make no such claim of American essentiality for their heroes. On the contrary, these figures are depicted as exotic and tangential to a nativist notion of Americanism.

Both Humphrey Bogart and James Cagney were born in New York in 1899. Bogart actually came from a family that saw itself as definitively American. He was a direct descendant of the original Dutch settlers of New Amsterdam, as New York was called before the British occupation of 1664. He belonged to the Holland Society and displayed the family coat of arms on his wall. His family was listed in *Who's Who in New York* from 1907 until 1933, and Bogart himself attended Andover and Harvard (Meyers 1997: 5). The image of American heritage did not, however, inform the cinematic figure of Humphrey Bogart. The most recent biography of Bogart depicts him as "a Hemingway hero in his gangster films" (Meyers 1997: 4). While he does embody twentieth century American notions of masculinity and independence, these are not articulated in the context of nostalgia or idyll. They are, on the contrary, highly ironized self-conscious images that presume as given the condition of modernity and decadence. This is the hero of conscious urban modernity, of resignation. When this figure is found in the odd natural setting, as in *The African Queen,* it must remain as if imported into and foreign to the natural environment. Bogart's accent is clearly that of New York, although not to an egregious extent. This particular accent has become fused with this particular icon of urban modernity.

James Cagney came from poor means in the lower east side of New York, of Irish descent, and was the son of a sometime bartender and saloonkeeper. His accent is also unmistakably that of New York and is not as mitigated as that of Bogart. He was exposed to Yiddish as a young boy, and claimed to have understood it and even to have had an affection for it (McCabe 1997: 24). This figures into a very telling scene in the 1932 film *Taxi!,* in which Cagney translates from Yiddish into English for the benefit of a monolingual Russian Jewish immigrant and an equally monolingual New York policeman who cannot communicate with each other. The Jew is saying, "Ich vil gayn tsu Ellis Island. Mein froy kimpt mit drei kinder fon Russland," which the policeman cannot understand. Cagney intercedes and translates, at which point the Jew asks, "Vu den– a Yiddischer yung?", to which Cagney responds, "Vu den, a shaygetz?" (McCabe 1997: 92). The scene is interesting in that it stereotypes the Russian Jew and connects him with Ellis Island. It also depicts Cagney as so native to the region that he can actually pass; the stranger asks him if he is Jewish, and Cagney responds, "What else, a gentile?"

Both Bogart and Cagney attempted to play cowboys in the unintentionally comical 1939 film *The Oklahoma Kid.* Bogart is supposed to represent the character Whip McCord from the Texas Panhandle, while still employing New York speech patterns, and Cagney attempts a Mexican lullaby. The most recent biography of Cagney describes the critical reaction to the film:

> There was much critical complaining, mostly humorous, about the dese-
> dem-dose kid becoming a cowboy by the two simplistic devices of donning
> a ten-gallon hat and mounting a horse ... *Variety* called the film "unbeliev-
> able," citing Cagney's playing "without variation of his Hell's Kitchen
> manner" and his incongruity in the chaps and spurs setting. (McCabe 1997:
> 167)

Cagney himself said of the film, "*The Oklahoma Kid* was something of a fiasco. Bogart and me on what you might call new territory, stalking around the set like a couple of city slickers dolled up in Western rigout" (101). In a *New York Times* interview, Bogart spoke disparagingly of the film: "I speak the same lines and do the same things as I do in any other Warner picture. The only difference is that I snarl at the Injuns from under a ten-gallon hat" (101).

Bogart, of the upper west side, and Cagney, of the lower east side, dovetail in utter incongruity in a Hollywood Oklahoma west-ern. Already firmly established as icons of the post-immigration me-tropolis in decline, their presence in the frontier evoked anything but romantic nostalgia. The nodal point of incongruity is where manner meets discourse, for both their affect and accent had become evoca-tive of and fully fused with the urban image. The attempt to trans-plant the ironic and problematized modern urban hero into the idyl-lic and nostalgic context that resisted modernization, urbanization, and immigration could yield only incongruity. Among the manner-isms associated with western and thus American identity are clearly to be found the speech patterns heard as western, which are also evocative of that identity; rhotic /r/ and the broad vowel /æ/ had be-come such markers, and the linguistic performance of Bogart and Cagney was no part of that identity. *The Oklahoma Kid* was Cag-ney's sole western film. Bogart played in one more, the even less fortunate *Virginia City* (1940), in which he was deemed miscast in several reviews.

By the end of the thirties, New York City speech had become dissonant with the notions of heartland American linguistic and eth-nic purity. Such a revolution was bound to effect a certain schizo-phrenia, a problematization of identity. Simultaneously, New York was and was not, and Boston was and was not a proper locus of American power and identity. Especially in the case of New York, this split was to express itself in concurrent self-images of pride and embarrassment, of chauvinism and self-deprecation. This split was also to become embodied in a certain linguistic schizophrenia as well, a decentering of speech, a heteroglossia of pronunciations competing for status, a scattering and stratifying of the postvocalic /r/.

Figure 1. Frederic Remington, *The Emigrants,* c. 1904. Oil on canvas. Museum of Fine Arts, Houston; The Hogg Brothers Collection, gift of Miss Ima Hogg.

Figure 2. Frederic Remington, *Fight for the Water Hole,* 1903. Oil on canvas. Museum of Fine Arts, Houston; The Hogg Brothers Collection, gift of Miss Ima Hogg.

Figure 3. Frederic Remington, *A Dash for the Timber,* 1889. Oil on canvas, 1961.381. Amon Carter Museum, Forth Worth, Texas.

Figure 4. Louis Dalrymple, *The High Tide of Immigration. Judge* 45 (August 22, 1903): center. Photo courtesy of Maryland Department, Enoch Pratt Free Library.

Figure 5. Charles M. Russell, *Caught in the Circle,* 1903. Oil on canvas, 75.20.09. National Cowboy and Western Heritage Museum, Oklahoma City, Oklahoma.

Figure 6. Frederic Remington, *Mounted Policemen Arresting Burglars Uptown in New York,* c. 1889. Photo courtesy of The Frederic Remington Art Museum, Ogdensburg, New York.

Figure 7. Charles Schreyvogel, *How, Kola!,* 1901. 89.69.17. Buffalo Bill Historical Center, Cody, Wyoming.

Figure 8. N. C. Wyeth, *The First Cargo,* 1910. Oil on canvas. From the collections of the Central Children's Room, Donnell Library Center, The New York Public Library. Photograph courtesy of the Brandywine River Museum.

3. Splitting the apple: schizoglossia in New York

The first systematic study of New York City speech that shows the problematization of the pronunciation of /r/ postvocalically is Allan Forbes Hubbell's *The Pronunciation of English in New York City.* Hubbell's data stems from the forties. He observes that "/r/ does not occur in the preconsonantal position within the word, just as it does not appear in the word-final position before a following initial consonant or before a pause," but he also reports that "some speakers– not very many–pronounce /r/ in the preconsonantal position as regularly and consistently as do speakers of General American" (Hubbel 1950: 48). Even more oddly, he also observes, in some speakers,

> the complete absence of any pattern. Such speakers pronounce /r/ before a consonant or a pause and sometimes omit it in a thoroughly haphazard fashion. In many cases this irregularity is a result of the conscious attempt, only partly successful, of originally "r-less" speakers to pronounce the consonant because they feel that it is more "correct" to do so. But often no conscious effort is involved. The speaker hears both types of pronunciation about him all the time, both seem almost equally natural to him, and it is a matter of pure chance which one comes first to his lips. (48)

On the other hand, the chronology of Hubbell's data overlaps with that of Hans Kurath, who, in the highly regarded *Pronunciation of English in the Atlantic States,* remarks that "the most important characteristics of the speech of Metropolitan New York are the loss of postvocalic /r/ as such and the consequent structural innovations" (Kurath 1961: 14). Kurath actually sees dropped postvocalic /r/ as in a state of growth. He states that "several of the most striking features of the speech of Metropolitan New York," notably the substitution of schwa for postvocalic /r/, "are now also current across the Hudson River in Jersey City and Newark and vicinity, and have been adopted by some cultured speakers in the Hudson Valley as far north as Albany" (15). In 1962, however, Arthur J. Bronstein, in "Let's take another look at New York City speech," notes an equal distribution of dropped and continuant postvocalic /r/. Also, Parslow (1971) observed a similar introduction of postvocalic /r/ into Boston speech in a study conducted in the sixties.

These contradictory phenomena originate in the general American reaction to New York City speech in the post-immigration era. There are two studies that document this very well. The first is "American speech preferences" by Walter H. Wilke and Joseph F. Snyder. This study, which was undertaken in 1942, proceeded with the three categories of American English that were still operative at that time: eastern, southern, and general American. The authors recorded the speech of thirty-two males from diverse regions of the country and played those recordings to 2700 listeners from eight different national areas. They then asked the listeners to rate the speech of each speaker, and they used a quite straightforward rating system. They asked three simple evaluative questions: "Do you like this type of pronunciation?", "Would it be an advantage for you to have this type of pronunciation in your everyday life?", and "Where do you think this type of speech is from?" (Wilke and Snyder 1942: 94). The speakers who occupied the five highest rating places all spoke "general American" (102–103). Of the speakers who occupied the three lowest rating places, two were speakers from the New York City area, and one was from Bombay, India, who also spoke Marathi. They ranked 30, 31, and 32 respectively. One of the speakers from the New York area was described as displaying "Yiddish Influence." It is interesting to note that, by the forties, the speech of New York City sounded to American listeners as exotic as that of someone from India. The two other speakers with New York and Yiddish influence were also ranked in the bottom half of the survey, and they were noted for the "unvoicing of z" (103). This would refer to the devoicing of the final alveolar fricative /z/, which is the product of Yiddish substratal influence, and which would display itself, for instance, in the pronunciation of *feels* /filz/ as /fils/. Not only is New York speech marked by the dropping of postvocalic /r/, but it is also marked by the devoicing of final obstruents.

Of the speakers who occupied the last six places in the survey, aside from the three already discussed, one was a speaker of British English, one was from Alaska, spoke Aleut, and displayed "noticeable foreign influence" (103), and one had a pronunciation that "suggests colored speaker" (103). The other "colored speaker" in the survey was also rated in the bottom half of the pool of speakers.

Thus one sees a ghettoizing of pronunciation that is associated with images of New York, of foreignness, and of black American culture. In addition, all of the speakers from the southern mountain or Appalachian region were ranked in the bottom third of the survey. Thus a pattern begins to emerge. The speech preferences of American listeners parallel their cultural and regional preferences, and the pronunciations that evoke images of marginalized cultures and regions become themselves marginalized and tabooed.

The marginalization of New York pronunciation also displays a surprising presence in this study. The authors are quick to note and emphasize this marginalization, while they are not as alarmed at the low rankings of some of the other regions. In addition, their experiments are set up in such a way so as to elicit a specific response to the New York area as a separate category. Wilke and Snyder include it as one of eight national regional categories and devote more explanatory space to the New York region than to any other. They observe that "the speech of New York city, that is, those local characteristics sometimes called New Yorkese, tends to rate low in proportion to its noticeability in the individual speaker" (104). One speaker who was described as having a "slight New Yorkese" (104) accent was ranked 18th. Similarly, they offer the following observations:

> A "speech conscious" individual who has eliminated most New Yorkisms, leaving a sort of Eastern "regional Standard" speech was up in 10th place, and a similar case of a New York City resident with speech training aimed at an r-less Eastern standard was ranked 8th. In second place was a New York City resident whose family background was probably responsible for his dominantly G. A. speech with few traces of New York influence. (104)

The authors also note that "there is some tendency for subjects to prefer the local type of speech (except in the New York metropolitan area where the opposite is true)" (109). This is another early record of the internalization of national preferences within the New York area and indicates that New York was starting to display a tendency to marginalize itself internally and to display a phonetically schizophrenic self-consciousness.

The results of the study by Wilke and Snyder appeared in the 1941 edition of *The World Almanac* under the title: "Midwest accent found preferred by U. S. public." The article begins with the follow-ing words, which indicate that the study had considerable elocution-ary influence: "The Eastern Public Speaking Conference advised campaign candidates (March 20, 1940) as follows: 'A man who talks with a Midwestern or general American accent is likely to have a larger voice-appeal than an Easterner or a Southerner'" (676).

In the study "White and Negro listeners' reactions to various American-English dialects," G. Richard Tucker and Wallace E. Lambert collected three groups of college students, whom they la-beled "northern white, southern white, and southern Negro" (Tucker and Lambert 1972: 175). To these groups of students, they played samples of the speech of six types of American English, which they labeled "Network, Educated White Southern, Educated Negro Southern, Mississippi Peer, Howard University, New York Alumni" (179–181). They asked the participants in the experiment to rate the speakers on a scale of the following fifteen character attributes: "up-bringing, intelligent, friendly, educated, disposition, speech, trust-worthy, ambitious, faith in God, talented, character, determination, honest, personality, considerate" (179–181). The participants were asked to assign numbers of one to eight to the speakers, with eight being the maximum quantity for the character attribute and one be-ing the minimum quantity. All three groups of participants–northern white, southern white, and southern black–gave the network speak-ers the highest ratings and consistently rated them higher than their own regional speech. The speakers from New York and Mississippi consistently received the lowest ratings from all participants. This data was collected in the sixties and initially presented in 1967. One can conclude that, by the decade of the sixties, if not sooner, net-work standard speech had become associated with positive personal-ity attributes. In other words, standard network speech patterns were thought to sound more friendly, educated, trustworthy, honest, and considerate and to indicate better upbringing, disposition, and faith in God.

It is important here to remember the Saussurean tenet that there is no natural or ontological connection between a sign and its referent, and that signs gain their value by virtue of their relationship to other signs. Sounds also acquire value by association with certain positive signs or images. Network standard speech was based on midwestern and western speech and came to evoke the valorized characteristics attributed to the speakers in that area, i.e. to "sound better." Thus the characteristic phonemes of that speech came to indicate these positive personality values. The sound of the fronted vowel /æ/ in the word *rather,* of the low central vowel /a/ in *god,* and of the rhotic postvocalic /r/ acquired precisely the values described in the experiment above. To say that the phonemes in themselves already carried these meanings *a priori* would be untenable. Any attempt to prove such an intrinsic connection and to hold, for instance, that /æ/ is an intrinsically trustworthy sound, or that it is the natural sound of great faith in God, could hardly be taken seriously.

The fact of the matter is that /æ/ and /r/ became signs of linguistic capital; they acquired the function of prestige markers of social unit and register. As Labov and others have noted, speech innovations are used to mark horizontal and vertical social separation: horizontal in the separating off of the group from other groups, and vertical in the imitation of speakers of higher status. The phonemes /æ/ and /r/ became markers of social and ethnic identity that served to mark standard American as separate from and superior to the pronunciations associated with those ethnic influences that were perceived as threatening to American identity.

A good example of the process underlying this phenomenon can be found in Labov's study "The social motivation of a sound change," which examines the speech of Martha's Vineyard, Massachusetts. Labov observes that

> the Vineyard is best known to linguists as an important relic area of American English: an island of r-pronouncers in a sea of r-lessness. With a 320–year history of continuous settlement, and a long record of resistance to Boston ways and manners, the island has preserved many archaic traits ... the most striking feature, still strongly entrenched, is the retention of final and preconsonantal /r/. (Labov 1972a: 6–7)

This may be the first observation of the dynamic that the present study describes. Postvocalic /r/ was maintained in an act of differentiation from urban speech and behavior, here that of Boston. Labov's study mentions the phoneme /r/ but concentrates, however, on the phenomenon of vowel centralization of the diphthongs /ay/ and /aw/ in the pronunciations, for instance, of *right* and *out* respectively. In the speech of the islanders, the first member of the diphthong, normally a mid low vowel, rises and centralizes to schwa. Labov found that this vowel shift correlated with the strong resistance of native islanders to the massive presence of tourists on the island. It had its highest incidence in the up-island area, which identifies itself as more native than the down-island area. The latter area displays signs of influence from the mainland (30). In addition, vowel centralization is present in teenagers who plan to stay on the island and absent in those who intend to pursue careers on the mainland. The centralization of the diphthongs /ay/ and /aw/ was a form of social bonding in order to secure the identity of the islanders against the presence of foreign elements that had invaded the traditional culture. Labov extracts some general rules for the process:

–A language feature used by group A is marked by contrast with another standard dialect.
–Group A is adopted as a reference group by group B, and the feature is adopted and exaggerated as a sign of social identity in response to pressure from outside forces. (39)

Thereupon, hypercorrection leads to generalization of the feature, and a norm is established that is then adopted by succeeding groups. Labov's scheme can be applied to the standardization of American English pronunciation and used to analyze the function of /r/ as a bonding member over and against coastal speech. Interestingly, the data to support this were also collected by Labov in his excellent and groundbreaking studies of the pronunciation of /r/ in New York City. Labov investigated New York pronunciation in the sixties and published his results in the 655–page study *The Social Stratification of English in New York City*. Part of Labov's investigations were published in *Sociolinguistic Patterns* as "The social stratification of (r) in New York City department stores." This inquiry makes use of the latter publication. Labov examined the pronunciation of postvocalic /r/ in New York as a function of socioeconomic class. He used the employees of three major New York department stores as samples: Saks Fifth Avenue, Macy's, and S. Klein, which he ranks in terms of price and prestige. Saks has the highest prestige, Macy's occupies the middle range, and S. Klein the lowest. He correlates them with the newspaper reading habits of the upper middle, middle, and working classes. The *New York Times* was read largely by the middle and upper middle classes, and the *Daily News* predominately by the working class. Saks advertised in the *Times* and not at all in the *Daily News,* Macy's had six pages of advertising in the *Times* and fifteen in the *Daily News,* and S. Klein only one-quarter page in the *Times* and ten pages in the *Daily News* (Labov 1972b: 46).

The employees of each store were enticed to utter the phrase "fourth floor" by an interviewer who asked for directions to a department that would be found on that floor. The interviewer then pretended not to hear the answer and said, "Excuse me," in order to elicit the utterance again. The interviewer then recorded the number of instances of continuant and dropped postvocalic /r/. The results "showed clear and consistent stratification of (r) in the three stores" (51): thirty percent of the Saks employees, twenty percent of Macy's, and only four percent of S. Klein's used postvocalic /r/ all the time. Sixty-two percent of the Saks employees, fifty-one percent of Macy's, and only twenty-one percent of S Klein's used postvocalic /r/ either some or all of the time (51). These figures increased at each store when the control group was limited to white saleswomen.

This demonstrates that, by the sixties, the use of postvocalic /r/ had become a prestige marker that correlated with class and economic status. This occurred, however, in an incomplete fashion, as forty-eight percent of the Saks employees still dropped the /r/. The standardization of radio speech had problematized the pronunciation of /r/ in New York; it established a class correlation, but did so in an uneven fashion and produced a certain discursive insecurity. In general, however, rhotic /r/ became a marker of upward class mobility. It is interesting and fascinating to note that the phenomenon of upward mobility actually manifests itself here spatially. Concrete physical location correlates with level of discourse. Labov observes:

> Another interesting comparison may be made at Saks, where there is a great discrepancy between the ground floor and the upper floors. The ground floor of Saks looks very much like Macy's: many crowded count-

ers, salesgirls leaning over the counters, almost elbow to elbow, and a great deal of merchandise displayed. But the upper floors of Saks are far more spacious: there are long vistas of empty carpeting, and on the floors devoted to high fashion, there are models who display the individual garments to the customers. Receptionists are stationed at strategic points to screen out the casual spectators from the serious buyers. It would seem logical, then, to compare the ground floor of Saks with the upper floors. (56–57)

The comparison of floors reveals that continuant postvocalic /r/ is used more on the upper floors than on the lower ones. On the ground floor, twenty-three percent of the employees used continuant /r/ in all points of articulation. On the upper floors, the number rose to thirty percent. The regular absence of postvocalic /r/ was exhibited in fifty-four percent of the employees on the ground floor, but only in twenty-six percent on the upper floors (57). Thus the use of continuant /r/ actually rises with vertical spatial progress, paralleling the implicit vertical economic progress.

The study also collected information on the substitution of interdental stops for interdental fricatives: (t) for (th), as in fourth, think, through, etc., and found similar social stratification. There were no instances of this at Saks, while fifteen percent of the subjects at S. Klein substituted (t) for (th) (57).

A very important factor for the tracing of the recession of dropped postvocalic /r/ in New York speech is the inclusion of age as a determining factor. At Saks, the consistent use of continuant /r/ occurred in sixty-seven percent of the employees between the ages of fifteen and thirty, twenty-six percent of those between thirty-five and fifty, and only thirteen percent of those between fifty-five and seventy. The speech patterns of the youngest age group would have been established after the advent of regular radio broadcasts, beginning in the thirties, at the earliest. The youngest in that age group would have been exposed to television broadcast speech, as well. The speech patterns of the oldest group would have been established well before regular radio broadcasts occurred. Labov posits that "the shift from the influence of the New England prestige pattern (r-less) to the Midwestern prestige pattern (r-full) is felt most completely at Saks. The younger people at Saks are under the influence of the r-pronouncing pattern, and the older ones are not" (59). The younger group seems to be more aware of the prestige dynamics of regional speech than are the older speakers. Thus they appear to apply the already considerable class awareness present at Saks more to the social vigilance of discourse than do the older speakers. Labov observes that the prestige norm before World War II prescribed the dropped /r/.

The introduction of postvocalic /r/ into New York speech as a prestige marker also parallels the recession of the diphthong (oy). This became known in the vernacular as the "Brooklynese" sound in "toity-toid street." This was once a marker of cultivated speech in New York, but it survives consistently only in the speech of those born before World War I. Among those born after World War II, it is found only in lower class speakers (Labov 1972c: 314–315). A similar diphthong is found in Tidewater speech, where it serves as a marker dividing the generations before and after World War II. It is rarely found in the speech of those born after World War II, but it appears to function comfortably in the pre-war generation either inoffensively or as a prestige marker.

Labov's methodology is fundamentally linguistic and secondarily social. In his study of the speech of Martha's Vineyard, there was a close correlation between the linguistic data and the microsocial dynamics of the island's population. This enabled the study to ask and answer the question as to what the islanders were protecting and avoiding when they centralized the diphthongs /ay/ and /aw/ and to locate the foreign irritant that the islanders were trying to resist. The case of New York speech and its macrosocial context, however, is a different matter. The question of the influences and presences that New Yorkers are avoiding in their progressive adoption of postvocalic /r/ and the sources of their anxiety lies beyond the scope of a quantitative linguistic inquiry, such as Labov's, which can offer little in the way of etiology.

While acknowledging that, within this methodology, "there is comparatively little that can be said about the particular social or linguistic events that trigger a particular change" (Labov 1972c: 317), Labov does observe that "the reversal of New York City attitudes towards r-pronunciation can be seen as merely one prominent

feature of a general shift away from British and New England models in favor of a general American broadcast standard" (317). He is
correct in correlating the sound shift with New England pronunciation and broadcast standard speech, for the latter was indeed the
missionary of phonetic change, but the inclusion of British in the
process changes the trajectory of the shift in such a way so as to
mask the actual social factors that account for the standardization of
(mid)western speech. Labov does perceive, however, that major
shifts in social consciousness must be linked to speech and discourse, and he does attempt to sketch out a broad causal relationship
between the sociohistorical and the linguistic:

> At some point in time, the older prestige dialect was redefined; instead of
> an "international standard" it became a "regional peculiarity." This event
> seems to coincide with the period of World War II, and one might argue
> that the experience of men in the service was somehow involved. It would
> be difficult to prove; all we can do at this time is to point to the war as the
> most prominent social disturbance which coincided with the period of the
> linguistic change. (317)

This actually locates the moment of change in a decade that is later
than the ones in which the pertinent catalysts became active and thus
posits a correspondence with unrelated social phenomena. The period of the onset of the linguistic change was the decades of the
twenties and thirties. The structural dynamics of the shift had already become operative by the forties. Augmenting Labov's inquiry
with a broader sociohistorical view brings the pieces of this puzzle
into a clearer *Gestalt,* one that correlates the linguistic change with
the profound triadic impact of the closing of the American western
frontier, eastern urban immigration, and the emergence of radio.

Network standard pronunciation provided New Yorkers with
acoustic images that differed from their own. This effected a sort of
phonetic mirror stage, in which the listener became confronted with
the discrepancy between the speech patterns of self and other and
experienced the form of implicit social coercion that Bourdieu discusses: "The recognition extorted by this invisible, silent violence is
expressed in explicit statements, such as those which enable Labov
to establish that one finds the same *evaluation* of the phoneme 'r'

among speakers who come from different classes and who therefore differ in their actual *production* of 'r'" (Bourdieu 1991: 52). The psychological effect of this discrepancy was intensified by the fact that the discourse of the other, in this case, was perceived as standard, norm, or ideal, and the discourse of the self was perceived as non-standard. This resulted in a decentering of speech, a form of discursive schizophrenia or schizoglossia that scattered and restratified speech patterns. Labov has noted that "when most New Yorkers say that outsiders dislike New York City speech, they are describing an attitude which is actually their own ... New Yorkers show a general hostility towards New York City speech which emerges in countless ways. The term 'linguistic self-hatred' is not too extreme to apply to the situation" (Labov 1966: 488–489).

More than thirty years later, the educated cultivated speech of New York and Boston indicates that Labov's findings have become systemic. Recent artifacts of popular culture display the prestige patterns of rhotic /r/ in New York City speech. In the popular television program *Law and Order,* which takes place in New York, and which is consciously constructed in an unmistakably New York milieu, the distribution of rhotic and non-rhotic /r/ seems to be largely a function of who is wearing a suit and who is not. Dropped /r/ is not used by lawyers, suited detectives, and middle class characters in general. It is used by police patrolmen and patrolwomen, criminals, apartment superintendents, and the working class. In the case of Boston and the New England coast, generational differences in the speech of the Kennedy family indicate a change in the older prestige pattern. Senator Edward Kennedy's speech now contains continuant /r/ in almost all postvocalic instances, although he cannot seem to insert it before the final voiceless fricative /s/, with the result that he pronounces *farce* as /faːs/. Robert Kennedy's speech can be seen as transitional, displaying both non-rhotic and rhotic /r/ after vowels. The speech of John F. Kennedy, however, was consistently classical New England coastal and confidently displayed dropped, linking, and intrusive /r/. The latter was very salient in his pronunciation of *Cuba* and *Russia* with a final non-etymological /r/. The former president's speech was one of the last instances of the unproblematized prestige pattern of the New England coast.

Thus the speech of the cultural and economic center of the United States experienced a crisis of linguistic capital. While seemingly paradoxical, this is nonetheless a good example of James Milroy's observation that the group with the highest social prestige is not necessarily the group with the highest linguistic prestige (J. Milroy 1999: 37–39). The fundamental constituents of American identity in the twentieth century were grounded in folkish notions of ethnicity and race that stood in opposition to the perception of the ethnic composition of New York. These ideologies overrode the formidable status of the influential societal and economic classes in that city. Thus national linguistic capital had to be divested from the area seen as alien and had to be invested in regions more consonant with race-based notions of proper identity. The decentered phonetic patterns of New York can be seen as records of linguistic archaeology that echo the problematic relationship between national and local identity.

Conclusion

Judgmental evaluations of pronunciation and elocution are invariably supralingusitic. While they often present themselves as descriptive statements on speech, they nonetheless surpass, at the instant of
qualitative evaluation, the domain of language in itself and enter the
sphere of social behavior, where their ideological bases become
manifest and articulate social divisions, such as those of class, race,
ethnicity, religion, and morality. They then import those ideologies
back into the theater of language, where pronunciation becomes a
forum for the performance of social empowerment and disempowerment. The dynamics of power are not always readily visible in the
evaluative discourses of pronunciation; they are there nonetheless,
even in the apparently innocuous interpersonal situations that juxtapose standard and non-standard speakers. Bourdieu has illuminated
the implicit violence and coercion that exist in such cases, which
tend to communicate the tacit authority of the standard speaker vis-
à-vis the nonstandard speaker and thus a kind of implied prescrip-
tiveness. The abstraction and generalization of prescriptions on pronunciation and their rise to a standard–de facto and otherwise–
present the most potent and damaging instances of power and exclusion.

English pronunciation in the United States standardized in an exceptional and anomalous fashion in comparison with other western
countries. First, a consciousness of race and ethnicity was present
from the onset in conceptions of the American language, which escalated to an outright xenophobia in the twentieth century and constituted a major motivational factor in the standardization process.
Second, the centers of urban power did not become the geographical
sources for the standard pronunciation, as they generally did elsewhere in the industrialized world; instead, the norm arose from a
primarily rural area, the midwest and west, a region that acquired the
meanings of *heartland.* Third, the standard congealed in an indelib-
erate and unplanned manner that lent it a natural, even populist appearance. When it emerged as the broadcast standard in the second

quarter of the twentieth century, its status seemed self-evident, and its transparent, seemingly non-ideological form rendered it resistant to criticism. Finally, three major historical phenomena coincided to determine the rise of the *heartland* accent to the standard: the closing of the frontier, the massive importation of immigrant labor to the eastern seaboard, and the emergence of radio broadcasting in the twenties.

In the United States, a fundamental ideology of a Teutonic and northern European essence has been present in conceptions of the American language since the eighteenth century. The consciousness of race and ethnicity within the ideology of language tends to surface in the presence of alterity and congeal around the distinct and definable other(s) existing at a particular time. For Benjamin Franklin, the German was constructed as the other; for Thomas Jefferson, it was the black American; and for Noah Webster, it was the British. This caused Webster to represent the American language as "more Teutonic" than British English. In the early nineteenth century, when immigration to the United States was relatively minimal, the absence of a readily definable immigrant other necessitated a reconfiguration of alterity, and the ideological hierarchy of language became rearticulated on the basis of class and morality. This continued into the postbellum period, when a waxing white anxiety of race began again to inform the discourses of pronunciation and elocution. This anxiety was coordinate with the northern migration of blacks from former southern slave states.

The ideology of race was extremely active in the early decades of the twentieth century and informed the discussions of proper speech and elocution during that era. It was difficult, if not undesirable, for the prescriptivists of that period to avoid the issues of race and ethnicity in discussions of proper pronunciation. American attitudes on race, class, and ethnicity were very different at that time. The unabashed prejudice seems almost unimaginable to those whose experience is limited to the last half of the twentieth century. The axis of race and pronunciation converged most acutely upon the characteristic phonemes of the eastern seaboard, especially the non-rhotic postvocalic /r/.

and *southern* were constructed as exotic to that identity. Consequently, the dominant (mid)western phonemes acquired the prestige associated with proper identity and geography, and the marginalized phonemes of the east and south came to indicate difference from that prestige. The overgeneralization present in the category of *southern,* i.e. that it subsumes very different speech areas, indicates such an ideological move of cultural and ethnic marginalization.

The phenomenon known as the closing of the frontier also had a considerable effect on immigration and the formation of national identity. The impression that there was no longer an open frontier to the west intensified the anxiety over immigration, for the presence of the other could no longer be neutralized by absorption into the western infinity. The closing of the western frontier and the closing of eastern immigration were thus interlocutors in the discourse of the crisis of national language and identity and engendered the figure of the western hero as an instantiation of the proper American male. This hero was, however, always a nostalgic and sentimental figure who was to recover a romanticized frontier lost. Thus his speech patterns came to function as phonetic metonymies of the condition of nostalgia, sentimentality, and tradition. These speech patterns of the American plains states then became iconic and evoked the positive personality characteristics that were reported to Wilke and Snyder (1942). It was for this reason that they became the preferred broadcast standard. When they were initially advocated as the proper radio pronunciation, the ethnic and racial preferences and associations of the accents involved were explicit, as is evident in the discourse of Vizetelly, who marshals the general American pronunciation as a bulwark against the ethnic associations of the speech patterns of New York. Thus the primary characteristic of race and the secondary characteristic of accent were concurrent. After the desired accent had become established and iconic, however, the juxtaposition of both accent and race was not necessary, and the secondary characteristic alone–the proper accent–sufficed to evoke, implicitly, the preferred ethnicity. Thus accent came to serve as a displacement of race and functioned as a metonymy that lost its ostensible connection to the race conscious infrastructure. Hence, when James Bender recommends general American as the broadcast standard, the choice appears to be transparent and self-evident: the preferred accent is pleasant, reasonable, inoffensive, etc.

A similar dissimulation informs the conventional narratives of the standardization of American pronunciation. They are structurally and thematically akin to the ideologies of American identity that supply their own self-justifying histories. These appear as myriad retellings of myths of national origin, as mythological accounts that invest their narratives with historical and nationalistic value and then justify present behavior as the logical result of historical progress. Roosevelt's and Turner's narratives of the American west are cases in point. Similarly, fundamental American stories inform the accounts of the standardization of continuant /r/, such as Mencken's patriotic tale of the nationalist origin of American pronunciation in an act of independence from England. Another common explanation invokes America's status as a populist democracy of majority rule that seeks maximum geographical representation. In this explanation, no ideology at all is presumed to exist; the standard is simply the way most people speak. There is also the individualist argument that the United States has no official language and therefore no official standard, and that one is free to speak as one wishes without being judged, which invokes an ideal, almost utopian myth of democracy that, when believed, suppresses the awareness of the real material dynamics of pronunciation, prestige, and prejudice. Also, the argument that the (mid)western accent simply sounds better, and that radio stations merely selected broadcasters who sounded most pleasant and least offensive, slips into a phonetic referentiality that conceals the origin, evolution, and dynamics of the exclusion of certain accents. These misprisions all function to suppress the discussion of language as an instrument of social division and stratification based on a consciousness of race and class. In doing so, these misprisions serve to sustain the linguistic strategies of social empowerment and disempowerment.

Afterword

The conclusions of this study raise the question as to whether the phenomena described here are still operative and, if so, in which regions they would be transpiring. The metonymic processes of stigmatization between accent and behavior are clearly a part of the ontology of spoken language; this study has explored a subset of these dynamics and endeavored to demonstrate the power of the consciousness of race and ethnicity in the transformation of accent. The era investigated in these pages exhibited a pronounced racism that clearly abated in the last half of the twentieth century, but it would be erroneous to hold that this racism has disappeared entirely, or that a certain surreptitious consciousness of race no longer influences American social behavior. This being true, one may ask if there are cases in which these biases are currently effecting accentual changes.

The phonetic patterns that characterize the accent of any given speech area are not all of equal perceptibility and value; some phonemes are much more salient than others, and often, the accent of a region will be flagged by one peculiarity in accent. The dropped postvocalic /r/ examined in this study is one such case in point: it is the major phoneme elicited in satires of the speech of New York, coastal New England, and the southern coast. Also, the continuant postvocalic /r/ is arguably the most perceptible difference between British and American speech. Similarly, the panorama of Canadian speech is, for American audiences, generally reduced to the synecdoche of the centralized diphthong /aw/, such as in the pronunciation of *about* and *house*. Most Americans are unaware of the other patterns that distinguish Canadian speech from American, such as the more constricted /r/, the lesser presence of offglides, and the rounded vowel /ɔ/ in *god, hot, don,* etc., making *don* and *dawn* homophonous. When Canadian speech becomes self-consciously adjusted to adapt to this external perception, as in the case of Canadian television programs broadcast to the United States, the centralized diphthong /aw/ is the first sound to go.

An interesting development has emerged recently in the pronunciation of the southern regions of the United States. As described in the body of this study, the pronunciation of the southern states falls into two general groupings: the southern mountain and plain area–which includes Appalachia, the south midland, and Texas–, and the southern coastal. At this writing, it seems that the southern coastal accent is undergoing changes that the southern mountain and plain is not; in short, it seems to be disappearing. One tends to hear it among the generation born before WWII, while it is becoming less and less present in the post-war generation, especially among the college and college-educated populations. Moreover, it is used neither in the media nor in film to represent a generic southern accent. When it is depicted, it tends to appear as caricature; a good example is the representation of southern coastal speakers in the recent film *Midnight in the Garden of Good and Evil,* which is clearly stylized and satirical. Once dominant in Richmond, the Tidewater area, Savannah, Charleston, and other coastal cities, it is now yielding to speech patterns that approximate network standard. A prominent feature of the accent, the dropped postvocalic /r/, is being systemically replaced by the rhotic variant.

The same cannot be said of the southern mountain and plains accent. It thrives in the speech of white social classes from the eastern Carolinas through Texas. Its salient features, such as the highly constricted retroflex /r/, the monophthongized vowels, and the homophony of *pin* and *pen,* may become mitigated in the educated population, but they are rarely eradicated; they are quite audible in the pronunciations of the major political figures who come from that region, such as Bill Clinton, Al Gore, and George W. Bush. In films, this accent is used quite confidently by regional speakers such as Julia Roberts and Sissy Spacek. Throughout the south, it is heard in the speech of advertising that is intended to sound southern, while its counterpart, the southern coastal variant, is not. Basically, non-coastal southern speech has risen to the status of representative southern speech in general. Clearly, there are many factors that one could name as probable contributors to this phenomenon. The accent is the voice of a large geographical area, of an ethnically homogenous white population, and of a clearly identifiable culture with its own music and manners. The tremendous cultural power of country and western music may be the most significant agent contributing to the stability of the accent. This particular musical genre is highly codified and ritualized, as is evident in its uniformity of dress, which offers the performer a color choice of either white or black for the perfectly blocked cowboy hat. This high degree of codification may have a regularizing effect on pronunciation. Also, the fact that these speech patterns have been and are used by major national political figures certainly does not hurt the status of the accent.

The question remains as to why one kind of southern speech should be thriving and another on the wane. It is difficult to argue that the power and scope of the mountain variety is causing it to dominate over coastal speech, because the latter is not being replaced by the former, it is instead being supplanted by approximations to network standard. One could also offer the possible explanation that there is a certain schism within the larger southern speech area, and that the coastal region is avoiding the stigmas associated with Appalachian speech. This explanation seems unlikely; in the southern states that contain both mountain and coastal speech patterns, such as Virginia, the Carolinas, and Georgia, both accents pass and are perceived as properly southern and native to the state. Moreover, this account leaves unanswered the initial question as to why coastal pronunciation should shift in the first place, and noncoastal speech should not. Perhaps the phenomenon in question has more to do with the associative and metonymic evocations of each of the southern accents.

Southern mountain speech is unmistakably white, as are its culture and music. Within the major genres of popular American music, country and western clearly ranks among those most evocative of white European culture. The same cannot be said of southern coastal speech. It is the source of black American English pronunciation and is often evocative of and even confused with that accent. The narrator in Henry James's *The Bostonians* (1886) says of the central character, Basil Ransom, a southern coastal speaker, "that he prolonged his consonants and swallowed his vowels, that he was guilty of elisions and interpolations which were equally unexpected, and that his discourse was pervaded by something sultry and vast, something almost African in its rich, basking tone, something that almost African in its rich, basking tone, something that suggested the teeming expanse of the cotton-field" (James 1985: 804). Black American English and southern coastal speech patterns share common features of monophthongization, vowel lengthening, and dropping of postvocalic /r/. This study has also discussed the difficulties that some northern listeners have distinguishing between black and southern white coastal speakers. Moreover, the speech patterns in question are generally present throughout the manifestations of black American culture; they are consistently used in comedy and are iconically fused with popular music of black origin, such as blues, jazz, motown, soul, rap, and especially rock, the accent of which is also used in the performance of white artists from Elvis Presley to the Rolling Stones.

It may indeed be possible that the southern coastal accent is waning because it is subject to stigmatic associations with black American English. Southern mountain speech contains no such associations; on the contrary, it is distinctly monocultural, and it is perhaps for this reason that it has come to represent white southern culture in general. The phonetic patterns of the southern coastal accent may be ambiguously evocative and may stimulate race-conscious metonymic associations that motivate the cultivated white speakers of that area to gravitate toward "neutral" and unstigmatized speech patterns. There is also present in the southern coastal area an interesting folk linguistic belief that may be symptomatic of this associative process: it is the idea that white southern coastal speech was changed by the influence of black American English, and that these changes are of African origin. Such misconceptions, which actually reverse the true causal process, have been properly dismantled by linguistic scholarship (Poplack 2000).

The recent examples of white reactions to minority languages in the United States–the "English Only" anti-Hispanic movement and the opposition to the teaching of Ebonics–indicate that a connection between consciousness of race and consciousness of language does indeed persist. The opposition to the use of Spanish on an official basis in states such as California and Colorado is ostensibly based on reasons of intelligible communication; the opponents see heteroglossia as an impediment to effective, unified government. Behind this apparently reasonable justification, however, their looms a surreptitious agenda of race that is elusive and difficult to bring to light, but that does occasionally manifest itself. In 1988, *the Arizona Republic* published parts of a confidential memo written by John Tanton, the chairman and cofounder of U.S. English, an organization that petitions to make English the official language of the United States:

> *Gobernar es poblar* translates "to govern is to populate." In this society where the majority rules, does this hold? Will the present majority peaceably hand over its political power to a group that is simply more fertile? Can *homo contraceptivus* compete with *homo progenitiva* [sic] if borders aren't controlled? Or is advice to limit one's family simply advice to move over and let someone else with greater reproductive powers occupy the space? ... Perhaps this is the first instance in which those with their pants up are going to get caught by those with their pants down! (Crawford 1992: 151)

This surprising passage actually seems to configure language legislation as a means of population control, namely the limitation, restraint and containment of a group perceived as alien, excessively sexual, lacking in self-control, and undomesticated.

The presence of race consciousness is more difficult to cloak, however, in the opposition to the teaching of Ebonics–also referred to as black English or, in linguistic circles, as African American Vernacular English. As one is dealing with differences within the same language, objections based on reasons of intelligibility become awkward and precarious. In 1996, the Oakland California schoolboard decided to implement the teaching of Ebonics in schools. The Linguistic Society of America endorsed the Oakland resolution in 1997. In the same year, the decision was suppressed by a meeting of the California State Legislature, which characterized it as teaching "slang" and "poor communication skills" (Baugh 2000: 129). Oakland's initial decision elicited a flurry of parodies and jokes within the white community. Robin Lakoff surveyed the internet jokes about Ebonics and found that they represent blacks as ignorant, sexually promiscuous, as drug abusers, and as criminals. The jokes use parodied black English to describe drug deals ("one joint, two joint, three joint") and maternal prostitution ("what you say about my mama?") (Lakoff 2000: 240). Lakoff makes some valuable insights on the dynamics of power, exclusion, and racism in the Ebonics issue. She observes that the suppression of Ebonics is a method of controlling speech and thus controlling behavior. "Our" language stays in power, "theirs" becomes marginalized, ghettoized, and never mainstreamed, and so do "they." Effectively, when Americans speak of excluding Ebonics, they are speaking of excluding blacks. Similarly, Smitherman sees the resistance as a "backlash against People of Color masquerading as linguistic patriotism" (Smitherman 2000: 293).

The discourse of ethnic and racial prejudice in "polite" society in the last half of the twentieth century has progressively displaced physical expressions onto peripheral associations. Instead of stigmatizing the physical characteristics of blacks–which is the essence of racism–one stigmatizes the characteristics of their speech. Thus language becomes a surrogate theater for the disguised performance of racial prejudice. Black English then becomes, at its moment of inception, nonstandardized and, consequently, substandardized. There is no question of its becoming *the* standard; it must be denied the status of another or alternative standard altogether. Clearly, there is a white fear of contamination at work here, which Smitherman has characterized as a fear of "the browning of America" (Smitherman 2000: 293).

Within this complex of anxiety, black English occupies a space next to some traditional neighbors stigmatized as other. A letter to the *San Francisco Chronicle* opposing the teaching of Ebonics predicted "that very shortly we will see New York punks being taught in Brooklynese, Georgia rednecks in Ya'allonics ..." (Lakoff 2000: 242). Here, black English is related to other groups traditionally configured in ethnic, geographical, and linguistic marginalization.

It is clear from these examples that a connection between consciousness of race and consciousness of language does indeed persist. What remains to be demonstrated is whether the prejudices against black English are precipitating accentual shifts in the white English of speech areas associated with black culture and pronunciation. Investigations in perceptual dialectology, however, such as those conducted by Preston in the inland northern area, could assess

the presence of such misconceptions and stigr
illuminate the extent to which the accentu
coastal speech are being determined by a consc

References

Aléong, Stanley
    1983   Normes linguistiques, normes sociales, une perspective anthro-pologique. In Bédard, Edith and Jacques Maurais, *La norme linguistique*. Paris: Le Robert, 255–280.

Alden, Abner
    1802   *The Reader*. Boston: Thomas & Andrews.

Algeo, John, James W. Hartman and A. M. Kinloch
    1970   American speech looks ahead. *American Speech* 45: 6–7.

Allison, Burgess
    1815   *The American Standard of Orthography and Pronunciation, and Improved Dictionary of the English Language*. Burlington: John S. Meehan.

Annual Report of the Commissioner of Indian Affairs to the Secretary of the
    1878   *Interior*. Washington, D.C.: U.S. Government Printing Office.

Ayers, Alfred
    1880   *The Orthoepist*. New York: Appleton & Company.

Babbitt, Eugene H.
    1896   *The English Pronunciation of the Lower Classes in New York and Vicinity*. Norwood: American Dialect Society.

Bailey, Richard W.
    1996   *Nineteenth-Century English*. Ann Arbor: The University of Michigan Press.

Bakhtin, Mikhail Mikhailovich
    1981   *The Dialogic Imagination*. Austin: The University of Texas Press.

Baugh, John
    2000   *Beyond Ebonics: Linguistic Pride and Racial Prejudice*. Oxford and New York: Oxford University Press.

Bell, Alexander Melville
    1887   *Elocutionary Manual: The Principles of Elocution, with Exercises and Notations for Pronunciation, Intonation, Emphasis, Gesture, and Emotional Expression*. Washington: John C. Parker.
    1896   *The Sounds of R*. Washington: Volta Bureau.

Bender, James F.
    1939   *The Personality Structure of Stuttering*. New York: Pitman.
    1943   *NBC Handbook of Pronunciation*. New York: Thomas Crowell.
    1945   *Salesman's Mispronunciations*. Roslyn Heights: Sales Training Publishing Company.
    1949   *How to Talk Well*. New York: McGraw-Hill.

1961   *How to Sell Well: the Art and Science of Professional Salesman-ship*. New York: McGraw-Hill.
Better-English Institute of America
1930   *Practical English and Effective Speech*. Chicago: Better-English Institute of America.
Bloom, Harold
1979   The breaking of form. In Bloom, Harold, *Deconstruction and Criticism*. New York: Seabury Press, 1–37.
Bonacich, Edna
1984   Some basic facts: patterns of Asian immigration and exclusion. In Cheng, Lucie and Edna Bonacich (eds.), *Labor Immigration under Capitalism*. Berkeley: University of California Press, 60–78.
Bourdieu, Pierre
1982   *Ce que parler veut dire: l'économie des échanges linguistiques*. Paris: Fayard.
1991   *Language and Symbolic Power*. Cambridge: Harvard University Press.
Bowen, Edwin W.
1905   Authority in English pronunciation. *The Popular Science Monthly* April 1905: 544–555.
Brigance, William N. and Ray K. Immel
1938   *Speechmaking. Principles and Practice*. New York: E. S. Crofts.
Bronstein, Arthur J.
1962   Let's take another look at New York City speech. *American Speech* 37: 13–26.
1990   The development of pronunciation in English language dictionaries. In Ramsaran, Susan (ed.), *Studies in the Pronunciation of English: A Commemorative Volume in Honour of A. C. Gimson*. London: Routledge, 137–154.
Brown, William R.
1970   *Imagemaker: Will Rogers and the American Dream*. Columbia: University of Missouri Press.
Burke, Kenneth
1969   *A Grammar of Motives*. Berkeley: The University of California Press.
Bynack, V. P.
1984   Noah Webster's linguistic thought and the idea of an American national culture. *Journal of the History of Ideas* 45: 99–114.
Chamberlain, Houston Stewart
1977   *Foundations of the Twentieth Century*. New York: Howard Fertig (Translation of *Die Grundlagen des 19. Jahrhunderts*).
Chermayeff, Ivan
1991   *Ellis Island. An Illustrated History of the Immigrant Experience*. New York: MacMillan.
Clark, Barret H.

1930   *Speak the Speech. Reflections on Good English and the Reformers.*
        Seattle: University of Washington Bookstore.
Cohen, Mark Nathan
1998   Culture, not race, explains human diversity. *The Chronicle of
        Higher Education* 17 April: B4–B5.
Cole, Jeffrey Ian
1985   *Born to the New Art: CBS Correspondents and the Emergence of
        Broadcast News, 1930–1941.* Ph. D. diss. UCLA.
Combs, Josia
1931   The radio and pronunciation. *American Speech* 7(2): 124–129.
Crawford, James (ed.)
1992   *Language Loyalties: A Source Book on the Official English
        Controversy.* Chicago and London: University of Chicago Press.
Crawford, James
2000   *Hold Your Tongue: Bilingualism and the Politics of "English
        Only."* Reading, Mass.: Addison-Wesley Publishing.
DeWitt, Margaret E.
1924   *EuphonEnglish in America.* London and Toronto: J. M. Dent.
1928   *Our Oral Word As Social and Economic Factor.* London and
        Toronto: J. M. Dent.
Dillard, J. L.
1980   *Perspectives on American English.* (Contributions to the Sociology
        of Language 29.) The Hague: Mouton de Gruyter.
1985   *Toward a Social History of American English.* (Contributions to the
        Sociology of Language 39.) Berlin: Mouton de Gruyter.
1992   *A History of American English.* (Longman Linguistics Library.)
        London: Longman.
Dinnerstein, Leonard
1994   *Antisemitism in America.* New York: Oxford.
Donahue, Thomas S.
1993   On inland northern and the factors for dialect spread and shift.
        In Frazer, Timothy C. (ed.), *Heartland English: Variation and
        Transition in the American Midwest.* Tuscaloosa: The University of
        Alabama Press, 23–49.
Douglas, George H.
1987   *The Early Days of Radio Broadcasting.* Jefferson: McFarland and
        Company.
Douglas, William
1809   *A Key to Pronunciation, in which is shown the true pronunciation
        of a large number of English words as also, the erroneous manner
        in which they are most frequently pronounced by the illiterate.*
        Philadelphia: Bouvier.
Drake, Glendon F.
1977   *The Role of Prescriptivism in American Linguistics, 1820–1970.*
        (Studies in the History of Linguistics 13.) Amsterdam and

Philadelphia: J. Benjamins.

Durham, Phillip and Everett L. Jones
1965   *The Negro Cowboys.* New York: Dodd, Mead, and Company.

Emerson, B. D.
1828   *The National Spelling Book and Pronouncing Tutor.* Boston: Jenks and Palmer.

Etulain, Richard W.
1996   *Re-Imagining the Modern American West.* Tucson: The University of Arizona Press.

Fliegelman, Jay
1993   *Jefferson, National Language, and the Culture of Performance.* Stanford: Stanford University Press.

Franklin, Benjamin
1961   *The Papers of Benjamin Franklin,* vol. 4. Ed. Leonard W. Labaree. New Haven: Yale University Press.
1967   *The Papers of Benjamin Franklin,* vol. 11. Ed. Leonard W. Labaree. New Haven: Yale University Press.
1970   *The Papers of Benjamin Franklin,* vol. 14. Ed. Leonard W. Labaree. New Haven: Yale University Press.

Frazer, Timothy C.
1993a   Problems in Midwest English: introduction and overview. In Frazer, Timothy C. (ed.), *Heartland English: Variation and Transition in the American Midwest.* Tuscaloosa: The University of Alabama Press, 1–22.
1993b   The language of Yankee cultural imperialism: pioneer ideology and "general American." In Frazer, Timothy C. (ed.), *Heartland English: Variation and Transition in the American Midwest.* Tuscaloosa: The University of Alabama Press, 59–66.

Fromkin, Victoria and Robert Rodman
1983   *An Introduction to Language.* New York: Holt, Rinehart, and Winston.

Graham, Stephen
1914   *With Poor Immigrants to America.* New York: MacMillan.
1927   *New York Nights.* New York: Doran.

Grandgent, Charles H.
1920   The dog's letter. In Grandgent, Charles H., *Old and New Sundry Papers.* Cambridge: Harvard University Press, 31–56.

Grant, Madison
1917   *The Passing of the Great Race, or, the Racial Basis of European History.* New York: C. Scribner's Sons.

Grey, Zane
1990   *Riders of the Purple Sage.* New York: Penguin Books.

Halberstam, David
1989   *Summer of '49.* New York: Morrow.

Harbaugh, William H.

1975   *Power and Responsibility: The Life and Times of Theodore Roosevelt.* New York: Octagon Books.

Harrison, Ralph
1804   *Rudiments of English Grammar.* Philadelphia: John Bioren.

Hartley, Laura C.
1999   A view from the west: perceptions of U.S. dialects by Oregon residents. In Preston, Dennis R. (ed.), *Handbook of Perceptual Dialectology.* Amsterdam and Philadelphia: John Benjamins, 315–322.

Hartley, Laura C. and Dennis R. Preston
1999   The names of US English: valley girl, cowboy, Yankee, normal, nasal and ignorant. In Bex, Tony and Richard J. Watts (eds.), *Standard English: The widening debate.* London and New York: Routledge, 207–238.

Harvard University
1923   Report of the committee appointed to "consider and report to the governing boards principles and methods for more effective sifting of candidates for admission to the university" April.

Haskins, Frederic J.
1919   Here at last is a professor of Americanese. *Minneapolis Tribune,* 24 August.

Haugen, Einar
1968   The Scandinavian languages as cultural artifacts. In Fishman, J. A., C. A. Ferguson and J. Das Gupta (eds.), *Language Problems of Developing Nations.* New York: Wiley, 267–284.
1972   *The Ecology of Language.* Stanford: Stanford University Press.

Henderson, Ellen Clark
1911   The Necessity for an Uniform Accurate Pronunciation of the English Language. B. A. Thesis, University of Utah.

Hendrick, Burton
1923   *The Jews in America.* New York: Doubleday.
1907   The great Jewish invasion. *McClure's Magazine* 28: 307–321.
1913   The Jewish invasion of America. *McClure's Magazine* 40: 125–165.

Hill, Archibald A.
1940   Early loss of [r] before dentals. *PMLA* 55: 308–321.

Hill, Thomas Wright
1860   A lecture on the articulation of speech (January 29, 1821). In *Selections from the Papers of the Late Thomas Wright Hill.* London: John W. Parker and Son, 8–34.

Hobson, Fred
1994   *Mencken: A Life.* Baltimore: Johns Hopkins University Press.

Holt, Alfred H.
1937   *You Don't Say! A Guide to Pronunciation.* New York: Thomas Y. Crowell.

Honey, John
  1989   *Does Accent Matter?* London: Faber and Faber.
  1997   *Language is Power.* London: Faber and Faber.
Howren, Robert
  1962   The speech of Okracoke, North Carolina. *American Speech* 37:
           161–175.
Hubbell, Allan Forbes
  1950   *The Pronunciation of English in New York City.* New York:
           Octagon Books.
Hurd, Seth T.
  1848   *A Grammatical Corrector; or, Vocabulary of the Common Errors
           of Speech: being a collection of nearly two thousand barbarisms,
           cant phrases, colloquialisms, quaint expressions, provincialisms,
           false pronunciation, perversions, misapplication of terms, and other
           kindred errors of the English language, peculiar to the different
           states of the union.* Philadelphia: E. H. Butler.
Jackson, Kenneth T.
  1985   *Crabgrass Frontier. The Suburbanization of the United States.* New
           York and Oxford: Oxford University Press.
James, Henry
  1985   *The Bostonians.* In James, Henry, *Novels 1881–1806.* New York:
           The Library of America, 801–1219.
  1999a   The question of our speech. In Walker, Pierre A. (ed.), *Henry James
           on Culture.* Lincoln and London: University of Nebraska Press, 42–
           57.
  1999b   The speech of American women. In Walker, Pierre A. (ed.), *Henry
           James on Culture.* Lincoln and London: University of Nebraska
           Press, 58–81.
Jefferson, Thomas
  1972   *Notes on the State of Virginia.* Ed. William Peden. New York:
           Norton.
Jenkins, Virginia Scott
  1994   *The Lawn: A History of an American Obsession.* Washington:
           Smithsonian Institution.
Jespersen, Otto
  1923   *Language. Its Nature, Development, and Origin.* New York: Henry
           Holt.
Johnson, H. P.
  1928   Who lost the southern r? *American Speech* 3(5): 377–383.
Joseph, John E.
  1987   *Eloquence and Power.* London: Frances Pinter.
Kennedy, Arthur G.
  1935   *Current English.* Boston: Ginn.
Kenyon, John S.
  1926   Some notes on American r. *American Speech* 1(6): 329–339.

King, Samuel Arthur
    1926   *Graduated Exercises in Articulation.* Philadelphia: John C. Winston Company.

Krapp, George P.
    1919   *The Pronunciation of Standard English in America.* New York: Oxford.
    1925   *The English Language in America.* New York: MLA.

Kurath, Hans
    1961   *The Pronunciation of English in the Atlantic States.* Ann Arbor: The University of Michigan Press.
    1971a   The origin of dialectical differences in spoken American English. In Williamson, J. V. and V. M. Burke (eds.), *A Various Language: Perspectives on American Dialects.* New York: Holt, Rinehart, and Winston, 12–21.
    1971b   Some aspects of Atlantic seaboard English considered in their connection with British English. In Williamson, J. V. and V. M. Burke (eds.), *A Various Language: Perspectives on American Dialects.* New York: Holt, Rinehart, and Winston, 101–107.

Labov, William
    1966   *The Social Stratification of English in New York City.* Washington: Center for Applied Linguistics.
    1971   The effect of social mobility on linguistic behavior. In Williamson, J. V. and V. M. Burke (eds.), *A Various Language: Perspectives on American Dialects.* New York: Holt, Rinehart, and Winston, 640–662.
    1972a   The social motivation of a sound change. In Labov, William, *Sociolinguistic Patterns.* Philadelphia: The University of Pennsylvania Press, 1–42.
    1972b   The social stratification of (r) in New York City department stores. In Labov, William, *Sociolinguistic Patterns.* Philadelphia: The University of Pennsylvania Press, 43–69.
    1972c   The social setting of linguistic change. In Labov, William, *Sociolinguistic Patterns.* Philadelphia: The University of Pennsylvania Press, 260–326.

Lakoff, Robin
    2000   *The Language War.* Berkeley: The University of California Press.

Larsen, Thorleif
    1931   *Pronunciation. A Practical Guide to American Standards.* London: Oxford University Press.

Levine, David
    1983   *The American College and the Culture of Aspiration, 1915–1940.* Ithaca: Cornell University Press.

Lewis, William D. and Mabel Dodge Holmes
    1917   *Knowing and Using Words.* Boston: Allyn and Bacon.

Lippi-Green, Rosina

1997   *English With an Accent: Language, Ideology, and Discrimination in the United States.* New York: Routledge.

Lounsbury, Thomas R.

1904   *The Standard of Pronunciation in English.* New York: Harper & Brothers.

Marx, Karl

1960   *Die Deutsche Ideologie.* Berlin: Dietz.

1976   *The German Ideology.* In Marx, Karl and Friedrich Engels, *Collected Works,* vol. 5. New York: International Publishers.

Matthews, Brander

1910   The American of the future. In Matthews, Brander, *The American of the Future and Other Essays.* New York: Charles Scribner's Sons, 3–24.

1921a   Is the English language degenerating? In Matthews, Brander, *Essays on English.* New York: Charles Scribner's Sons, 1–30.

1921b   One world language or two? In Matthews, Brander, *Essays on English.* New York: Charles Scribner's Sons, 269–281.

1921c   A standard of spoken English. In Matthews, Brander, *Essays on English.* New York: Charles Scribner's Sons, 205–222.

McCabe, John

1997   *Cagney.* New York: Alfred A. Knopf.

McDavid, Raven

1966   Sense and nonsense about American dialects. *PMLA* 82(2): 7–17.

1981   Webster, Mencken, and Avis: Spokesmen for linguistic autonomy. *Canadian Journal of Linguistics-Revue Canadienne de Linguistique* 26(1): 118–125.

McLean, Margaret P.

1928   *Good American Speech.* New York: Dutton.

Mead, Theodore H.

1890   *Our Mother Tongue.* New York: Dodd, Mead, and Company.

Mearns, Hugh

1916   Our own, our native speech. *McClure's Magazine* 47: 43.

Mencken, Henry Louis

1923   *The American Language. An Inquiry into the Development of English in the United States.* New York: Alfred A. Knopf.

1948   *The American Language. An Inquiry into the Development of English in the United States.* Supplement II. New York: Alfred A. Knopf.

1963   *The American Language. An Inquiry into the Development of English in the United States* (One-Volume Abridged Edition). Ed. Raven I. McDavid. New York: Alfred A. Knopf.

Meyers, Jeffrey

1997   *Bogart: A Life in Hollywood.* Boston: Houghton Mifflin.

Milroy, James

1999   The consequences of standardisation in descriptive linguistics. In

Bex, Tony and Richard J. Watts (eds.), *Standard English: The widening debate*. London and New York: Routledge, 16–39.

Milroy, James and Lesley Milroy
1985   *Authority in Language*. London: Routledge.

Milroy, Lesley
1999   Standard English and language ideology in Britain and the United States. In Bex, Tony and Richard J. Watts (eds.), *Standard English: The widening debate*. London and New York: Routledge, 173–206.

Mugglestone, Lynda
1997   *"Talking Proper:" The Rise of Accent as Social Symbol*. Oxford: Oxford University Press.

Nemerov, Alex
1991   Doing the "old America:" the image of the American west, 1880–1920. In Truettner, William H. (ed.), *The West as America: Reinterpreting Images of the Frontier, 1820–1920*. Washington: Smithsonian Institution, 285–343.

New Pennsylvania Primer: being an approved selection of words, the most easy of pronunciation, adapted to the capacities of young children. N. d. Harrisburg: G. S. Peters.

New York Times
1923   Language by law established. Editorial, 7 February.

Nietzsche, Friedrich
1980   *Zur Genealogie der Moral*. In Nietzsche, Friedrich, *Sämtliche Werke. Kritische Studienausgabe in 15 Bänden*, Bd. 5. München: Deutscher Taschenbuch Verlag, 245–412.

1998   *On the Genealogy of Morality*. Translated by Maudemarie Clark and Alan J. Swensen. Indianapolis and Cambridge: Hackett Publishing Company.

Oliver, Laurence J.
1992   *Brander Matthews, Theodore Roosevelt, and the Politics of American Literature, 1880–1920*. Knoxville: University of Tennessee Press.

Parslow, Robert L.
1971   The pronunciation of English in Boston, Massachusetts: vowels and consonants. In Williamson , J. V. and V. M. Burke (eds.), *A Various Language: Perspectives on American Dialects*. New York: Holt, Rinehart, and Winston, 610–624.

Payson, Thomas
1816   *Address delivered before the Associated Instructors of Boston and Its Vicinity, on their anniversary, Oct. 10, 1816*. Boston: John Eliot.

Pederson, Lee
1977   Studies of American pronunciation since 1945. *American Speech* 52 (3–4): 262–327.

Peirce, John
1808   *The New, American Spelling Book*. Philadelphia: Joseph Crukshank.

Phillips, Arthur E.
    1920   *Natural Drills in Expression.* Chicago: Newton.
Phyfe, William H.
    1897   *How Should I Pronounce?* New York: G. P. Putnam's Sons.
Pollak, Oliver B.
    1983   Antisemitism, the Harvard plan, and the roots of reverse
            discrimination. *Jewish Social Studies* 45(2): 113–122.
Poplack, Shana
    2000   *The English History of African-American English.* Oxford:
            Blackwell Publishers.
Preston, Dennis R.
    1999   *Handbook of Perceptual Dialectology.* Amsterdam and Phila-
            delphia: John Benjamins.
    1993   Two heartland perceptions of language variety. In Frazer, Timothy
            C. (ed.), *Heartland English: Variation and Transition in the
            American Midwest.* Tuscaloosa: The University of Alabama Press,
            23–48.
    1989   *Perceptual Dialectology: Nonlinguists' Views of Areal Linguistics.*
            (Topics in Sociolinguistics 7.) Dordrecht and Providence: Forris
            Publications.
Pyles, Thomas
    1952   *Words and Ways of American English.* New York: Random House.
Ramsaran, Susan
    1990   RP: fact *and* fiction. In Ramsaran, Susan (ed.), *Studies in the
            Pronunciation of English: A Commemorative Volume in Honour of
            A. C. Gimson.* London: Routledge, 178–190.
Randolph, Vance
    1929   Is there an Ozark dialect? *American Speech* 4(3): 203–204.
Raubincheck, Letitia
    1934   *Improving Your Speech. A Pupil's Practice Book in Speech
            Training.* New York: Noble and Noble.
Reith, J. C. W.
    1924   *Broadcast over Britain.* London: Hodder and Stoughton Limited
Reyhner, John
    1992   Policies toward American Indian languages: a historical sketch. In
            Crawford, James (ed.), *Language Loyalties: A Source Book on the
            Official English Controversy.* Chicago and London: University of
            Chicago Press, 41–47.
Roberts, Randy and James S. Olson
    1995   *John Wayne: American.* New York: The Free Press.
Roosevelt, Theodore
    1905   *The Winning of the West.* Vol. 1, *The Spread of English-Speaking
            Peoples.* New York: Current Literature.
Russel, William
    1830   *Lessons in Enunciation, Comprising a Statement of Common Errors*

in Articulation, and the Rules for Correct Usage in Pronouncing; with a Course of Elementary Exercises in these Branches of Elocution. Boston: Richardson, Lord, and Holbrook.

Salisbury, Albert
1879   *Phonology and Orthoepy: An Elementary Treatise on Pronunciation for the Use of Teachers and Schools.* Madison: Wm. J. Park & Sons.

Sanford, William P. and Willard H. Yeager
1934   *Principles of Effective Speaking.* New York: Thomas Nelson.

Savage, William
1979   *The Cowboy Hero.* Norman: University of Oklahoma Press.

Scott, John Rutledge
1915   *The Technic of the Speaking Voice.* Columbia: Stephens Publishing Co.

Sevareid, Eric
1946   *Not So Wild A Dream.* New York: Alfred A. Knopf.

Shakespeare, William
1964   *The Tragedy of Romeo and Juliet.* New Haven: Yale University Press.

Shapiro, Michael J.
1989   A political approach to language purism. In Jernudd, Björn H. and Michael J. Shapiro (eds.), *The Politics of Language Purism.* (Contributions to the Sociology of Language 54.) Berlin and New York: Mouton de Gruyter, 21–29.

Shaw, Ronald E.
1966   *Erie Water West: A History of the Erie Canal 1792–1854.* Lexington: The University of Kentucky Press.

Sherman, Lewis
1885   *A Handbook of Pronunciation.* Milwaukee: Cramer, Aikens & Cramer.

Shingawa, Larry Hajime and Michael Jang
1998   *Atlas of American Diversity.* Walnut Creek: AltaMira Press.

Slotkin, Richard
1981   Nostalgia and progress: Theodore Roosevelt's myth of the frontier. *American Quarterly* 35: 608–637.

1986   *The Fatal Environment: The Myth of the Frontier in the Age of Industrialization, 1800–1890.* Middletown: Wesleyan University Press.

Smitherman, Geneva
2000   *Talkin That Talk: Language, Culture, and Education in African America.* London and New York: Routledge.

Snyder, Joseph F. and Walter H. Wilke
1940   *Effective Pronunciation: A Phonetic Analysis of American Speech.* New York: New York University Bookstore.

Soule, Richard and William Wheeler

1874   *Manual of Pronunciation and Spelling.* Boston and New York: Lee and Shepard.
Stockdell, Helen
1930   *Speech Made Beautiful. Practical Lessons in English Diction.* New York: Abingdon Press.
Sutton, V.
1933   Speech at the National Broadcasting Company. *The English Journal* 22(6): 456–460.
Tatalovich, Raymond
1995   *Nativism Reborn? The Official Language Movement in the United States.* Lexington: University of Kentucky Press.
Taylor, Hanni U.
1989   *Standard English, Black English, and Bidialectism.* (American University Studies XIII: Linguistics, vol. 9.) New York: Peter Lang.
Thomas, George
1991   *Linguistic Purism.* London: Longman.
Thomas, C. K.
1945   A symposium on phonetics and standards of pronunciation. *Quarterly Journal of Speech* 31(3): 318–327.
Tower, David B.
1851   *The Gradual Reader.* New York: Cady and Burgess.
Toynbee, Arnold Joseph
1935   *A Study of History.* London: Oxford University Press.
Trudgill, Peter
1999   Standard English: what it isn't. In Bex, Tony and Richard J. Watts (eds.), *Standard English: The widening debate.* London and New York: Routledge, 117–128.
Trudgill, P. and J. Hannah
1982   *International English.* London: Edward Arnold.
Tucker, G. Richard and Wallace E. Lambert
1972   White and Negro listeners' reactions to various American-English dialects. In Fishman, Joshua A. (ed.), *Advances in the Sociology of Language.* Vol. 2, *Selected Studies and Applications.* The Hague: Mouton, 175–184.
Turner, Frederick Jackson
1901a   Jewish immigration. *The Herald-Tribune.* Chicago: 16 October.
1901b   Editorial, *The Chicago Record-Herald.* Chicago: 25 September.
1967a   The significance of the frontier in American history. In Turner, Frederick Jackson, *The Frontier in American History.* New York: Holt, Rinehart, and Winston, 1–38.
1967b   Social forces in American history. In Turner, Frederick Jackson, *The Frontier in American History.* New York: Holt, Rinehart, and Winston, 311–334.
Utter, Robert Paltry

1918   *Every-Day Pronunciation.* New York and London: Harper & Brothers.

Vizetelly, Frank H.
1920   *Mend Your Speech.* New York: Funk and Wagnall's.
1932   *A Guide to Correct Speech and Writing.* New York: Funk and Wagnall's.
1933   *How to Speak English Effectively.* New York: Funk and Wagnall's.

The Vulgarities of Speech Corrected; with Elegant Expressions for Provincial and
1829   *Vulgar English, Scots, and Irish; for Those Who are Unacquainted with Grammar.* London: F. C. Westley.

Voorsanger, Catherine H. and John K. Howat
2000   *Art and the Empire City: New York, 1825–1861.* New Haven and London: Yale University Press.

Walker, John
1791   *A Critical Pronouncing Dictionary and Expositor of the English Language.* London: G. Robinson.

Webster, Noah
1789   *Dissertations on the English Language.* Boston: Isaiah Thomas.
1828   *An American Dictionary of the English Language.* New York: S. Converse.
1831   *The American Spelling Book.* Middletown: Niles.

White, Ray
1996   The good guys wore white hats: The B western in American culture. In Aquila, Richard (ed.), *Wanted Dead or Alive: The American West in Popular Culture.* Urbana: University of Illinois Press, 135–159.

White, Richard
1994   Frederick Jackson Turner and Buffalo Bill. In White, Richard, *The Frontier in American Culture.* Berkeley: The University of California Press, 7–66.

White, Richard Grant
1872   *Words and Their Uses.* New York: Sheldon.

Wilke, Walter H. and Joseph F. Snyder
1942   American speech preferences. *Speech Monographs* 9: 91–110.

Winter, Irvah L.
1912   *Public Speaking, Principles and Practice.* New York: Macmillan.

The World Almanac and Book of Facts. New York: The New York World-
1941   Telegram.

Wolfram, Walt and Natalie Schilling-Estes
1997   *Hoi Toide on the Outer Banks: The Story of the Ocracoke Brogue.* Chapel Hill: The University of North Carolina Press.

Wrobel, David M.
1993   *The End of American Exceptionalism: Frontier Anxiety from the Old West to the New Deal.* Lawrence: The University Press of Kansas.

Yeomans, Henry A.
   1948   *Abbott Lawrence Lowell.* Cambridge: Harvard University Press.

Index